FRANZ KAFKA

A BIOGRAPHY

Franz
KAFKA

A Biography by Max Brod

SCHOCKEN BOOKS · NEW YORK

With a few minor omissions,
this paperback edition is identical
with the second enlarged cloth
edition published in 1960.

First Schocken Paperback edition, 1963

10 9 8   85 86 87 88

Translated from the German
by G. Humphreys Roberts (chapter I to VII)
and by Richard Winston (chapter VIII)
Copyright 1937 by Heinr. Mercy Sohn, Prague
Copyright 1947 by Schocken Books Inc.
Copyright © 1960 by Schocken Books Inc.
Copyright renewed © 1975 by Schocken Books Inc.
Library of Congress Catalogue Card Number: 60–14601
Manufactured in the United States of America
ISBN 0-8052-0047-9

CONTENTS

P. 8 *et passim:* "Contemplation" was published under the title "Meditation" in *The Penal Colony, Stories and Short Pieces,* New York 1948.

P. 8 *et passim:* The diary was published under the title *The Diaries of Franz Kafka,* edited by Max Brod, two volumes, New York 1948–1949.

P. 8, line 22: "The Merchant" was published under the title "The Tradesman," in *The Penal Colony,* pp. 31 ff.

P. 15 *et passim:* "Letter to My Father" appeared under the title "Letter to His Father," in *Dearest Father, Stories and Other Writings,* New York 1954. (The reasons for withholding the publication of the "Letter" are no longer valid.)

P. 60, line 6 from the bottom: "Preparations for a Wedding in the Country" was published under the title "Wedding Preparations in the Country" in *Dearest Father.*

P. 61, note 1, line 2: "Description of a Battle" was issued under the title "Description of a Struggle" in the volume *Description of a Struggle,* New York 1958.

P. 62, lines 21–22: "At the Window," "At Night" were published under the titles "Absent-minded Window-gazing," "Passers-by," "Clothes," "The Passenger," "Thoughts for Gentlemen Riders" appeared under the titles "Clothes," "On the Tram," "Reflections for Gentlemen-Jockeys" in *The Penal Colony.* (Lines 24–28 to be changed accordingly.)

P. 105, lines 19–20: "The Aeroplanes at Brescia" was published in the Appendix to *The Penal Colony.*

P. 132, line 3: "Children on the Post Road" appeared under the title "Children on a Country Road" in *The Penal Colony.*

P. 164, lines 15–17: A volume of letters by Kafka appeared under the title *Briefe 1902–1924,* New York 1958.

P. 178, line 19: The letter to Oskar Pollak (Fall 1902) appeared in *Briefe 1902–1924,* p. 14.

CHAPTER I

PARENTS AND CHILDHOOD

FRANZ KAFKA, son of Hermann and Julie Kafka, was born in Prague, July 3, 1883. The name Kafka is Czech by origin and—in its correct spelling of "Kavka"—literally means "Jackdaw." This bird, with its big head and beautiful tail, was embossed on the business envelopes of the firm of Hermann Kafka in which Franz in the old days often used to enclose his letters to me.

Kafka is not an uncommon surname among Jews whose families came from Czech districts, that is to say, Jews whose families lived in Czech districts at the time that the Emperor Joseph II ordered a census of all Jews. It provides no clue to the bearer's political or national sympathies. Franz's father, it is true, seems to have had a certain sympathy—though one could hardly call it a marked one—with the fighting Czech parties of Old Austria, and memories of his Czech home town may well have contributed to it. But Franz went only to German schools, was brought up as a German, and only later, led by his own inclinations, acquired a thorough knowledge of Czech and a deep understanding of its literature—without, of course, neglecting his close connection with German culture. The importance of his Jewish background, of which he later became conscious, will be discussed in due course. A second cousin of Franz's very like him in appearance, in fact a sort of sturdier, stronger edition of Franz, whom Franz much admired for his systematic energy and organizing ability, was a leading figure in German liberal circles when he was still a student, as well as later as a university don and member of the Czech parliament. This was Professor Bruno Kafka, who, although he died young, could point to ample evidence of a fruitful life as a critic and creative collaborator in drawing up bills of parliament, as a politician, as the editor of the posthumous scientific writings of

3

Krasnopolski, and by his own work in jurisprudence. Franz's and Bruno's fathers were first cousins.

This is what Kafka writes about his parentage in his diary:

"In Hebrew my name is Amschel, the same as my grandfather's on my mother's side, whom my mother, who was six years old when he died, can just remember as a very pious and learned man, with a long white beard. She remembers she had to take hold of the corpse by the toes and beg her grandfather's forgiveness for any wrong she might possibly have done him. She remembers, too, what a quantity of books her grandfather had, and how they filled all the wall space. He used to bathe in the river every day, even in winter, when he would cut a hole in the ice to bathe in. My mother's mother died at an early age of typhoid fever. After her death her grandmother succumbed to low spirits, refused to eat, and would not speak to anyone. One day, a year after her daughter's death, she went for a walk and never came back. They dragged her body out of the Elbe. My mother's great-grandfather was an even greater scholar than her grandfather, and enjoyed an equal respect among Christians and Jews. His piety was such that a miracle took place during a big fire, when the fire passed over his house, and spared it, though all the other houses round about were burnt down. He had four sons; one turned Christian and became a doctor. All of them except my mother's grandfather died young. He had a son whom my mother knew as mad Uncle Nathan, and a daughter who was, of course, my mother's mother."

From Franz's mother, whom I often used to talk to until her death in 1934—she outlived her son by ten years—and who was a quiet, pleasant, extremely clever, not to say wise, woman, I was able to get details to complete the picture. According to her, the Kafkas on the father's side came from Wossek near Strakonic (South Bohemia). Hermann Kafka's father was a butcher. Hermann's youth was hard and full of hard work; obviously his capacity for work and endurance was boundless. The rest of the family, too—three brothers and two sisters—were, in the words of Mrs. Julie Kafka, Franz's mother, "giants." All his life Franz was over-

4

shadowed by the figure of his powerful and extraordinarily imposing father—tall, broad-shouldered—who, at the end of a life full of work and success in business, but also full of worries and illness, succeeded in leaving a large family, children and nephews, in whom he took a patriarchal pride and (after selling a wholesale business in the Old Town Square, which still[1] exists) a block of flats in the center of Prague. The way this firm was founded by a widely ramified family and kept with great sacrifice and effort in good middle-class style by nothing but its founder's own hard, thorough, careful work, always remained a shining example for Franz's imagination and creative genius. His admiration for his father in this respect was endless—it had a touch of the heroic in it; in fact, an impartial onlooker who was not under the spell of the family circle could not but feel that it contained, alongside right and proper elements, something of exaggeration too. Anyhow, it was fundamental in Franz's emotional development. How much so can be seen from the following— critical—entries in the diary which I quote because they give a good picture of how his father began life.

Franz writes:

"It's unpleasant to listen to father talking about what he had to go through as a child, with his constant digs at how lucky people are nowadays, especially his own children. Nobody denies that for years he had sores on his legs because his winter clothes were too light; that he was often hungry; that when he was only ten he had to push a handcart round the villages, in winter too, and very early in the morning— but, a thing he will never understand, from these undeniable facts, together with the equally undeniable fact that I have not been through all this, it doesn't in the least follow that I have been luckier than he; that he can preen himself on these sores on his legs; that he should take it absolutely for granted, and insist on it; that I can't appreciate what he went through then; and that finally I must be unboundedly grateful to him just because I never went through the same. How I should

[1] [This and succeeding references to a present time are references to the year 1937, when this biography was written.]

5

like to hear him talking on forever about his childhood and his parents, but to hear all this in a boastful and quarrelsome tone is distressing. He is forever beating his hands together: 'Who nowadays knows anything about it! What do the children know about it! Nobody else has been through it! Is there one of you children knows anything about it?' Today Aunt Julie was here, and there was the same kind of talk. She has that enormous face that all our relations on father's side have. There's just a tiny upsetting something about either the set or the color of her eyes. When she was ten she had to go into service as a kitchen-maid. When it was freezing cold she had to run about in a wet skirt; the skin on her legs used to chap; the skirt used to freeze, and didn't get dry until she got to bed in the evening."

I am now going back to what Franz's mother told me. His grandmother on his father's side, a Platovsky, was described as very kindhearted; she had a great reputation among the people of the village for her medical knowledge. In general, on the father's side the predominant hereditary character-istics would seem to be a fighting capacity for living and getting the better of life, even physical strength, too. Her-mann did three years' military service, and liked to talk about his soldiering even when he was an old man—used to sing soldiers' songs when he was in a good mood—which was not very often, admittedly. His father, Franz's grandfather that is, could lift a sack of flour from the ground with his teeth. Once when some gipsies went into a lonely little inn, the terrified landlord sent for Kafka's grandfather. It was not long before he had beaten the unwelcome guests out of the place.

When we turn to the mother's family we are presented with quite a different picture. Here we find scholars, dreamers, inclined to eccentricity, and others driven by this inclination to the adventurous, the exotic, or the freakish and reclusive.

The passage from Franz's diary quoted above hints at the piety and scholarly reputation—in rabbinical lore—of his mother's grandfather and great-grandfather. Bathing in the

6

icy river is to be regarded, too, as a rite practiced by an exceptionally pious man, and not as part of a "back-to-nature" health cult which did not exist at that time, or at any rate was unknown among the Jews. These two men belonged to the Porias family and lived at Poděbrady. The great-grandfather always wore the fringes that his religion ordained over his clothes, not under them. Children used to run after him and mock him, but were later spoken to in the—Christian—school, and told they mustn't make fun of such a pious man. The grandfather's only child, who died so young and thus probably caused her mother's suicide, was Esther Porias, and she married a Jakob Löwy. There were six children, the second eldest (Julie Löwy) became Franz Kafka's mother. The eldest brother (Alfred) went abroad as a young man, and rose, covered with decorations, to be general manager of the Spanish railways. He stayed a bachelor, often came to Prague, and had a certain influence on Franz's boyhood, chiefly because Franz hoped he would give him his start in practical life. Franz longed for far-off lands, to which in fact another of his mother's brothers had been led by his career—Joseph—who was in charge of a trading-station in the Congo, and had fitted out caravans sometimes as many as a hundred and fifty strong. He lived later in Paris, married to a Frenchwoman. What was life in their case became literature in Kafka's work, became all the exotic countries which formed the scenes of Kafka's completed works and drafts. Uncle Alfred in Madrid was reputed to be reserved, but kindly, and to have a strong feeling for the family. (I met him but retain no clear-cut impression.) How disappointed Kafka was in him can be seen in a letter to a friend of his boyhood, Oskar Pollak. Franz had asked him "if he couldn't somehow help me to get out of all this, and if he couldn't take me somewhere where I could at last set my hand to something fresh." Franz had always looked on his legal profession solely as a make-shift, and dreamed of other activities. His relations with his uncle, to whom, we may be sure, he had only shyly hinted his youthful desires, nevertheless remained not unfriendly, within the general family coolness.

7

Another of his mother's brothers (Rudolf) lived a lonely crank in a little bookkeeper's office in the Košiř brewery, and went over to Catholicism out of conviction. The youngest brother (Siegfried) was a country doctor in Triesch, also a bachelor, came later to Prague and settled in the house that belonged to the Kafka family, and played an active part in Franz's fate in the last stage of his life through his medical treatment of him.

Franz was born, according to his mother, in the house on the corner of Maislgasse and Karpfengasse (now Kaprová). Other childhood scenes were the Lämel Institute in the Geistgasse (Dušní), the house called "Minuta," and the house on the corner of Wenzelsplatz and Smečky. When I first went to see him, the Kafkas lived in the narrow, twisty, ancient, but friendly building next to the Thein church, in the Zeltnergasse (No. 3 Celetna). His father's warehouse was also in the Zeltnergasse before it was transferred to premises in the Kinsky Palace in the Old Town Square. In Kafka's "Contemplation" and other works of his early period, and of course in the diary, you can see the manifold impressions left by the sights and situation of this warehouse. You have only to read the sketch "The Merchant." Who are these "unapproachable people from the country" whose fashions the "merchant" must cater to—"different from those that reign among the people in my circle"? Hermann Kafka's wholesale warehouse stocked haberdashery for sale to retailers in villages and country towns. I remember with particular distinctness the quantities of warm slippers I saw in the warehouse when Franz, accompanied by me, made yet another vain attempt somehow to help his father, groaning under the amount of work he had, or at least to show his good will, to win without making a great fuss a friendly glance or a word of recognition from him. His mother herself was untiringly busy helping his father in the business, and most probably irreplaceable. I even saw one of Franz's sisters there for some time. But that was not nearly enough for his father, whose domineering character would best have liked to have his family round him all the time. How far back, and how dimly these recollections stretch! But two other homes where I often went to see Franz are quite clear in my memory—Niklasstrasse 36 (now Pařiška), overlooking the quay, the Moldava, the baths, the bridges, and the green slope of the Belvedere; and the Oppelt house on the corner of Niklasstrasse and the Old Town Square. Kafka's study was on the Niklas street side, with its window right on the left of the top floor. You looked down on a more-than-lifesize baroque figure on the Russian church.

Franz was the eldest. Two brothers (Heinrich and George) died in infancy (one was two, the other a year and a half old). Six years later came the series of three sisters, who always held together and were conscious of the gap between them and their brother. Later, after Franz's illness, the youngest sister closed up this distance with the greatest firmness. She was and remained for Franz one of the most trusted and intimate of human beings—but Franz's childhood, by all accounts, must have been indescribably lonely. As his mother was busy all day in the warehouse, and his father couldn't do without her company—particularly for a game of cards—in the evenings either, Franz's education was entrusted chiefly to governesses and soulless schools. His first memories of erotic awakening are connected with a French governess or some Frenchwoman.

The sadness and awkwardness of his early years—"earthweight" Kafka calls this characteristic in another connection—are described in pages in the diary like the following from 1911, a long way back, that is to say:

"While I sometimes believe that all through my secondary schooldays and even earlier I could think unusually clearly, and that it is only because my memory later became weaker that this cannot be appraised correctly, at other times I admit that my bad memory only wants to flatter me and that I was mentally extremely lazy in things which are unimportant in themselves but fraught with consequences. Thus I can remember, anyhow, that when I was at my secondary school I often debated, even if not very thoroughly—I got tired easily even then, probably—with Bergmann in some fashion either following my own inward reasoning or following the Talmud, in a way I copied from him, about God and the possibility of His existence. At that time I used to like tacking the debate on to an article I had found in some Christian paper—I think *Die christliche Welt*—in which a clock and the world were compared to a watchmaker and God, and the existence of the watchmaker was supposed to prove that of God. I thought I could refute this very well as far as Bergmann was concerned, although the refutation was not firmly founded in me myself, and I had first, before I could produce it, to fit it together like a jigsaw puzzle. But the refutation did once take place as we were walking round the Town Hall clock. I remember it so exactly because we reminded one another of it a few years ago. But while I believed I excelled in that—it was only through the urge to excel, and the pleasure in producing an effect, and in the effect itself, that I could bring myself to do it—it was through not thinking deeply enough that I always walked about in bad clothes which my parents had made for me first by one customer, then by another, but longest of all by a tailor in Nusle. I noticed, of course, as it was only too easy to do, that I was particularly badly dressed, and even had an eye for others who were well dressed, but my brain didn't discover for years that my clothes were responsible for my miserable appearance. As I was already on the way, more in apprehension than in reality, to underestimate myself, I was convinced that it was only on me that clothes looked either as stiff as boards or hung in creases. I didn't want any new clothes at all; because if I had to look ugly anyway, I wanted at least to be comfortable, and further, since people were accustomed to my old clothes, to avoid demonstrating to the world the ugliness of new ones. These constant refusals when my mother wanted to have these new clothes made for me, for she, with the eye of a grown-up, could after all see the difference between the old and the new clothes, also had their effect on me, as, with my parents confirming it, I couldn't help telling myself I didn't care about my appearance. In consequence, I let my badly cut clothes govern my carriage, walked about with my back bent, my shoulders crooked, and my arms and hands all over the place; I was afraid of mirrors because, according to one of my ways of looking at it, they showed an inescapable ugliness, which moreover could not be absolutely faithfully mirrored, because if I had really looked like that I must have excited even greater attention. I put up with gentle pokes in the back from my mother on our Sunday walks, and with warnings and prophecies which were much too remote for me to be able to connect them with the sufferings I was then enduring. In general, my worst defect was an incapacity for taking the least thought for the actual future. I stayed with my thoughts firmly on the present circumstances, not out of thoroughness or from any too firmly held interest in them, but from sadness and fear—from sadness because, since the present was so sad I believed I dare not leave it until it turned into happiness; from fear, because, afraid as I was of the smallest present step, I considered myself unworthy, with my contemptible childish behavior, seriously and responsibly to form an opinion about the great adult future, which, in any case, generally appeared to me so impossible that every tiny advance seemed a fraud, and the next impossible of achievement. Miracles I could admit more easily than any real progress, but was too unconcerned not to leave miracles in their sphere and real progress in its. As a result I could spend a long time before going to sleep, imagining myself one day driving into the ghetto as a rich man in a coach-and-four, and with one word rescuing a beautiful girl who was being unjustly beaten, and taking her away with me in my carriage; but undisturbed by all this make-believe which probably fed on nothing more than a sexuality which was already unhealthy, the conviction remained that I should not get through the end-of-year exam, and even if I did I should make no headway in the next class; and even if by some swindle that could be avoided, I was bound to fail matriculation completely, and anyhow, it was quite certain, no matter at what particular moment it might happen, my parents, so far lulled by my, to all appearances, regular progress, and the rest of the

world with them, would suddenly be surprised by the revelation of some unheard-of incapacity. But seeing that the only fingerpost to the future I ever looked at was my incapacity—only very seldom my feeble literary work—thinking over the future brought me no profit; it was merely a drawing-out of my present sadness. If I wanted to, I could hold myself straight enough, but it made me tired, and I couldn't see what difference round shoulders could make to my future. If I am to have a future, my feeling was, everything will come right of itself. Such a principle I didn't choose because it gave me any confidence in the future, in the existence of which I didn't believe anyway, but rather for the purpose of making life easier. My principle was to walk, to dress, to wash, to read, above all to shut myself up in my room in the way that caused me the least trouble, and that demanded the least courage. If I departed from this principle, I only landed in some ridiculous evasion. There was a time when it seemed it was impossible for me to manage any longer without some kind of evening clothes, particularly as I had to make up my mind whether I should join a dancing class or not. The tailor from Nusle was summoned and the style of the suit was discussed. As always in such cases I couldn't make up my mind, because I was always afraid that if I made a definite statement I might be rushed not only into some unpleasant next step but even further along into something still more frightful. So first of all I decided I wouldn't have a black suit; but when I was put to shame in front of the stranger by its being pointed out to me that I had no evening wear at all, I allowed the question of an evening dress suit to be brought up; but as I felt that evening dress was a revolution of my habits that one could just bear to hear mentioned, but could never allow to be realized, we decided on a dinner jacket, which I thought I might at least be able to wear, because it was so like an ordinary jacket. But when I heard that the jacket had to be low-cut, which meant I should have to wear a boiled shirt, I almost overstrained myself to decide against it, knowing that this kind of thing could be warded off. I didn't want that kind of dinner jacket; I was prepared to have one lined
12

with silk and with silk facings, if that had to be, but the jacket must button high. Such a dinner jacket the tailor had never heard of, but he remarked that whatever kind of suit I was thinking of, it certainly couldn't be for going to dances in. Very well, then it wasn't for going to dances I wanted it, I didn't want to dance at all in fact; that was a question which was far from being settled, but I did want to have a suit made like the one I described. What made the tailor even less capable of grasping my meaning was that hitherto I had had myself measured and fitted for new clothes in a kind of ashamed haste, without expressing any comments or desires. So the only thing left for me to do, particularly as my mother was insistent, was, embarrassing as it might be, to go with him across the Old Town Square to a shop window where I had seen a harmless dinner jacket of this kind displayed for quite a long time, and had recognized it as the right thing for me. But unluckily it had already been taken out of the window, I couldn't see it anywhere inside, even after trying my hardest to peer into the shop; to walk into the shop solely to look at the dinner jacket I didn't dare, so we had to go back in the same state of indecision. But I had the feeling that the futility of this journey had already cast a curse on the future dinner jacket; at least I used the annoyance of all this hemming and hawing as an excuse for sending the tailor away with some small order or other, and a few words of comfort about the dinner jacket, and stayed behind, tired, to listen to my mother's reproaches, shut out forever—everything that happened to me was forever—from girls, making an elegant appearance, and balls. The happiness which I felt about it at the same time made me feel miserable, and besides I was afraid I had made a bigger fool of myself in front of my tailor than any of his customers had ever done."

Franz attended the German elementary school in the Fleischmarkt, and then the German grammar school in the Old Town Square. The latter was considered the most severe in Prague. The attendance was small. In its roomy classrooms, as there were not many pupils, naturally each one's turn came quicker and each one was asked more questions than in other luckier, lazier secondary schools. The masters were feared. I went to St. Stephen's grammar school, and didn't know Kafka at that time, but dark rumors reached me by other routes. I saw the chillingly elegant rooms when I went to the optional French lessons, which were given for us pupils from St. Stephen's grammar school also in the Kinsky Palace, where the premises of the Old Town grammar school were. Years afterwards Franz sometimes told me he passed in mathematics only "by crying during the examination," and thanks to the Hugo Bergmann mentioned above in the excerpt from the diary, who let him copy his homework. Otherwise he seems to have been a really good pupil. At the Old Town grammar school there were only good pupils, the others were mercilessly weeded out in the lower classes.

According to his mother, he was a weak, delicate child, generally serious, but nevertheless ready for an occasional prank—a child who read a lot, and didn't want to take any exercise—this last is in contrast with the older Kafka's strong interest in games and physical training.

A photograph of him as a child shows a little boy of about five, slender, with big, questioning eyes, and a dour, tight-lipped, self-willed mouth. His black hair combed straight down nearly to his eyebrows strengthens the impression of an almost threatening peevishness, with which the limp way he lets his hands droop is in keeping, but not the carefully chosen sailor suit, the big hat, and the walking stick.

Franz played very little with his sisters, the difference in their ages was too great and seems rather to have led to occasional quarrels. Only for his parents' birthdays little Franz wrote plays for his sisters. They were acted in the family circle, the custom lasted until they were adolescent, the sisters remember some of the plays and some of the lines to this day. One of the plays was called "The Equilibrist," another one "George of Poděbrady," another "The Photographs Speak"—of which the family photographs standing on the console table form the subject. Franz never acted in them, he was only the author and stage manager. Later he suggested to his sisters that instead of his things they should do short plays of Hans Sachs which he arranged for them.

It is among the boys he went to school with that we must look for young Franz's real associates. The small class contained a few figures whose importance will appear later. There was besides Kafka, Hugo Bergmann, of whom we have already spoken, who in years to come became a famous philosopher; at present he is professor and rector of the Hebrew University at Jerusalem. While they were at school together, although they were in close relationship with each other, Kafka and Bergmann seem never to have recognized each other's true worth. The same is true of Emil Utitz, later professor of philosophy at Halle and Prague, and of Paul Kisch, literary historian, and editor of the *Neue Freie Presse*. Oskar Pollak was the only one with whom he developed a more intimate friendship, which we shall have to go into later.

Of all the impressions of Kafka's childhood the one that is of outstanding importance is the grand image of his father— exaggerated in its grandeur as it undoubtedly is by Kafka's natural genius. One of Kafka's last writings deals with this. In November 1919, when we were living together in Schelesen near Liboch—that is why I can reconstruct the mood of those days fairly exactly—he wrote a very circumstantial "Letter to My Father." It is hardly a work that one can call a letter any more, it is a short book, but one that cannot yet be published—at the same time it is certainly one of the most remarkable and, for all its simplicity of style, one of the most difficult of documents dealing with a life-struggle. It is not easy to get to the bottom of the whole affair; in some passages it is easy, naturally, to find some correspondence with the theses of psychoanalysis, but they are confined rather to the surface of the facts and do not go down to their deeper implications. For reasons of a personal nature this "Letter to My Father" cannot yet be given wide publicity. But the few excerpts and quotations I am able to produce already contribute something indispensable to the understanding of Kafka's development.

Although it is more than a hundred pages long, the letter,

15

as I can testify from my conversations with Kafka, was intended actually to be handed to his father, through his mother, and Kafka was for some time of the opinion that by this letter he was doing something towards clearing up his relationship with his father which had become distressingly stagnant and painfully scabbed over. In reality the opposite would probably have happened. The explanation of himself to his father that the letter aimed at would never have been achieved. And Franz's mother did not pass on the letter but gave it back to him, probably with a few comforting words. Afterwards we never mentioned the whole affair again.

"Dearest Father," it begins, "you once asked me why I maintain I am afraid of you. As usual, I didn't know how to answer you, partly because of this very fear I have of you, and partly because the explanation of this fear involves so many details that when I am talking I can't keep half of them together." After this there follows a most detailed analysis of the relations of this peculiar father to this peculiar child, and vice versa; then comes a most severe self-analysis which grows, episode by episode, into a short autobiography, with special reference, arising naturally from his theme, to the years of his childhood. That is why this is just the place to quote some passages from the letter.

Kafka always set very great store by autobiographical sketches, as one can see not only from the fact that he kept a diary over long periods of his life, but also from remarks such as the following: "My urge to write my autobiography would be the first thing I should set to work and obey the moment I managed to get free of office work. Some such drastic change I should have to have in view as a temporary goal, when I begin to write, to be able to give some direction to the mass of events. Any other change than this, which is itself so terribly unlikely, that would lift me out of the rut, I cannot foresee. But after that the writing of my autobiography would be sheer pleasure, because it would go so easily, just like writing down one's dreams, and yet would have an entirely different result, a great result that would influence me forever, and that would at the same time be accessible to the understanding and feeling of everyone else." A letter to me, in which the idea of "tracing the outline of my [i.e. Kafka's] life with complete decisiveness" was very favorably considered, points in the same direction: "The next step would be that I would hold myself together, not fritter myself away in meaningless speculation, keep a clear vision." Thus in the case of Kafka, the desire to set his extremely complex soul in order far outweighed the ordinary pleasure a writer feels in revealing his most intimate feelings, which Thomas Mann, in his essay "Goethe and Tolstoy" once so beautifully described as a writer's inevitable failing and unconditional claim on the world, to be loved with his weaknesses as well as with his virtues. "The remarkable thing is that the world acknowledges and admits his claim." The fight that Kafka himself fought for his own perfection (he would have said against his egregious imperfection) was so hard, that he could not dream of dramatizing or "arranging" things for the outside world.

True as it is that the "Letter to My Father" was written solely for the sake of the matter in hand, just as true is it that its contents, its subjective truth when confronted with the sober facts, remains in spite of everything ambiguous and ambuscaded. Here and there I feel the perspective is distorted, unsupported assumptions are occasionally dragged in and made to fit the facts; on what appear to be negligible, immediate reactions, a whole edifice is built up, the ramifications of which it is impossible to grasp as a whole, which in fact in the end definitely turns on its own axis and contradicts itself, and yet manages to stand erect on its own foundation. At the end, indeed, the letter pretends the father himself is speaking and answering the letter in these words: "While I put the whole blame on you as frankly as I mean it, you on the other hand insist you are 'over-clever' and 'over-sensitive' and want to declare me, too, free from any blame. Naturally you are only seemingly successful in the latter—which is all you want—and reading between the lines, despite all your fine words about being, and nature, and opposition, and helplessness, it appears that I am really the aggressor

17

and everything you did was only in self-defense. So now by your dishonesty you have already achieved enough, for you have proved three things; firstly, that you are innocent; secondly, that I am guilty; and thirdly, that out of sheer greatness of heart you are prepared not only to forgive me, but, what is much more, and much less, even to go further and prove, and try and convince yourself, that I—contrary to the truth of course—am also innocent. That ought to be enough for you, but it isn't. You have in fact made up your mind that you want to live on me altogether. I admit we fight each other, but there are two kinds of fight. There is the chivalrous fight, where two independent opponents test their strength against each other, each stands on his own, loses for himself, wins for himself. And there is the fight of the vermin, which not only bite, but at the same time suck the blood on which they live. They are really the professional soldier, and that is what you are. You cannot stand up to life, but in order to set yourself up in it comfortably, free from care, and without self-reproach, you prove that I robbed you of your capacity to stand up to life, and shoved it in my pocket." (This, by the way, is an exposition in the light of which the genesis of Franz Kafka's "vermin story"—*The Metamorphosis*—becomes clearer, as also that of the short story "The Verdict.")

Just as in these lines of the last paragraph, the main theme of the whole letter remains unchangedly the same—it is only the question of who is guilty that takes on a different aspect in the last paragraph—and might be formulated thus: the weakness of the son is opposed to the strength of the father, who made himself entirely, and who in the consciousness of his achievement and of his strong, unbroken self through which this achievement was made, regards himself as the standard measure of the world, and that with the right of a naïve man who has never thought things out, and followed only his own instincts as far as principles are concerned—in fact to some extent a man of instinct. But a constant awareness that the opposites are not so glaring and clear-cut as the "Letter," for all its efforts to do justice to the complexities of life, cannot help but portray them—this awareness which is
18

something one takes for granted in any work of Kafka's—pervades the whole text, and stands out clearest in the words of the last sentence, which are the most reconciliatory in the discussion: "Naturally, in reality things cannot fit together so neatly as the examples in my letter, life is more than a game of patience; but were the proofs to be corrected on the lines suggested in my objection, a proof-reading which I am unable and unwilling myself to carry out in detail, something so near the truth would be arrived at that it might comfort us both a little, and make our lives and our deaths easier."

Apart from this reservation, the contrast between the two characters is sharply drawn. The characteristics Franz Kafka inherited from the two families he was born into, the odd, shy, quiet people of his mother's side (Löwy) and the realistic father's family, he himself describes as follows: "Just compare us! Myself, to put it as briefly as possible, a Löwy with a certain amount of Kafka at the bottom, which however can just not be got going by the Kafka will-to-live, to do business, to conquer. . . . You, on the other hand, a real Kafka with your strength, health, appetite, decision, eloquence, self-satisfaction, superiority over the world, endurance, presence of mind, knowledge of the world, a certain largeness, and naturally with all the weaknesses and failings that go with these qualities, and in which your temperament and sometimes your temper encourage you." Compare with this the characteristics listed in another passage of what Franz considered he inherited from his mother's family: "Obstinacy, sensitivity, a sense of justice, restlessness." What a gamut of contrasts, that can only be described as tragic, from this point to the vital portrait of the father that appears once more towards the end of the "Letter," in the passage where Kafka speaks of the failure of his attempts to get married. A comparison is made between the father and the son, according to which the father has everything he wants and the son nothing: "The chief obstacle to my marriage is the conviction, which I can no longer eradicate, that to keep a family, particularly to be the head of one, what is necessary is just what I recognize you have—just everything together,

19

good and bad, just as it is organically united in you, viz. strength and contempt for others, health and a certain excess, eloquence and stand-offishness, self-confidence and dissatisfaction with everybody else, superiority to the world and tyranny, knowledge of the world and distrust of most people in it, and then advantages with no disadvantage attached, such as industry, endurance, presence of mind, fearlessness. Of all these qualities I had comparatively almost nothing, or only very little, so how should I dare to marry under such conditions when I saw that even you had a hard struggle in your married life, and even failed, as far as your children were concerned? Of course I didn't put this question to myself in so many words, nor answer it in so many words, otherwise I should have fallen into the ordinary way of thinking on the subject, and discovered other men who are different from you—Uncle R., to mention one in your own circle— and who have married all the same, and at least not collapsed under the strain, which is already a great deal, and would have been enough for me. But I just didn't ask myself this question, but lived it ever since my childhood. I didn't, in fact, examine myself from the standpoint of marriage, but from the standpoint of every little thing; from the standpoint of every little thing you convinced me, as I have tried to explain, both by your example and by the way you brought me up, of my incapacity, and what turned out to be true for every little thing, and proved you were right, was bound of course, to be monstrously true for the greatest thing— marriage."

Here it seems impossible any longer to reject the connection with Freud's theories, particularly with his explanation of the "subconscious."

And yet I hesitate and must utter my protests against finding connections in this facile way, not least of all because Franz Kafka knew these theories very well and considered them always as a very rough and ready explanation which didn't do justice to detail, or rather to the real heartbeat of the conflict. In the following lines I shall therefore try to give a different slant on the facts, and refer to the example of

20

Kleist. First of all it must be admitted that Kafka's own remark that he had never put into so many words or into the "ordinary way of thinking," but rather "lived ever since childhood" the question that was bound up with the superiority of the father which the son so tremendously felt, seems to confirm the psychoanalyst in his usual method of approach. The same thing applies to the picture he gives of his father's "method of bringing up children," and the many entries in Franz Kafka's diary on the subject of how badly he was brought up, and the letters in the appendix on the bringing up of children written with reference to an essay of Swift's ("children should be brought up only away from their families, not by their parents") represent the further thematic development of this subject.

Almost the whole of the letter is devoted to the way his father brought him up. "I was a nervous child," said Kafka, "but I was certainly sulky, too, as children are; it is also true that my mother spoiled me, but I can't believe that I was a particularly difficult child, I can't believe that a friendly word, taking me quietly by the hand, a friendly glance, would not have got me to do anything that was wanted. Now at bottom you are a kind and gentle man (what I am about to say doesn't contradict this; I am talking only of the appearance you presented to the child), but not every child has the patience and the courage to go on looking until it has found the good side. You can only handle a child in the way you were created yourself, with violence, noise, and temper, and in this case moreover you thought this was the most suitable way, because you wanted to bring me up to be a strong, brave boy."

The "Letter" recalls with uncanny penetration an insignificant punishment in earliest childhood, which was concerned anyhow with the child's moral rather than bodily welfare, and yet made an ineradicable impression on the son, because he recognized "that I was such a mere nothing to him." The slighting criticisms that the father let drop of the child's little pleasures, of the friends he went about with, of his whole way of living and behavior, came to be felt as an enormous burden, and led finally to the child's despising himself. The father himself didn't follow his own criticisms and rules too strictly, and this very lack of logic appears to the son, on looking back, as a sign of unruly zest for life and unbreakable will-power. "You had worked yourself up to such a position by your own strength, that you had unlimited confidence in your own opinion. . . . From your armchair you ruled the world. Your opinion was right, everybody else's was mad, eccentric, *meshuggah,* not normal. At the same time your self-confidence was so great that there was no need for you to be consistent, and yet you were always right. You often even happened to have no opinion whatever on a subject, in which case any possible opinion on the subject must, without exception, be wrong. You could swear at the Czechs, for example, and then at the Germans, and then at the Jews, not for any particular reason but for every reason, and in the end there was nobody left but yourself. For me you developed the bewildering effect that all tyrants have whose might is founded not on reason, but on their own person."

It must be pointed out here how great a role for Kafka the principle of authority played, alongside elements of the dignity of man, that is to say democracy, in *The Trial,* in *The Castle,* in all the short stories and fragments that belong to *The Great Wall of China.* One may well know from personal experience what a spell can be exerted by self-confident and irrational personalities, who aren't troubled about their principles or their self-contradictions, so long as (*a*) one doesn't see through these contradictions, or (*b*) one needs the person as he or she is—as for example a woman one is in love with—and therefore has to put up with him or her under all circumstances. The question arises, posed in sober arrogance, "What did Kafka need his father for?" Or, better put, "Why was he not able to break away from him, although he adopted a critical attitude towards him in so far as (*a*) of the above reasons for feeling dependent on a person doesn't apply—why didn't he seek refuge in that distance which so many children feel obliged to put between themselves and their parents; or rather, since he did manage to put that

22

distance between himself and his father, and in later years hardly spoke to him, why did he suffer so from this distance and coldness? Must he not have said to himself that between two such entirely different characters as his and his father's an intimate union was just impossible?" It is true Franz could understand his father, and not only value him according to his deserts, but also look on him with loving admiration. But his father was by his very nature, and of course through no fault of his own, as Kafka emphasizes again and again in the "Letter," but just because of his nature, that is to say, unconditionally and finally, barred from any understanding attempt to probe his son's peculiar character. In how many talks did I not try and make clear to my friend—whose deepest wound, I knew, without yet having seen the diary, was just this—how he overestimated his father, and how stupid it is to despise oneself. It was all useless, the torrent of arguments that Kafka produced (when he didn't prefer, as he frequently did, to keep quiet) could really shatter and repel me for a moment.

Still today I feel that the fundamental question, "What difference could his father's approval make to Kafka?" is put not from Kafka's point of view but from an outsider's. The fact that he did need it existed once and for all as an innate, irrefutable feeling, and its effects lasted to the end of his life as "a general load of fear, weakness, and self-contempt." In the "Letter" his father's verdict is given a wholly disproportionate power of deciding the life or death of all Kafka's efforts (cf. the short story "The Verdict"). The "Letter" says, "Courage, decision, confidence, pleasure in this or that could not hold out to the end, if you were opposed to it, or even if your opposition were only presumed—and presumed it might well be almost whatever I did. . . . In your presence—you are an excellent orator, the moment it is a question of anything that concerns you—I began to stammer and stutter, even that was too much for you, so finally I shut up, at first probably out of pig-headedness, later because I could neither think nor speak in front of you. And as it was you who really brought me up, it affected my whole life in all its aspects."

At this point a remarkable parallel forces itself on one's attention which one might do well to consider before going on to the next stage—"infantile complex": it seems that Kleist, too, suffered from the same affliction of stuttering. Kafka's remark that he stuttered, can, in any case, *only* refer to his dealings with his father. When talking to anyone else, when he did bring himself to talk, that is, and broke his usual silence, he talked absolutely freely, easily, elegantly, and with a winning wealth and flow of ideas that was often playful, always astoundingly natural, and anything but "stammering."

The result of his father's upbringing was, according to the "Letter" (and in this passage Kafka provides his own commentary to the conclusion of his novel *The Trial*): "In front of you I lost my self-confidence and exchanged it for an infinite sense of guilt. In the recollection of this infinity I once wrote about someone, quite truly, 'He is afraid the shame will even live on after him.'" Kafka goes on to construe his life after this as a series of efforts to break loose from his father's sphere, to reach fields where he would be safe from his father's influence. It is worth noting that Kafka, who when passing judgment on literary work condemned nothing so severely as "constructions placed on things" which, lacking any breath of organic life that blossoms forth in ever unexpected directions, cling desperately to arbitrarily rigid and abstract combinations, himself falls into placing "constructions" on things, and dovetails into them, alongside what is genuine, also things that are half-true or exaggerated. That is why he wants to lump all his literary work together as an "attempt to get away from my father," as though his pleasure in art and his joy in creating would not have grown of their own accord out of his own powers. To those who knew him closely, at least, he presented quite a different picture from that of a man haunted by the "father-image"; they had the picture of a man glowingly under the impulsion of form, the desire and power to mold things, the urge to know, interest in observing life, and the love of humanity. One must admit, of course, that part

24

of the picture was what he thus describes, in deeply moving terms, in the "Letter to My Father": "My writings were about you, in them I merely poured out the lamentations I could not pour out on your breast. It was a farewell deliberately drawn out, save that, although you, it is true, imposed it, the direction it was given *I* determined."

It is under this same aspect, of an attempt at escape, that Kafka, in the "Letter" looks at other spheres of his life—the family, friendship, Judaism, profession, finally the two attempts he made at getting married. "My opinion of myself depended more on you than on anything else, such as, for example, on any outward success. . . . Where I lived I was an outcast, condemned, defeated, and although I struggled my utmost to flee elsewhere, it was labor in vain, because I was trying to do something that was impossible, that was beyond my strength except for a few insignificant exceptions." After a general survey of the conditions of his boyhood, Kafka arrived at the following depressing characteristic of himself, a characteristic described probably much too pessimistically through retrospection, and under the influence of the "father-construction" he so stubbornly clings to in the "Letter." He asserts he learnt little or nothing while at his secondary school—an assertion I cannot but dispute from my own private knowledge, for example of his knowledge of Greek, for we read Plato together at the university—and then continues, "Ever since I can remember I was so concerned about the problem of defending my spiritual existence that everything else was indifferent to me. Jewish schoolboys in our country are often peculiar, you can find the most improbable things among them, but my cool, hardly hidden, imperturbable, childishly helpless, at times almost ridiculous, self-satisfied animal indifference of a child 'sufficient unto himself,' and yet coolly fantastic, I have never seen anywhere else, but all the same ιt was my only protection against my nerves collapsing through fear and my sense of guilt."

The "attempts to escape" will be dealt with in their proper place, though not altogether from the standpoint of the "Letter to My Father." Only his accounts of how he tried

25

Judaism as a way of escape from his father's domination might find room here, because they are of vital importance for his youth, and have a further general significance both for Kafka's recognition of Judaism during that period of transition, and for his later religious development. "I found just as little escape from you in the Jewish faith. Here, in itself, was a possible escape, nay more, it would have been possible for us to have found each other in Judaism, or at least for us to have found in it a point from which we could have traveled the same road. But what kind of Judaism did I get from you! In the course of the years, I have had three different attitudes towards it.

"When I was a child I agreed with you, and reproached myself for not going often enough to the synagogue, not keeping the fasts, etc. . . . I thought I was doing you an injustice, not myself, and the feeling of guilt, which was always ready to hand, overwhelmed me.

"Later, when I was a young man, I couldn't understand how you, with the insignificant fragments of Judaism you possessed, could reproach me—out of godliness, as you put it—with not making an effort to put the same insignificant fragments into practice. It was really, as far as I could see, nothing, a joke, not even a joke. On four days in the year you went to the synagogue, where you were at least nearer in spirit to the indifferent than to those who took it all seriously, went through the prayers patiently as a formality, sometimes astonished me by being able to show me in the prayer book the place which was just being chanted, otherwise, provided—that was the chief thing—I was only in the synagogue, I could twist and turn about as much as I liked. So I used to yawn and fiddle the long hours away—the only place where I have been as bored later on was, I believe, when I went to dancing lessons—and tried my best to enjoy the few little distractions there were, such as, for example, the opening of the Ark of the Covenant, which always reminded me of a shooting-range at a fair, where there was also a box with a door which opened if you hit the bull's-eye, except that there something interesting came out, whereas here there were always just the same old dolls with no heads. Apart from everything else I was also always terrified there, not only, as you can understand, of the crowds of people one had to come into close contact with, but also because you once casually mentioned that I myself might be called on to read the Torah. For years I trembled at the thought of it. Otherwise I was not essentially disturbed in my boredom, except perhaps by the Bar Mitzvah, which anyhow only meant a lot of silly learning by heart, in other words led only to a ridiculous kind of examination; and again, as far as you were concerned, when you were called on to read the Torah, which as far as I could feel was a purely social affair, and got through it well, or when you stayed on in the synagogue for the Memorial Service, and I was sent away, which for a long time, obviously owing to my being sent away, and a complete lack of any deeper interest in it, left one with the feeling, of which I was hardly conscious even, that there was something indecent about it. That is how it was in the synagogue. At home it was even more miserable, and confined itself to the first Seder night, which always turned rather into a comedy with fits of laughter, brought about it is true by the influence of the elder children. (Why did you have to give in to this influence? Because you yourself had produced it, of course.) So that was the stuff that was handed on to me to build my faith out of, except perhaps your hand pointing to 'the sons of F. the millionaire,' who were in the synagogue with their father on the High Holy Days. What better there was to do with such material than get rid of it as quickly as possible I couldn't imagine; in fact, just getting rid of it seemed to me the most godly thing to do with it.

"But still later in my life I saw things differently again, and understood how you could believe I was wickedly betraying you in this matter too. You really did bring something of Judaism with you out of your tiny little ghetto-like country parish; it wasn't much, and a little of that got lost in the city and in the army, but all the same there was just enough left of impressions and memories of youth to satisfy your kind of Judaism, particularly as you didn't need much help of that kind, seeing that you came of a very sturdy stock, and, as far as you were concerned, could hardly be shaken by religious doubts unless they got mixed up too much with social doubts. Fundamentally the faith that guided your life was that you believed in the absolute rightness of the opinions of a certain class of Jewish businessmen, and really, since these opinions were part of your origin, it was but belief in yourself. There was enough Judaism in that, too, but as far as your child was concerned, it was not enough to be passed on, it trickled away drop by drop as you tried to hand it on. Partly they were impressions of childhood, which are incommunicable, partly it was your dreaded person. It was impossible, too, to make a child driven to over-critical observation by sheer fear understand that the few insignificant details you performed in the name of Judaism, with an indifference which matched their insignificance, could have a higher meaning. For you they had a meaning, as little memories of old times, and that is why you wanted to hand them on to me, but could do so, since they had no more intrinsic value for you yourself, only by persuasion or threats; that could not succeed, on the one hand, and on the other hand, couldn't fail, since you didn't realize the weakness of your position in this matter, to make you furious with me for what you thought was my intransigeance.

"Anyway, the whole business is no isolated phenomenon, it's the same with most of this Jewish generation of the transition period, that has migrated from the country, which is still comparatively religious, into the towns; it was a natural result, only that just in our case, where there is certainly no lack of bitternesses, just this one more, which is painful enough, had to be added. On the other hand, you must believe, just as I do, in your innocence in this point, too, but you must explain your innocence by your nature and the state of the times, but not simply by outward circumstances, and say for example that you had too much other work and too many other worries to have been able to bother your head about such things. In this way you always manage to twist your undoubted innocence into an undeserved reproach against

28

other people. The argument can in this case, as in all the others, very easily be refuted. It wouldn't have been a question of giving your children any particular lessons, but of the example of your own life. Had your Judaism been stronger, your example would have been more compelling, that is obvious, and this again is not at all a reproach but only a warding off of your reproaches. You have lately been reading Franklin's memoirs of his youth. I really gave it you to read on purpose, not, as you ironically remarked, for the sake of a short passage on vegetarianism, but because of the description it contains of the relationship between the author and his father, and the relationship between the author and his son, as it finds expression precisely in these memoirs written for the son. I don't want to call particular attention to any details here.

"I got a certain delayed confirmation of this conception of your Judaism from your attitude in the last few years, when it seemed to you that I was taking more interest in Jewish questions. Since you have as a matter of course a dislike for any of my occupations, and particularly for the nature of my interest in anything, you developed a dislike in this case too. And yet for all that, one might have expected you would make a little exception in this case. It was, after all, the Judaism of your Jewish faith that was occupying my attention, and therefore there was a chance of establishing new points of contact between us. I don't deny that if you had shown any interest in them, these things would immediately have become suspect in my eyes for that reason. I haven't the slightest intention of affirming that I am any better than you in this respect. But it never came to the test. Through my agency Judaism became revolting to you, Jewish writings unreadable, they 'disgusted' you—that might have meant that you were insisting that that form of Judaism which you revealed to me in my childhood was the only right one, one must go no further. But that you should insist on this point was hardly imaginable. In that case your 'disgust'—apart from the fact that it was felt not against Judaism, but against my own person—could only mean that you unconsciously realized the

29

weakness of your Judaism and my Jewish upbringing, did not wish to be reminded of it in any shape or form, and reacted to all reminders with frank hatred. In any case, your negative high opinion of my new interest in things Jewish was very exaggerated; in the first place, it brought your curse with it; and secondly, what was vital to its growth was the fundamental relationship with my fellow-men, in my case, in fact, it was fatal."

Alongside the father, the mother appears "in the turmoil of childhood as the emblem of reason." Her un-self-assertive attitude towards the father the son complains of, but also fully understands, just as much from the point of view of love for her husband as from the point of view of the common sense of giving way to a man who anyhow cannot stand being gainsaid. But the idea that by doing this the parents formed a unity, a common front against their son, which the mother could leave only secretly even to show her love for him, that idea has left a deep mark on all Kafka's work. You can find it everywhere, look at the short story *The Married Couple;* if you look at it from this angle, it becomes one of Kafka's most inspiring and personal works. Every word in it, rightly understood, is full of clues, from the complaints about business in the beginning to the words towards the end in which Mr. N.'s wife reminds the visitor, or rather intruder, of his own mother, and causes him to utter these words: "Whatever you may say, a mother can do wonders. She puts together again what we have wrecked. I lost her when I was a child." And the final note, "Oh, how many business calls come to nothing, and yet we must continue to shoulder the burden."

The odd thing is not that Kafka very early in life felt his father's character was something foreign to his own, although at the same time something highly worthy of admiration for its vitality and strength. The odd thing is that even as he was growing older he still wished above all for his father's approval, which *could* never be granted. "You have an unusually beautiful kind of quiet, satisfied smile, such as one seldom sees, which can make the recipient quite happy," says Kafka in the "Letter." He reckons up the moments when he felt close to his father: "It was not often, of course, but it was wonderful. For example, when I used to see you on a hot summer afternoon tired after lunch, sleeping a little in the shop, with your elbow on the desk, or when you came on a Sunday, worn out, to have a little fresh air with us in the country; or when mother was dangerously ill and you clung to the bookcase, shaken with sobs; or when, during my last illness, you came softly to my room to see me, stopped at the door, just stuck your head in, and out of consideration for me, only waved a hand to me. On occasions like this one lay down and cried for joy, and is crying now as one writes about it." . . . He dedicated one of his books, *The Country Doctor*, to his father. Franz often recounted the reply with which his father received the book—he certainly meant no harm by it —his father said nothing but, "Put it on the table by my bed."

And what a melancholy ring the sentence in the diary has, with which Franz closes a description of an evening, of an act with which he was for once completely satisfied: after a great deal of trouble he had arranged, he thought with a great deal of prudence and success, a recitation evening in the Jewish town hall for a poor Polish Jewish actor. He himself made the introductory—and significant—speech. (It was the only lecture he ever gave—otherwise one can only record a reading from his own works at Munich, and a reading from Kleist's *Michael Kohlhaas* in the Toynbee Hall in Prague.) But he ends the description sadly with the words in brackets, as though spoken from the depth of his soul, "My parents were not there."

Life in Kafka's parents' house has many resemblances to that in Proust's house (Léon Pierre-Quint: *Marcel Proust, sa vie, son œuvre*). "Son père, parti tôt le matin, ne voyait presque pas son fils." On the other hand, the mother: "une femme douce . . . . elle veillait avec soin sur lui, lui pardonnait d'avance ses fantaisies, les habitudes de nonchalance auxquelles il s'abandonnait." If one were to investigate what they had in common in the way their parents brought them

31

up, one might perhaps also come upon the common roots of the similarity of outlook and style of two authors who were contemporaries, and yet never heard of one another—a fact that refers an investigator trying to co-ordinate his facts back to the darkness of the general world chaos. The unusual preciseness of the descriptions, the love of detail, a peculiarity I might describe as "copy fever" (*Akribismus*)—the feeling of being spellbound in the family circle, even certain analogies of race (Proust's mother was a Jewess) and even of outward fate—all this challenges one again and again to make the comparison, although of course Proust's cosmopolitan surroundings and Kafka's bourgeois Prague led to important differences in their development.

For cases such as those of Proust, Kleist, and Kafka, who all their life long never grew out of the impressions of their childhood, and the dominating factor of their family and the family tradition, the psychoanalysts have their scheme of a subconscious erotic mother-complex, and a subconscious hate of the father. But for the infantile complex there is surely—not that I wish to exclude the co-responsibility of motives which are relevant from the psychoanalytical side—the simpler explanation that the parents are the *first* problem a child comes up against, the first resistance he has to assert himself against; his arguments with them are the model for all his later fights in life. A man begins his duel with life and the world. First round: his parents. Then life sends other opponents for him to stand up to; school-fellows, teachers, fellow-citizens, the public, the unfathomable world of women. Nothing but enemies—or at least nothing but opponents, among whom it is hard to find those who mean well; and finding them is already itself a battle, an activity, a task, a life-test imposed upon men. The way in which the man and fighter is able to get through his first round is an indication of his future, and can be considered as a symbol of the future. By the researcher the beginnings will rightly be regarded as the real roughcasts or representations of further phases of his life, and in fact of his life as a whole altogether. While the psychoanalyst supposes that a man draws the picture he has of God involuntarily after his own father, the opposite possibility (which Heinz Politzer was the first to point out) cannot be excluded that it is just sensitive people like Kafka who have their idea of "father" enriched, enlarged, and their horizon filled by their experience of God (or rather, as I have tried to show here, by the experience of the universe which opposes and fights against them as they grow older).

"Oh, that I knew the way, the dear way back to the land of childhood," sings Klaus Groth in a poem set to music by Brahms. This longing occurs only as an occasional episode in the case of the average man, perhaps as a sign of weariness at the end of a hard day—which raises the question as to whether a man who is tired doesn't perhaps show his character more truly than an ambitious man, or a man keyed up by the necessity of earning his living. But alongside this episodic "back to the land of childhood," there exists too the true infantile complex, the deciding of a man's fate by the events of his young days, from which a certain type of man never breaks loose for the whole of his life.

The child trusts his parents and wants his parents to trust him too. This is the point out of which arises one of the first great conflicts to which the soul of man is exposed. Instead of mutual trust, the world offers something entirely different—struggle, war. Of how deep and glowing an emotional experience this first collision with parents and the family may be, the life of a typical infantile poet, Kleist, is an example in the grand manner. All Kleist's days the thought hung over him, "What will the family—the extension of the parent-milieu—say about my way of life? Will they trust me?" Of course, the discrepancy between Kleist's old Prussian family, which considered fame could be won only on the field of battle or in the seats of government, and the delicate, emotional, unstable poet who was at the same time, one can only say, tyrannized by the highest ethic principles, was enormous. He knew that in the eyes of his family his verses and dramas meant not much more than an immoral excess, the work of a ne'er-do-well. Kafka read Kleist's letters with

33

special interest, and made note of the passages which show that Kleist's family looked on the poet as "a completely useless member of the human community, who deserved no further consideration," and remarked with silent irony that on the centenary of his death, the family laid on Kleist's grave a wreath with the inscription, "To the best of his breed."

The hearty man is inclined, shrugging his shoulders and rather disdainfully, to gloss over how intensely the sensitive man looks for confirmation of himself, and of his innermost being, for faith and acceptance, to his own family and breaks down when he feels that he isn't understood in his own home. The hearty man, you see, soon reaches a point in his development when he says to himself—rightly or wrongly—"Oh, what do I care; my family is unteachable, incorrigible. But the world is wide. There are other courts of appeal after all. I shall show them what I am worth, and not give a damn what that lot at home think of me. . . ." Here again, though, we have a glimpse of the tragi-comedy of life. For in fact your hearty man, who gives up trying to win the trust of his family, has not gained anything very much over the sensitive man. The conflicts that the "wide world"—alas, it soon becomes so narrow—holds in store for him, are the same, almost to a *t*, as the first one, in which one begs for trust and doesn't get it. Whether it is your friend or your boss, the one you love above everything else, or simply your neighbor that has just one little matter to settle with you; over and over, you would like to be recognized according to your own self, your own person, your own heart's inclination—but they always ask only what you have done, and really, if you look at it rationally, they have nothing else by which they can judge your state of mind except the manifestations of that state of mind. But you don't want to be judged, you want people to have faith in you. For every man—just like every god—demands faith on every side of him. The soul can only blossom forth to its sublime and rare capacities when it feels it is being met with faith.

This question of faith is so much the hub of things, that one philosopher—Felix Weltsch—has described the "decision of faith" as the foundation of all ethics. One cannot prove that the world as a whole has any meaning, or that it is the work of a good spirit, or that it is meaningless and wicked. This is a thing that one has only to believe or reject, with no proof whatsoever. In exactly the same way, essentially, the being, the virtue of every man is either believed or rejected, without any proof. For just in this field exact proof cannot be produced: what a man has done is subject to conflicting judgments, and often what is most useful comes from the most corrupt soul. Thus the first conflict—the vain striving to win the faith of the family—is the pre-formation of all the conflicts of life that follow it and at the same time includes them all. This shrugging of shoulders over the infantiles who are caught up in this very first conflict, in the van of the battle as one might say, is nevertheless not so entirely justified, as it appears to be at first sight. These "unpractical" people perhaps curtail many a long chain of doubt and distress which would only lead into the void; they are, as it turns out in the end, not only more delicately sensitive, but also nearer truth and the deepest understanding. That is why the picture of the world given by an "infantile" poet such as Kleist was, moves us so: infantilism is no weakness in his case; it is only a more honest, a more serious comprehension of the fatal fundamental constellation of existence, in which we all stand opposed to one another, all mistrusting one another, each one with the secret plea in his heart that one should after all have faith in him, even though he can give no proof of himself. What a number of moving situations Kleist [1] found to work up this one eternal situation, in which someone has fallen into the most shameful disgrace, in which every outward circumstance tells against him, and in which nevertheless with the utter self-surrender of a clear conscience he demands that we do not condemn him. I even have the feeling that all Kleist's work is centered round this *one* point. The ideal image of his faith is Käthchen von Heilbronn. But just as Kätchen has faith in her knight, Penthesilea wants Achilles to sense her love though all the appearances condemn her.

[1] And Kafka also: cf. *Amerika*.

"If only you had not mistrusted me" are her last words. And Alkmene before the husband who spurns her, Eve (in *The Broken Jug*) before her fiancé, the apparently so cruel elector before the Prince of Homburg—they all stand there burdened with acts difficult to explain away; dark, guilty, at the very least not good acts, and yet they are innocent and have no more heartfelt wish than that their lovers should recognize their enormous love. It is the fundamental situation of humanity with which, in Kleist's case, the situation of his own purely personal life grew commensurate. He had the wickedness to write verse instead of legal documents—but underneath this naughtiness and levity his family should recognize that he was a proper fellow after all. The most moving symbol he created is this: the Marquise von O. becomes pregnant (just as genius inspires a work in the soul of the artist), she doesn't know how it happened, medical evidence is to the most positive degree against her, and yet she is innocent. Kleist is extremely inventive in piling up the evidence of guilt around his heroine with every possible argument, like the faggots round the stake of a martyr. The lightning that tears the clouds to rags and reveals blinding, snow-white innocence is all the brighter. Hence the overpowering pathos of the scene in which the father of the Marquise von O. realizes the full purity of her soul, and begs her forgiveness. What boldness guided the writer's pen, and made him—long before Freud—set down these words which one cannot read without being shaken to the core of one's being:

"The daughter motionless, her head leaning back, her eyes shut fast, in her father's arms . . . while the latter, sitting in his armchair, his wide eyes full of shining tears, pressed long, hot, and hungry kisses on her mouth, just like a lover! The daughter said nothing; he said nothing; but he sat with his face bent over her, as over the face of the first girl he ever loved, and set her mouth right and kissed her. . . ."

How often may Kleist have had visions of such a scene with all the magic of wishes come true. How often has every "infantile" shared such or similar dreams with him! That

Franz Kafka's writing has several important features in common with Kleist's work, particularly as far as his prose style is concerned, which cannot at all be explained as a mere emotional echo, has often been pointed out before. But so far as I know no one has ever pointed to the spiritual nearness of their fundamental outlook. This fundamental standpoint is in the truest sense of the word so much a part of them both that even in their portraits they resemble each other, at least in so far as boyishness and purity of features are concerned. In Kafka's work, too, one finds the center-point is "responsibility towards the family"! This is the key to short stories like *The Metamorphosis,* "The Verdict," "The Stoker," and to many a detail in other works. Also the peculiar trick of setting up symbols, which are at the same time absolutely real life, is a trait common to both writers. The vision of a lady who before the eyes of her high-born family suffers the sea-change into a dishonored woman-with-child is by no means so far from that of the picture of a family son whose fate is a metamorphosis into a despised species of vermin— *The Metamorphosis.*

Ties with the experiences of boyhood, ties with the family, and a strict tradition that had unconscious after-effects— which in Kleist's case was Prussian, refreshed by Kant's sys- tem—in Kafka's case Jewish ethics of justice, brought to new life by later studies. On the question of the childlike air of Kleist's portrait I put forward for comparison what Kafka once said to me: "I shall never grow up to be a man, from being a child I shall immediately become a white-haired ancient." He often emphasized and noted in his diary how young he was always taken to be. A certain temporary mis- trust of his sexual capacity is part of the same story—Kleist reports the same of himself. Further, the overstrain of the demands they made on themselves, as though both of them were under an obligation to prove to their families that they were not good-for-nothings. Franz's dislike of any kind of "tutelage," which plagued him during the last year of his life in Berlin, when he had parcels of food sent him by his par- ents in Prague during the starvation winter of 1923. And

Kafka's highest aim in life could not be better described than by Kleist's cry full of yearning: "To farm a field, to plant a tree, to father a child." For both of them, one must admit, life ran far from the farmer's life and the simple constructive outlook they desired. The analogy can be carried still further, and shown to go right into their way of writing, in doing which sight must naturally not be lost of the fact that Kafka consciously learned from Kleist's style. But apart from that, the community of a special kind of fairy-story-like inventiveness and weaving of a story is certainly to be set down to their dependence on early days, in which the child casts a spell on and transforms into a dream-shape everything he plays with. Both of them really knew "the way back"—and passed along it often and with pleasure. The crystal-clear style and realism of detail of both thus turns out to be the counterbalance and defense of strong natures against this inclination to dreams and childhood. In the case of both writers what is fundamentally insoluble, most secret, most obscure, is related in the clearest, simplest, most clear-cut words possible.

CHAPTER II

THE UNIVERSITY

"TALK comes straight out of his mouth like a walking stick"—that is the first remark of Kafka's that I find noted down in my diary. Kafka was describing with these words somebody or other—who it was I have long ago forgotten—who could never be stopped talking.

In this little note of mine I can still feel today my admiring astonishment at Kafka's manner. For him nothing was ordinary, always and everywhere he expressed himself with his own peculiar gift of pregnant observation and simile. And this he did in a completely unforced manner without preciosity, with the most charming naturalness.

Of any burden of strained, gloomy, boyhood impressions, of the decadence or snobbishness which might easily have offered themselves as escapes from so much depression, of a troubled or a contrite soul, no one who met Kafka could observe any trace. What Kafka set down in the "Letter to My Father" didn't seem to exist on the surface—or rather revealed itself only in hints, and then only in extremely confidential talks. I only learned of this great sorrow, and to understand it, by slow degrees. At first sight Kafka was a healthy young man, admittedly remarkably quiet, observant, reserved. His spiritual bent was not in the direction of the morbidly interesting, the bizarre or the grotesque, but in that of the greatness of nature, the curative, health-giving, sound, firmly established, simple things.

I have experienced over and over again that admirers of Kafka who know him only from his books have a completely false picture of him. They think he must have made a sad, even desperate impression in company too. The opposite is the case. One felt well when one was with him. The richness of his thoughts, which he generally uttered in a cheerful tone, made him, to put it on the lowest level, one of the most amus-

39

ing of men I ever met, in spite of his shyness, in spite of his quietness. He talked very little; when there were a lot of people he often didn't speak for hours on end. But when he did say something, everybody had to listen immediately, because it was always something full of meat, something that hit the nail on the head. And in an intimate conversation his tongue sometimes ran away with itself in the most astounding manner. He could be enthusiastic and carried away. There was no end to our joking and laughing—he liked a good, hearty laugh, and knew how to make his friends laugh too. More than that, if one were in a tight corner, one could unhesitatingly rely on his knowledge of the world, his tact, his advice, which hardly ever failed to be right. He was a wonderfully helpful friend. It was only in his own case that he was perplexed, helpless—an impression that, owing to his self-controlled bearing, one did not get in personal contact with him except in rare, extreme cases, but one which is undoubtedly deepened, all the same, when one reads his diary. The fact that from his books, and above all from his diary, such a totally different, much more depressing, picture may be drawn than when it is corrected and supplemented by the impressions one can add from having lived with him day by day—that is one of the reasons that persuaded me to write these memoirs. The portrait-from-life of Kafka that remains in the memory of our circle stands alongside his writings, and demands to be taken into account in any final judgment of him.

I got to know Franz Kafka in my first year at the university, that is to say in 1902–3, I suppose as early as the winter term, 1902. Franz, who was a year older than I, was beginning his second year. After leaving school he first studied chemistry for a whole fortnight, then he took German for one term, then law—this last only as a makeshift, with no preference for it, as with most of us. A plan to continue his German studies in Munich with Paul Kisch was never carried out. Law he took up with a sigh because it was the school that involved the least fixed goal, or the largest choice of goals—the bar, the civil service—that is to say, the school that put off longest taking a decision and anyhow didn't demand any great preference. On the subject of Kafka's dislike of the study of law, which he never attempted to conceal, I find the following entry in his diary (1911): "Out of an old notebook: Now in the evening, after studying since six o'clock this morning, I noticed how my left hand clasped the fingers of my right hand for a few moments, in sympathy."

In the "Letter to My Father" he connects his choice of profession, too, with his feeling of being defeated by his father, with the "chief thing." I consider this a later interpretation; but the kernel, the haziness and aimlessness of our youth can be clearly glimpsed in Kafka's words, behind the scaffolding of interpretation. He writes: "There was no real freedom of choice of profession for me, I knew: compared with the main point everything will be as indifferent to me as the subjects I took in my secondary school, and so the only thing is to find a profession which will give the widest scope for this indifference, without hurting my vanity too much. So the law was the obvious thing. Feeble oppositional attempts of my vanity, of senseless optimism, like my fourteen days' study of chemistry, my half-year of reading German, served only to strengthen my fundamental conviction. So I read law. That meant that in the few months before the examinations, while wearing out my nerves at a great rate, intellectually I fed myself exclusively on sawdust—sawdust, too, which had already been chewed by thousands of jaws before me. But in one sense, this was just to my taste, as in one sense my schooling had been, and later my civil service, because it all fitted in exactly with my position. In any case, I showed remarkable foresight in this case; when I was a mere child I already had sufficiently clear presentiments about my education and my profession. I didn't expect any deliverance in this direction, I had already abandoned all hope of any."

At bottom the state of affairs was this: both of us felt ourselves honestly drawn only to creative art, but that we did not yet admit; furthermore, we had far too high a regard for art to care to connect it with all the sordidness that lay in the words and idea of "earning one's living"—besides we had no one to guide us, no one who could show us the way, if there

41

was a way at all. We were so without guidance that to both of us the idea that there could be any other refuge than our hated studies never occurred seriously. Least of all to me. Kafka, it is true, had something more like a vague idea—which recurred in later periods of his life—that one "should get away from Prague and start on something altogether different."

The place of our first meeting was the "Reading and Lecture Hall for German Students"—the clubroom at that time was in Ferdinand street, now Národní. Everyone who matriculated at a German secondary school in Prague—and in many places in the provinces—became a member of this big students' union as a matter of course unless he was an anti-Semitic nationalist or a professed Jew. (I myself didn't take up Zionism till much later, some ten years after.) The "Hall" belonged to the German Freedom Party. We didn't wear any caps, it is true, but we did wear the black, red, and gold ribbon, with the date of the revolution, 1848. But how faded, how lukewarm was the memory of this revolution; indeed it never rose above the horizon. The most important component of the "Hall" was the Hall Committee, between it and the members there existed a certain antagonism, in fact at times a kind of "battle," which, however, invariably ended in the crushing and utter defeat of the members; for at the general meeting there always turned up in a body the "couleurs," the corporations that wore colors, and which belonged to the "Hall" by a very loose tie, and never otherwise bothered their heads about the life of the club. For the voting however they were there in full number and voted unanimously for the committee list—to our disgust, which we felt afresh each time, against this voting-machine which was run according to an exact, preconceived plan by the committee's great tactician, Bruno Kafka. They never took any part whatsoever in the debates, and complaints made by the despised "chaffinches"—that is to say, those who wore no colors—against the committee, however justified they might be, didn't interest them; they contented themselves with making their irrevocable wishes known through the mouths

42

of their doughty whips. And the committee remained unshaken in their seats as always.

Franz took no interest in this childishly ambitious game, it was not until his later years that I first heard him mention even that he was related to Bruno Kafka—to the accompaniment of his admiration for the man's energy. And yet it was the conduct of this Batrachomyomachia that brought us together for the first time. The center of resistance to the committee was, in fact, the "Section for Literature and Art," which led an independent life in some respects, and was dependent on the vote of the committee only in matters of finance—which led to specially violent quarrels; I remember, for example, that the committee refused to approve the fee, or at any rate to approve a sufficiently high fee for Detlev von Liliencron, whom we had invited to lecture in Prague. As opposed to the committee with its ball-committees and its "Winers," we in our section, whether rightly or wrongly, considered ourselves the bearers of the spirit. The section held its regular debates and read papers regularly in its own circle. On one of these evenings I, straight from school, made my debut with a paper on "Schopenhauer and Nietzsche" which created some stir. As the bitter and fanatical adherent of Schopenhauer that I then was, and as such I considered the slightest contradiction of the tenets of the philosopher I worshipped as nothing less than lèse-majesté, I spoke of Nietzsche quite simply and baldly as a "swindler." (I have, by the way, remained to this day true to my antipathy to Nietzsche, even if with reservations and in a different sense.)

After this paper Kafka, who was a year older, saw me home. He used to take part in every meeting of the "section," but until then we had hardly taken any notice of each other. It would indeed have been difficult to notice him, because he so seldom opened his mouth, and because his outward appearance was above all deeply unobtrusive—even his elegant suits, which were mostly dark blue, were as unobtrusive and reserved as himself. But that evening something about me seems to have attracted him, he was more communicative than usual; anyhow the endless conversation that went on

while he was seeing me home began with a strong protest
against the extreme uncouthness of my way of putting things.
From that we went on to talking about our favorite authors,
and defended them against one another. I was enthusiastic
about Meyrink. At school I modeled myself on the classics,
and rejected everything "modern," but in one of the upper
classes I swung round, and at this time in a proper "storm
and stress" mood, I welcomed everything that was out-
of-the-way, unbridled, shameless, cynical, extreme, over-
caustic. Kafka opposed me with calm and wisdom. For Meyrink he had no time.[1] Well, I quoted him "purple passages"
by heart. One from Meyrink's "Purple Death" compared butterflies to great opened-out books of magic. Kafka turned up
his nose. That sort of thing he considered too farfetched and
much too importunate; everything that suggested that it was
planned for effect, intellectual, or artificially thought up, he
rejected—although he himself never used labels of this kind.
In him there was something of the "softly murmuring voice
of Nature" of which Goethe spoke, and it was that he liked
to hear in other writers. As a contrasting example—as what he
himself liked—Kafka quoted a passage from Hoffmannsthal,
"the smell of damp flags in a hall." And he kept silent for a
long while, said no more, as if this hidden, improbable thing
must speak for itself. This made so deep an impression on me
that I remember to this day the street and the house in front
of which this conversation took place. There may be a number of people who manage to find in Kafka's work an affinity
with writers like Poe, Kubin, and Baudelaire, writers of the
"night side of life," who will be astonished to hear that it was
just to simplicity and naturalness of feeling that my friend

[1] He had just as little for Wedekind and Oscar Wilde—but he loved
Thomas Mann's *Tonio Kröger*, and reverently searched out every line
of this author's in the *Neue Rundschau;* he read Hamsun, Hesse, Flaubert, and Kassner with enthusiasm. Among favorite authors of his later
years I can name Emil Strauss, Wilhelm Schäfer, Carossa (in saying this
I have no wish to express approval of their development after Kafka's
death), also Hebel's "Little Treasury," Fontane, Gogol, Stifter—and
above all, constantly, Goethe and the Bible. Other authors of Kafka's
preference are to be found in the appropriate passages in this biography.

guided me, and led me gradually out of my confused and corrupt state of mind, puffed up with childish pride and a completely false assumption of a blasé air. But that is how it was. Indisputable documentary evidence is the letter I quote below, I think the first Kafka ever wrote me. I can't give its exact date, because its envelope is missing, but it must be before 1906 (the year Kafka took his degree) because he mentions going to lectures still.[1]

It gives you some idea of Kafka's gracious character, ready to understand other people's views, tolerant, for all his severity about his own life, if you read how gently the letter puts me in my place, how he localizes the attitude he reproves—one of cheap romanticism and gross seeking after effect—which he describes as a "Wolves' Glen"—not in myself but in the people who surrounded me at that time, and who recognized a ringleader in me.

Dear Max

Particularly because I was not at lectures yesterday, I feel it is important to write to you to explain why I didn't come with you to the evening at the Redout, although I did perhaps promise to do so.

Forgive me, I wanted to give myself the pleasure of bringing you and Pr. together for one evening, because I thought there was bound to be some lovely combinations when you, carried away by the impulse of the moment, made hypersarcastic remarks—you do that when you are in company— and he on the other hand, with the sensible grasp he has

[1] The handwriting, too, points to the letter being from the earliest period of our acquaintance, it is written in Gothic characters—later Kafka used Latin characters. His handwriting went through various stages of development in the course of years. The Gothic flourishes in the beginning accord with the rich, rounded-off, decorated, occasionally precious, style of his prose. In accordance with this, the letters to Oskar Pollak, written in a still earlier period are written in a still more ornamental handwriting. The period of his spacious Latin handwriting is the period of comparatively peaceful maturity and mastery. Manuscripts from the last few years often reveal the use of a fine pen, tiny characters, speed, as though overwhelmed by the richness of his inspiration.

of almost every point except art, would give you the right answer.

But when I first thought of it, I forgot your crowd, the little crowd with whom you go around. To the first glance of a stranger it doesn't show you up to advantage. Because it is partly dependent on you, and partly independent. In so far as it is dependent, it stands around like a receptive mountain range with a ready echo. That puts the listener off. While his eyes would like to busy themselves peacefully with the object in front of him, he is attacked from the rear. In this case he cannot but lose his ability to enjoy either, especially if he doesn't happen to be more than usually agile.

In so far as your companions are independent, they do you still more harm, because they caricature you. Through them you are not seen in your proper perspective; as far as the listener is concerned, you are defeated through yourself, and the wonderful moment when your friends are consistent does not help; friendly crowds are only useful in revolution when they all play their parts simultaneously and simply, but when there is a small uprising by a straggling light at a table, they ruin it. This is what happens when you want to show your conversation piece "Landscape at Dawn" and put it up as the backcloth—but your friends think the "Wolves' Glen" would be more suitable, and they set your "Wolves' Glen" up in the wings. Of course you painted both pictures, and every onlooker can recognize that, but what disturbing shadows there are on the meadows of a "Landscape at Dawn" and foul birds fly over the field. That's what I think about it. It doesn't happen to you very often, but it does happen from time to time (and I still don't quite understand this) that you say, "Look at Flaubert! There you have nothing but discussions about facts, you see, there is no sentimental nonsense." How odious I could make you appear if *I* used it in this way some time or other. You say, "How beautiful *Werther* is!" I say, "But if we are prepared to tell the truth, there is a lot of sentimental nonsense in it after all." That is a ridiculous, unpleasant remark, but I am your friend when I say it, I don't wish to do you any harm, I only want to tell the listener your whole opinion on such matters. For it may often be a sign of friendship not to take a friend's pronouncements too seriously any more. But meanwhile the listener has become sad and tired.

I have written this because it would be still sadder if you didn't forgive me for not having spent the evening with you than if you don't forgive me for this letter; my love to you,

Your Franz K.

Don't put it away yet, I have read it through once more and see it is not clear. I wanted to write: What a wonderful stroke of luck for you that you can safely venture to grow careless when you are feeling tired, and yet be led to a point you are striving to reach without taking a step yourself, through the help of a friend who absolutely shares your thoughts; that is just the thing, when it is made a display of—that was what I thought to myself at Pr.'s—that shows you as I don't want you to be. That's enough of that now.

Absolute truthfulness was one of the most important and distinctive features of his character. Another distinguishing feature was his unimaginably precise conscientiousness. *Conscientia scrupulosa.* It revealed itself in all questions of a moral nature, where he could never overlook the slightest shadow of any injustice that occurred. From the very beginning one is reminded of debates in the Talmud; this method of reasoning was foreshadowed there too; at the same time, he didn't get to know the Talmud itself until much later on in life. Many of his works exhibit this trait, for example, "The Runners-by," in which the possibilities are discussed which could have led to one man's running behind another man in the night, but not running after him—or the great scene in *The Trial*, in which the legend "Before the Law" is discussed from various angles.

There were times when Franz himself could not get over tiny scruples, was afraid he had done this, that, or the other wrong, and admired, *e contrario*, every decision, particularly decisions concerning marriage, to an exaggerated degree. At the same time, as far as his own person was concerned, he

47

was brave, a good horseman, swimmer, and oarsman. His conscientiousness therefore arose from no cowardice, but from an unusually developed sense of responsibility. I remember going out for the evening with him once immediately after the news that Italy had declared war on Turkey (Tripoli) had been published. We were in the theater. Franz was unusually restless. During the interval he suddenly said, "Now the Italian battleships are taking up position before the undefended coasts." And the sad smile with which he said it! The condition of contemporary humanity seemed to him hopeless and desperate. And yet for all his deep pessimism one must not overlook his joy in everything that was healthy and growing, his interest in every kind of reform—e.g. in the methods of natural healing, in modern methods of education, such as the Montessori system. In the authors of the "night side," of the decadence, he felt as we have already said, not the slightest interest. It was to the simple positive forms of life that he was powerfully attracted. Among his favorite books were Stifter's "Indian Summer" and Hebel's "Little Treasury." In him there was a rare mixture of hopelessness and constructive urge which in his case did not cancel each other out but rose to endlessly complicated visions.

The artistic counterpart of the preciseness of his conscientiousness is the attention he gives to detail in his descriptions. You can see it in every one of his books. He loved detail. Under his influence I wrote a long descriptive novel which went into every detail, called "The Thousand Pleasures"—Franz and I sometimes called it also "The Happy Ones." Franz used to be enormously pleased every time I read him a new chapter I had finished, and urged me to go on with it (1909). I finished the book, but I never published more than one chapter of it, in a magazine, "Under the Intoxication of Books," a description of the university library—because in the end, despite lively protests from Kafka, the whole thing seemed to me too monstrous. Kafka's preference for thoroughness, for descriptions that ranged far and wide, was characteristically displayed in his life too. He was often late for appointments; not out of unpunctuality, but because he had felt the need to settle some other business absolutely exactly before leaving it. There was nothing that was unimportant, nothing that he would just "leave at that." He could no more be unjust to a thing or an everyday piece of work than he could to a human being. That was why when one was with him one had the impression strongly that nothing vulgar or "common" existed at all. Saints and founders of religions are said to have affected people similarly—and going about with Kafka has convinced me that such reports are based on real experience. The category of sacredness (and not really that of literature), is the only right category under which Kafka's life and work can be viewed. By this I do not wish to suggest that he was a perfect saint—that would be, even in his own sense, a thoroughly false, not to say iniquitous statement. But from the many indications, even taking all the proper caution that every step on this the last crest of human nature demands even from the observer himself, one may pose the thesis that Franz Kafka was on the road to becoming one. The explanation of his charming shyness and reserve, which seemed nothing less than supernatural—and yet so natural—and of his dismayingly severe self-criticism, lies in the fact that he measured himself by no ordinary standard, but simply measured himself up against the ultimate goal of human existence. Here, too, we can find one of the motives that held him back from publishing his works.

A characteristic that places him in the realm of the sacred was his absolute faith. He believed in a world of Rightness, he believed in "The Indestructible" of which so many of his aphorisms speak. We are too weak always to recognize this real world. But it is there. Truth is visible everywhere. It glints through the mesh of what we call "reality." This explains Kafka's deep interest in every detail, every wrinkle of this reality. In the diary there are to be found pages and pages of notes on the appearance, features, etc., of indifferent people, people sitting opposite him in the train, for instance. Immediately bound up with this interest is a pervading irony. Even the most gruesome episodes in Kafka's writings (*In* the Penal Colony, "The Whipper"—chapter v of *The Trial*) stand in a curious twilight of humor, an investigator's interest and tender irony. This humor, which is an essential ingredient of Kafka's writing (and of his manner of living), points through the meshes of reality to the divine existence beyond. His faith in this existence, never expressed in formulas, and never in a clumsy appeal to emotion, expressed itself in all his actions, made him at heart inwardly certain of himself, although he was fond of presenting himself and others with a picture of the uttermost uncertainty, made him above all spread around himself a sweet aura of certainty such as I have only very rarely felt elsewhere.

In everything he came into contact with Kafka looked for that which was important, that which came from this world of truth. That is why he was the best of listeners, the best of questioners, the best of readers and critics. How remote from his way of looking at things was all the talk about the "standards," "literary hallmarks," "distinction of rank." In every case he hit upon the essential. He could be carried away by a turn of speech in a newspaper article; with passionate enthusiasm he would dilate on the crowded life, the eye for drama, in some novel by some author or other who was generally sneered at as "cheap." I remember how, that time we were staying together in Schelesen in the Stüdl boarding-house, he produced a novel by Ohnet from the boarding-house library and, with great enthusiasm, read me a passage—a conversation—which he praised for its unforced liveliness. Odd passages in a musical comedy or a conventional film that had somehow come off and taken on organic shape as if by a miracle (the Muse had thrust the wretched author's pen on one side, and written a few lines herself) could move him to tears. He was an entirely independent explorer, who had not the faintest idea of being tied down by the insensitive classifications of histories of literature.

He passed judgment on people and conditions in exactly the same way. He had neither a prejudice in favor of going with conventional opinion, nor a prejudice in favor of going against it on principle. The most refreshing thing about him was that he was completely unparadoxical—in fact anti-paradoxical. His judgment had a certain elemental simplicity, naturalness, obviousness. It was easy and sure, although he delivered it with great care and was extremely, even passionately, ready to acknowledge a mistake.

In people, too, who were considered contemptible by the world in general, he saw admirable single qualities. He never lost patience, one might say, with any man. And in great men, whom he himself admired, he found ridiculous features. But when he emphasized comic details of this kind, there was never any suggestion of holding them up to derision in it, but rather a quiet tear and regret, or acknowledgment of something incomprehensible which passes our earthly understanding. The love he felt for Goethe and Flaubert never changed in all the two-and-twenty years I was a close friend of his. In the case of some writers, such as Hebbel and Grillparzer, Kafka liked their diaries better than their works—or so it seemed to me, at least. I have never heard him pass disrespectful remarks against the great, never heard him use the method of bluff which is so popular nowadays, and which consists in an impertinent and effectively delivered sneering reference to a writer's "youthful period" and his "puerilia." In this respect one may well say that Kafka had a very clear idea of the difference in rank there is among people. Only he also knew how easily the divine—and also the devilish—sparks overleap these classifications according to rank. And since he was too conscientious ever to simplify the picture of the world for himself, he watched this "overleaping" with a zeal for knowledge which one can only describe as fanatical.

His preciseness did not come from any cowardice which had to hide behind ideas, and was also not pedantic like Zola's preciseness. It was a quite special preciseness of genius, the peculiarity of which at first dumbfounded one, striking as it did a road which had previously lain hidden and which one had least expected, and then following this road with astonishing consistency right to the end—but in such a manner that one admitted that it was not capriciousness, it *was* a road of natural importance. Every chapter in *The Trial*,

51

in the other two novels *The Castle* and *Amerika,* and in the unfinished short stories demonstrates this astounding peculiarity of Kafka's plastic gift.

He never pointed the way out to you by saying: "Look, that is the right road"—or even by saying as much as, "That is a road, too." He simply marched on with firm step, realistically, without using philosophical terms (for his thinking, as his wonderful diary shows, was generally done in the form of images), absorbed only in observing the detail which the ever-changing vistas of the road crowded in on him.

The strangeness of Kafka's person and writing is only apparent. In fact, one should add, anyone who finds Kafka singular and attractive on account of his *bizarrerie* has not yet understood him, or perhaps may be in the first stages of understanding him. Kafka traced to their source the individual and the unobvious with such love and preciseness that things came to light which one had never before suspected, which seem strange indeed and yet are nothing but true. Such, too, was his way of looking at a moral duty, a fact of life, a journey, a work of art, a political movement—never bizarre, but only very exact, keen, right, and in consequence different from everyday talk, in consequence, perhaps, also quite often (though not perhaps always) unsuitable for what one calls "practical life."

There is no more pregnant contrast to Kafka than Balzac's sham preciseness, Balzac's superlatives and generalizations (something after this style: "She walked along with that light tread with which every Paris woman walks between ten and ten-fifteen in the morning").

It is superfluous to point out (superfluous that is for anyone who has even half followed the above) that Kafka found much to admire in Balzac. For he never lost the grand line in the mass of details nor the sweep of a way of life. Kafka once said: "Balzac carried a stick with the motto, 'I break every obstacle'—my motto would rather be, 'Every obstacle breaks me.'"

This would be the right place to drag in a long list of remarks on Kafka's weaknesses which, however, on the whole, spring in the most tragic fashion from his good qualities. By discussing the one feature of his character "preciseness," I have indicated only one side of his being. One could go on explaining and explaining (people will undoubtedly do so), but necessarily without coming to an end. It is like walking forever along a wall without a door—one can never penetrate the inside of the building. But even this endless and vain explaining does give some kind of picture of Kafka's personality, gives a picture at the same time of its force, its weight, its inexhaustibility. This is the same method, by the way, in which Kafka portrays his characters, without ever explaining them to the end.

Of course I can now no longer sort out exactly how my opinion of Kafka developed and was perfected in the course of the years—what was there from the very beginning and how gradually it grew. I know only this; in the beginning our relations developed very slowly, and it took some years before we became really intimate.

It began with a decision we made not to let the Greek we had picked up in our secondary schools get too rusty. Together we read Plato's *Protagoras* with the aid of translations and our school dictionary—often with a great deal of difficulty. At that time I never got as far as the real meaning which Plato was to have for me much later—long after Kafka's death; what we enjoyed chiefly was undoubtedly nothing more than the vivid and scurrilous description of the life of the Sophists, and the Plato-Socratic irony. If the reading of Plato was due to my inspiration (for I have been drawn to this great star at various periods in my life), it was Kafka who, to my gratitude, brought Flaubert to my attention. This great love I inherited from him. We read *A Sentimental Education* and the *Temptation of St. Anthony* in the original. As we could find time for these studies only two or three times a week, we went on together with this work for years, and it provided us with continual fresh material for a long time. Our reading parties generally took place in Kafka's little room in his parents' house (in Zeltner street) and sometimes at my place. Over Kafka's desk there hung a copy of the picture by Hans Thoma, "The Ploughmen." On the wall at the side there was a yellowing plaster cast of a little antique relief, a maenad brandishing a piece of meat—a leg of beef, to be precise. The graceful folds of her dress danced around the figure, which had no head. All that I still see before me just as my eyes swept over it countless times. I have described it in my novel *The Kingdom of Love*, in which Kafka appears as Richard Garta, together with the simple, almost miserly furnishings of the room which were of an almost provisory nature. "The whole not uninhabitable, but not perhaps comfortable for people who want the conventional ornaments and luxury." This modest furniture accompanied Franz to all his lodgings in Prague: a bed, a wardrobe, the little, old, dark brown, almost black, desk, with a few books and a lot of unarranged notebooks. His last room (in Niklas street) had at least a second entrance which Kafka generally used, through the kitchen and the bathroom. Otherwise he didn't live apart from the rest of the family, which was certainly not healthy for the conflicts that were ever inwardly consuming him. In later years he tried to get away from the spell of not being independent by taking a room of his own in a different district. (Proust lived in the room of his childhood until he died.)

The above-mentioned picture by Thoma, a *Kunstwart* print, bears witness to the great influence that a friend from his secondary schooldays, Oskar Pollak, had on Kafka at the time when I first got to know him. Pollak had gone deeply into the theories of the *Kunstwart* series of handbooks, which were edited by Avenarius, and out of which later the Dürer League grew. At the university Pollak began by reading chemistry; that Kafka, too, began with fourteen days of chemistry happened most probably for the sake of Pollak, whose special gifts of leadership are hinted at also in Franz's letters to him. Pollak afterwards went to Vienna and Rome as a historian of art; baroque and modern art, the architectural history of Prague and Rome were his chief fields of activity and he furthered them by important work of extraordinary scientific import, founded on meticulous studies of sources. The young professor fell on the Isonzo front as a volunteer in the Austrian army in 1915. Among the riches of his posthumous papers was found, ready for print, the manuscript of a two-volume work on "Art Activities under Pope Urban VII," which has since been published, as well as drafts of manuscripts on the papacies of Innocent II and Alexander VII, preliminary notes for a bibliography of the guidebooks of Rome, and the beginnings of a collection of material for a monograph on Pietro da Cortona, and other fragments. One of the wild ironies of war—the scholar who had devoted most of his life to the love of Italian art, must needs have his life ended by Italian bullets! In the *Neue Züricher Zeitung* of August 27, 1915, J. A. F. Orbaan, of Geneva, paid honor to the man who died "crowned with the halo of science." After praising several essays of his, e.g. the keenly critical tone of his "Architects' Fairy Stories," he goes on: "It is no wonder that we so tensely awaited the publication of the 'Sources of Baroque,' which he had planned in the grand manner, and the first volume of which, dealing with a section of the art life of Rome, he had reserved for himself, and which was to be followed in a reasonably short while by a critical edition of Baglione's *Careers of Artists*. We knew that our excellent colleague was, in the first place, on intimate terms with the actual works of art, through his many wanderings in Rome and about it, an advantage which not all art historians possess, because the libraries and the archives often claim all their strength. We knew it from our daily meetings with him when we saw his kindly, tanned face in the Vatican early in the morning, after he had the previous day collected together in out-of-the-way parts of Latium a rich booty of notes and negatives of the country seats and churches of the Barberini. With the same spirit of enterprise he would then sit down to a pile of books of the managing board of the Fabbrica di San Pietro, the Barberini library, the Papal Treasury, or of rare books of the seicento, completely at home with the bookkeeping of antiquity and able to decipher the cacography and technical language of master-builders and master-painters long since passed away. A learned conversation with the

55

ever-interested Pollak on the remote theme of the paleography of baroque was always worth while. He achieved astonishing results in the interpretation of entries written almost in shorthand, which you find here and there in some firm's books, where important information about Giovanni Lorenzo Bernini may be waiting round the corner at any moment. But with all this work, which demanded a severe daily dose of research into manuscript sources and other literature of the same kind, Pollak never had anything about him of the superfluous, and always awkward, self-importance of the savant. He was in deadly earnest, and he brought every ounce of effort and brain-power to bear on his work, but his studies did not make him any the less capable of enjoying the pleasures and excitement of the moment and these were offered him in plenty by his marriage with a witty and affectionate young wife, who showed a fine understanding for what he was striving to do, and by the time he spent in the company of a wide circle of friends and acquaintances including people of the country."

This, then, was the man who won a decisive influence over Kafka in his younger days. To complete the picture I shall quote from an obituary by Hugo Bergmann (*Bohemia,* July 4, 1915). "The richness of his interests was inexhaustible; but to whatever it might be that got hold of him and carried him away at one time or another, he devoted himself completely, forgot everything else for its sake, and in no time became a disciple and a gospeler. In this way he studied the Upanishad, the Bible, Luther, St. Francis of Assisi, the Italian short story tellers of the Renaissance—with what purity he could read the *Decameron* to us—in this way he took up playing the guitar, and sport of various kinds." I hear he was one of the first to take up skiing in Bohemia.

I myself remember Oskar Pollak as a young man who passed severe judgments and knew his own mind. Despite his nineteen years he wore a full beard. This, I now discover after my researches, he later discarded together with a certain abruptness and stand-offishness of manner, which at that time made any approach to him no easy matter. Him, too, I met in the "Hall." On that occasion he recommended to me the "Rembrandt-German." The most serious Jewish intellectualism, unconscious of its origin, revealed facets, at that time, which had many analogies with, and tried to take lessons from, a Teutonism that was groping into the past for its pure wells of strength. So far as I know, Oskar Pollak never bothered himself with truly Jewish questions, and it was not until very much later that Kafka and I came to this our home ground. The love of Teutonism led, in all honesty, and so to speak, innocence of heart, occasionally also to pure Teutomania. For example, in one of Kafka's letters to Oskar Pollak you may find the following passage, which sounds odd to the ear of a connoisseur of Kafka's later style:

"Just opposite the vineyard, on the road, deep in the valley, stands a tiny cottage, the first and the last in the village. There isn't much in it. Between you and me it's worth at the outside a miserable hundred shillings. And what is still worse not even Schultze-Naumburg could find a use for it, unless, at most, as a hideous warning. In all probability I and the owner are the only people who love it and weave our dreams about it. It is small and squat. It isn't even old. On the contrary, it's a modest five or ten years old at most. It has a tiled roof, a tiny door, through which one can obviously only crawl, and a window on either side. Everything is symmetrical, as though it had crept out of a school textbook. But—the door is of heavy wood, painted brown, the shutters are painted brown, and always shut, in sunshine or in rain. And yet the house is inhabited, too. And in front of the door is a broad, heavy, stone bench, which appears to be almost old. And when one day three apprentices come along with their sticks in their hands and their all-too-light knapsacks on their backs, and sit down on it to rest, and wipe the sweat from their brows, and then lean their heads together—I can see all this quite well from up above—then it is like a dear, old, peaceful German fairy story."

The influence of the works of art and art values which *Kunstwart* propagated is here clearly revealed in every detail. When it concerns a writer who, like Kafka, so early developed his own quite personal attitude in which scarcely a trace of outside influence can any longer be felt, to know of this beginner's stage of dependence strikes one as nothing less than grotesque, and, at the same time, touching, it seems to me.

The letters to Oskar Pollak are from the years 1902 till 1904. In this case Kafka wooed the friendship; in his friendship with me, which broke up this first strong spiritual tie, things were rather the other way round. At least, Kafka was the stronger partner in our friendship, if through nothing else than his calm and reserve, even though a foundation of equality of rights was cheerfully acknowledged on either side. It is with astonishment that I learn from Kafka's youthful letters to Pollak that he himself offered to send him his writings, or to read them to him. That never happened later—one had to plead hard with Kafka, and bring fervent pressure to bear on him before one could get him to show one anything in his manuscripts. This attitude was not, all the same, founded on pride, but on immoderate self-criticism. It began very early with him. Thus the fifth letter to Pollak is followed by an unpublished one, from which I quote, with the additional inducement that it tells us something about these first works of Kafka's which have not survived: "Of the few thousand lines I am giving you there might be perhaps ten that I could listen to patiently, the flourish of trumpets in my previous letter was unnecessary, instead of a revelation emerges childish scribbling. . . . The greatest part of it, I openly say, I find repulsive. 'Morning,' for example, and other bits, too—I find it impossible to read it all, and I am satisfied if you can stand odd samples. But you must remember I began at a time when one 'created work,' when one wrote high-flown stuff; there is no worse time to begin. And I was so mad about grand phrases. Among my papers there is a sheet on which are written all the uncommon and particularly impressive names I could find in the calendar. You see I needed two names for a novel, and chose finally two, underlined, Johannes and Beate—Renate had already been snatched
58

from under my nose [1]—because of the size of their halo. It is almost funny."

In this letter there are some mischievous remarks about another schoolfellow, who had an inexhaustible store of words—"they were bars of iron, and I was driven to despair when I saw how easily he threw them around. There was no hope of my approaching it, and I vowed never again in all my life to be so jealous as I was then." This is followed by even severer self-criticism. "There is one thing that is entirely missing in these copy-books, that is hard work, perseverance, and whatever all these strange things are called." In the next paragraph he writes again, "What I lack is discipline. That you half read the copy-books is the least I want from you today. You have a lovely room. The little lights from the shops below twinkle, tucked away, and busily. I want you to let me read to you there every Saturday, beginning from the very next Saturday ever, for half an hour. I am going to work hard for three months. Above all, I know this now: Art needs hard work more than hard work needs art. Of course I don't believe that one can force oneself to give birth, but one can force oneself to look after the children."

I don't know how Oskar Pollak received the works of Kafka which were submitted to his severe judgment, whether he admired him as I did from the very start; to be honest, as I felt I had to admire him. Oskar Pollak's interests certainly lay in rather a different direction from Kafka's fantastic microcosm, which, particularly at that period, had a specially whimsical air—it was just the extraordinariness, the unrepeatable newness of it that pleased me. The first friend of his youth, who left Prague very soon afterwards, was drawn to great things, to the laws of science. So Kafka's cry of longing fell at first on deaf ears—the cry that rings so movingly through the letters and thus early anticipates the later longing for community: "You will never do anything without other men"; "To become a hermit is abhorrent"; and the polemic, which affects one, one can only say like

[1] Allusion to an early work of Wassermann's.

prophecy, against "the Mole," which became a symbol in Kafka's late period. "I know that were a pair of stranger's eyes to look at it, they would make everything warmer and more alive"—for me that is the vital sentence of the young Kafka in this pursuit, in this friendship about which I first learned from a study of the letters, and to which, remarkably enough, Franz himself hardly ever made a definite allusion in my hearing. Perhaps it never got further than a trial friendship, and no real relationship ever came out of it; Kafka's later silence—there is no mention of it in the diary—would seem to me to point to this. But that does not in the least affect the greatness of the molding influence his first comrade had on him. He disappeared from our sight, first to take up a job as a tutor in the country, and then to his famous scientific work in Rome. From time to time we used to hear how he would show and explain the architectural monuments of Rome to friends, visitors to Rome from our circle, in a particularly kindly way, with no trace of gruffness any longer, and of course extraordinarily knowledgeably. Then the dreadful news of his death at far too early an age shocked us.

I went about with Kafka for several years without knowing that he wrote. I myself had already published several things in newspapers and magazines, and my first book appeared in 1906. Perhaps the first mention that my friend made to me of his literary activities was when he told me he had sent in a short story for a competition in the Vienna newspaper *Zeit*. He sent it in under the pseudonym "Heaven in Narrow Streets." That may possibly have been the title of the story as well, I can't remember exactly any longer. The entry did not gain a mention in the competition, and has disappeared.

Then one day, in 1909, he read me the beginning of a novel which was called "Preparations for a Wedding in the Country." Parts of the manuscript survive in unpublished form. The hero's name was Raban. Here, too, is a reference to the "ego," through the philological similarity of the two names Kafka and Raban,[1] like that which Franz himself analyzed in the

[1] Kafka, remember, means jackdaw, while Raban is similar to the German *Rabe*=raven. Note, too, the two *a*'s in Kafka and Raban.

name of the hero of his short story "The Verdict," which is Bendemann. Raban, as the first chapter tells us, leaves his workshop to go and see his fiancée who lives in the country. The first chapter describes, with great detail, in the twilight of humor, no more than the journey to the station, a rainy afternoon, and a few meetings with casual acquaintances. It is extraordinary. I was overpowered and delighted.[1]

I got the impression immediately that here was no ordinary talent speaking, but a genius. My efforts to bring Kafka's works before the public began from that moment—an endeavor that was stronger than myself, and which indeed I made no effort to fight against, because I considered it right and natural. Franz resisted sometimes with greater, sometimes with less violence, sometimes not at all: one cannot say that he always on principle adopted an attitude of disapproval (after all, apart from other things, his entering in the competition I mentioned above shows this). Naturally he, too, sometimes felt pleased over literary success. There was, I must admit, generally a deprecatory smile there at the same time; but once I saw him very angry at an unfavorable ununderstanding criticism in the "Almanack" of the Dürer League. In general his hopes and fears were directed towards quite other things than literary reputation, which was not exactly unpleasant to him, but unimportant. The whole business of publicity didn't interest him very much, did not occupy his feelings very much—so that his shrinking from publication (apart from certain later periods in his life) was a matter of no great fuss, no passion.

I mentioned his works, which had not yet been published at all, in the Berlin weekly *Die Gegenwart,* by adding his

[1] The impression this made on me was increased, if that were possible, when he read me his short story, "Description of a Battle." (The date of this in my diary is March 14, 1910.) The draft of this work, which Franz did not value very highly—in fact on March 18, 1910 he wrote to me, "Dear Max, the thing that pleases me most about the short story is that I have got rid of it"—and the manuscript of which I took home with me, because he wanted to destroy it, dates back several years I am sure, and points distinctly to the period of family dances, to the time he was at the university. On studying my diary closer, I discover that this was not the first of his works that Kafka showed me.

name to a list I gave of prominent authors (Blei, Mann, Wedekind, and Meyrink). This must have been the first public reference to Kafka's name (February 9, 1907). Kafka wrote me a letter full of humor about this "carnival-like" first appearance before the public. I was certainly displaying a certain amount of high spirits in thus offering to the public the name of a writer a single line of whose had not been printed at the time, in the same breath with very big names, as though everyone should have heard of him. A little joke, of no importance. "Very well, so I have had one dance this winter after all," Franz mocked.

It was not until 1909 that some of Kafka's prose works were printed for the first time, in Franz Blei's journal, *Hyperion*. (Blei had come out very warmly in favor of my first book, "Death to the Dead," and afterwards often came to Prague, and I introduced him to Kafka.) The second published work was "The Aeroplanes at Brescia" (September 28, 1909) which appeared in the Prague daily, *Bohemia*. The third was published in the Easter supplement to *Bohemia* on March 27, 1910. In it, under the general title of "Contemplations," will be found the following works: "At the Window," "At Night," "Clothes," "The Passenger," "Thoughts for Gentlemen Riders." Nobody took any notice of these writings which it cost me so much energy to get published. (In book form, entitled "Contemplation" [in the singular], these pieces are called "Distracted Gazing," "The Runners-by," and then as above, "Clothes," "The Passenger" and "Thoughts for Gentlemen Riders." Franz Blei had published two passages from the story "Description of a Battle."

In 1908 Max Bäuml, the friend of my childhood, died.

From then on my relations with Franz grew deeper. We met daily, sometimes even twice a day. The whole time Franz was in Prague (it was only later that his illness forced him to live in the country, in sanatoriums), we kept up this custom. When we had both achieved the longed-for post "with a single shift" (i.e. with no afternoon duty), as chance would have it, we both went the same way home from our offices. So I used to wait for Franz every day at two o'clock in the afternoon by the "Powder Tower"—how well and thoroughly I studied the beautifully wrought, old double-headed imperial eagle on the gable of the provincial head office of the internal revenue, on the corner of Hyberner lane, because Franz was always later than I—he had something extra to do in the office, or got lost in conversation with his colleagues—with my stomach rumbling, I used to stride up and down; but my anger was quickly forgotten, when the slim, tall figure of my friend hove in sight, generally with an embarrassed smile that was intended rather to simulate than really to express utter fright, nay horror, at being so frightfully late. At the same time he would hold his hand clasped to his heart. This gesture meant, "I am innocent." What is more, he came along at the run, so that one really couldn't say anything very furious to him. As we walked along together the same way from Zeltner street to the Old Town Square, there was always no end of things we had to tell each other, and when we did reach Franz's house, it was still a long time before we could finish talking. And in the afternoon or evening we were together again.

In my novel *The Kingdom of Love,* in the figure of Richard Garta I have set down very much of what remains of Kafka in my heart and memory. Write an objective biography of Kafka!—that I felt I could not do at that time, four years after his death. It is only now, after nine more years have passed, thirteen years, that is, after the catastrophe, that I can bring myself to do it. At that time, however, I *lived* still with my unforgettable friend, he was present with me in the truest sense of the word, always by my side, I knew exactly what he would have said in this or that situation, exactly how he would have thought about things that went on round about me. I asked him questions, and could answer myself in his name. That is how I came to feel the necessity of bringing my incomparable friend to life in the form of a living work of art, not in a historical study collecting dates and carefully piecing facts together, but as an epic figure. Above all, I wanted to bring him to life for myself in this new way. So long as I lived in this book, in working at it, he was not dead,

63

he still lived with me and still exerted his influence on my life. (You will find that the whole treatment of the novel serves this purpose.) But this was misunderstood just as everything else is—people found it odd, or even incompatible with my reverence for Kafka. Nobody remembered that Plato in a similar, although of course much more comprehensive way, defied Death and all his life long kept his friend and mentor Socrates alive and functioning still, as a companion who lived and thought together with him, by making him the protagonist of almost every dialogue he wrote after Socrates' death.

Here I shall take out of this novel (for otherwise I should have to repeat myself) the passage about the first books to which Kafka drew my attention. Apart from Flaubert, whom I have already mentioned, there were also Stefan George, two volumes of whose work Kafka gave me, one on each of two birthdays, the marvelous prose translation of Chinese lyrics by Heilmann, not to be mentioned in the same breath with later imitations in rhyme and watered-down versions by other authors, and further, Robert Walser. On the unobtrusive way Kafka had of making his friend (who is called Christof in the novel) fonder of his own favorite authors, on the whole spirit of the first years of our friendship, and on the way it was intensified after Max Bäuml's death, I could not find anything more apt to say than what I wrote in *The Kingdom of Love:*

"Garta does not persuade one, that is not his way, and he does not evolve a system—systems are not much in his line. What he does is read to you over and over again this or that passage from his favorite authors in his rapid, unemotional voice that, at the same time, creates a sense of rhythm and climax, with a throbbing chant in the background, with his eyes flashing, surrendering himself utterly to joy in human greatness; except that now and then he quietly curls his lip, not at all mischievously, but rather in gleeful skepticism— well, well!—when some bit seemed to him not quite to have come off, or to be painfully exaggerated. Anything forced, in any artistic expression, he always thrusts as far away from

64

him as possible, unless it be that as an effort it is at least genuine, and the writer cannot avoid it, in which case it ad-. mittedly betrays his occasional weaknesses and demands only sympathy with what his other deeds show him capable of. In short, he does not canvass for his chosen ones, he always sees clearly, there is clarity even in his most unbounded enthusiasm, he never attempts to rush Christof off his feet; on the contrary it often comes to Christof, being the one who is all aflame for the works that Garta revealed to him, and who even feels he must rush to the defense on behalf of some parts of them, against Garta. All this is done with the pleasantest earnestness, it is a gracious mutual education on the part of each; there is no breath of vanity or pretense; both have the feeling that at this very moment the whole world differentiates itself into purest truth and worthlessness. Not only that, but this feeling does not make them proud, or excessively worried, or crushed under responsibility. It is quite a simple feeling—the Good is there, and it lies in our power either to follow after it, or, which would be senseless folly, to reject it. But who, who would do that! So they enter joyfully into the land of 'The Spirit' which is otherwise hidden from the poor children of men by millions of reservations, chances, sorrows, passions, considerations; but in this case it has revealed itself for once quite simply in all the bright, health-giving light of its eternal splendor, it lies there—invitingly great.

"Then comes the decisive turn of events—Christof's first friend, who passed through all the eight classes of his secondary school with him, dies. A few days after the funeral Christof, sad unto death, goes for a walk with Richard Garta in the evening. It is the 'Kleinseite,' dark castle stairways rise above them. 'Will you . . . fill his place for me?' he asks, stammering, knowing in the deep distress of his heart that he is asking an impossible question—and yet feeling that there was something justifiable, courageous, and good about the question, and that this was fully recognized by Garta. Only there is no other way in which it can be recognized than by a long, deep silence. Then they walk through many a narrow, winding street, side by side, still in silence, and Christof thinks he can feel the presence of his good, loving friend who is dead, and with whom really his whole boyhood died—the memory of countless things they went through together at school, of first perceptions and sorrows, narrow but deep scars in the heart. When one is at school, friendship comes of itself, but afterwards it must be won, fought for indeed, and finally even this becomes impossible. That is the law of the world of men. . . . The question, and the answer that was never given, were never mentioned again. But from this night on the parting handshake of the two friends is heartier and longer."

Reading together and exchanging our favorite authors may have been the first thing that brought us clearly together, but alongside this great and noble circumstance there was from the beginning an immense number of little circumstances, almost unnoticeable, in which we formed the complement to one another. If I don't wish to pretend false modesty, I must at this point confess that Kafka felt he benefited just as much from me as I did from him. My initiative and energy were the characteristics that especially appealed to him in me. Looking at things objectively, I was not at all so unreflectively bold and unconcerned as he perhaps saw me. If I were writing my own biography now, I should know how to explain and illustrate that in great detail. As it is, it is enough to state that, in comparison with Kafka, it was I who was the adventurer and that I really was. What fascinated me about Kafka I am at liberty to explain in greater detail. He had an unusual aura of power about him, such as I have never met anywhere else, even when I met very important, famous men. I have often tried to analyze this peculiarity, after Kafka's death that is, because while he was alive it made itself felt in a way so naturally and so completely taken for granted, that the idea of thinking about it never struck one. Perhaps the best way to express this remarkable, extremely personal characteristic is this; the unintermittent compactness of his ideas could not endure a gap, he never spoke a meaningless word. Everything that came from him,

66

came in a way that became less and less forced as the years went on, a precious expression of his quite special way of looking at things—patient, life-loving, ironically considerate towards the follies of the world, and therefore full of sad humor, but never forgetful of the real kernel, "The Indestructible," and so always far from being blasé or cynical. Yes, that was it—in his presence the everyday world underwent a transformation, everything was new, new in a way that was often very sad, not to say shattering, but which never precluded the possibility of final consolation because it was never dull, and never flat. In a thousand easy ways, so it seemed, his powers of observation caught connections, of which one had never dreamed, but which had nothing arbitrary, nothing "surrealistic," [1] or wayward about them, but were true connections, minute but faithful perceptions, from which one felt a strong urge to build up a completely new system of knowledge—without failing to realize that the attempt to know the world and the souls of men in such meticulous detail is of course justified and even very essential and yet may easily have to be reckoned among those things which, like Kafka's *Great Wall of China,* or *The Trial,* can never, by their very nature, come to an end.

In addition, it was not only on me, but on many others that Kafka had the effect I have described. Among the friends and in the hospitable house of Mrs. Bertha Franta, where precise philosophy was discussed, with the lady of the house taking a zealous part in the discussions, Kafka had a very high reputation—simply by virtue of his personality, his occasional remarks, and his conversation—because no one at that time beyond myself knew his literary work. There was no need of his works, the man produced his own effect himself, and despite all the shyness of his behavior, he was always quickly recognized by men of worth as someone out of the ordinary. At all periods of his life women felt themselves drawn to Franz—he himself doubted he had this effect, but the fact cannot be disputed.

[1] The word did not exist at that time. The surrealists of today claim Kafka as one of themselves without foundation.

How markedly a special spell pervaded every living utterance of Kafka's, how you can except from this not a word, not a line that he wrote—be it on a casual picture postcard, or just wishing someone many happy returns, or dedicating a book—appears from the following express messages and short notes which he wrote to me. Generally they contain only cancellations of a rendezvous, or apologies—as we saw each other every day there was no other reason for writing to each other, except when one of us occasionally failed to turn up. Even for these everyday bits of information, Franz never had a conventional, ready formula. And that is why just these writings hastily tossed off (they deal with the period of our studies, the law examinations and then first work in the office) appear to me to be especially characteristic documents of a boundlessly rich spirit which never succumbed to routine or convention. Here are some specimens:

1

I am now half delighted that I am actually studying at last, and for that reason will not come to our café this week. I would very much like to be there, because I never study after 7 o'clock; but if I do take a little change of this kind, it disturbs my studies all day the next day. And I daren't waste any time. So it's better for me to read my *Kügelgen* [1] in the evening, a splendid occupation for a little mind and for sleep when it comes. Love to you.

Franz

2

Dear Max

Now I was nearly forgetting it after all. To write and tell you, I can't go to the exhibition tomorrow, I can't go at all any more. You see I've let myself be led astray, and elected to sit for my finals at a stupidly early date, while my knowledge is not even infinitesimal. Now that would be irrespon-

[1] A famous book of memoirs by Wilhelm von Kügelgen.

68

sible, and for that reason very nice, if I didn't keep on thinking of the doctor's certificate that I shall soon have made out for me, to enable me to withdraw. How are things with the *Amethyst?* [*Note.*—A periodical published by Franz Blei that we subscribed to between us.] I've got my money prepared already.—So take a look round at the exhibition, and see if there isn't anything attractive that you can buy for a small sum. Perhaps it might do for a wedding present.

Your Franz

3

Now, dear fellow, I shan't be able to go out anywhere for a bit. The Dean has been so irresponsible as to fix my finals a little earlier and as I was ashamed to be more cautious than he, I've made no protest. All my love.

Franz

4

Dear Max

Forgive me for yesterday evening, please! I shall come to your place at five o'clock. My excuse will be a little comic, so you are quite sure to believe it.

Your Franz

5

My dear Max

I am a completely useless person, really, but nothing can be done about it. Yesterday afternoon I sent you a letter by special messenger: "Here in the tobacconist's in the Graben I beg you to forgive me for not being able to come tonight. I have a headache, my teeth are falling out, my razor is blunt, I am an unpleasant object to look at.—*Your F.*"

And now in the evening I go and lie down on my sofa and reflect that I have made my excuses anyhow, and that there is again a little order in the world, but as I am thinking it over, I suddenly remember that I wrote Wladislaw street [*Note.*—Oskar Pollak's address. I was living in Schalen street at that time], instead of Schalen street.

Now, please, I beg of you, be annoyed about it, and don't speak to me any more because of it. I am utterly on the downward path, and—I can see far enough for that—I can't help going to the dogs. Also I should love to cut myself, but as that is impossible, there is only one thing I can rejoice about, and that is that I have no pity on myself, and so I have at last become egoistic to that extent. We should celebrate achieving this height—you and I, I mean; just as a future enemy, you should celebrate it.

It is late. I should like you to know that I wished you a very good night tonight.

Your Franz

6

By speedy work in the office, we have earned our lunch. Forgive me if I don't come today, I should have done something on Sunday, and neglected to do it, because Sunday is short. In the morning one sleeps, in the afternoon one washes one's hair, and in the evening one goes for a stroll as though one were a lounge lizard. I always use Sunday as a springboard for pleasure, which is rather ridiculous. Write and tell me when you are free except for Thursday and Friday. All the best.

Your Franz

7

My dear Max

We are beginning a race for unreliability and unpunctuality. Of course I don't hope to be first in this race, because I am only simply unpunctual through Italian industry,[1] but you through your lust for pleasure. But since you are trying to make it up by being ready to come and see me (Wednesday, I believe?) that is all right with me again. But perhaps you are only doing it because it is easier to put off a visit than a visitor.

Your Franz

[1] He was taking Italian lessons before going on his journey to Riva.

70

My Max

I am in such a bad way that I think I can only get over it
by not speaking to anyone for a week, or as long as may be
necessary. From the fact that you won't try to answer this
postcard in any way, I shall see that you are fond of me.

Your Franz

My dearest Max

This, a soiled, but my most beautiful picture postcard,
is a kiss from me to you—and in front of the whole populace! As I believe you much more than I do myself, I
thought yesterday it was really my fault, only I considered it
didn't make so much difference, because we still have a long
time to live. But if things are as you write, and I am already
again convinced that they are, then it is all the better, and
you will soon be coming up in the lift after all. Besides, I am
in such a good mood today, as though I were beginning to
live, and your card fits in so nicely too, for what a nice friendship it must be if it begins in such a way. You don't frighten
me at all with the date, because after all you will get your
job before then, and if not, "The Maid" [1] is coming out—it is
coming out in any case, apart from everything else, so what
more do you want, I ask you? In the night one can wish for
still more: but in the morning?

10

My dear Max

It looks as if I shall not be able to come. This morning, just
as I was looking forward to the afternoon and evening, I was
told I must go to the office in the afternoon; lunch time, as I
was looking forward to the evening only, I was told I must be
in the shop in the afternoon and the evening. There is a lot to
do, one of the assistants is ill, and father is not too well.

[1] A short novel by me, "A Czech Maidservant."

There would be murder if I didn't stay in the shop till eight, and probably there would be if I went away at night.

So forgive me nicely, please!

11

My dearest Max

Look, if I go on like this, all the people I like will be angry with me except the one, and she doesn't love me anyhow. The story of my life yesterday is simple. I was there until 10 o'clock, and in the bar until 1 o'clock. At half-past seven, when your music had already begun, I suppose, I still heard the clock strike. My mother and my father are not feeling well, my grandfather is ill, they are distempering the dining-room, and the whole family is living in my room as though it were a gipsy caravan. This afternoon I must go to the shop. I haven't the courage to make my excuses to Baum. Don't desert me.

Your Franz

12

But your memory, dear Max! I remember so exactly. In front of your house on Sunday night, I shook myself and said, "Tuesday, I am going to such-and-such a place." You said, "Come on Wednesday." I, "I shall be tired, and I want to go and see Pr. . . ." "Come on Thursday then." "All right." So Thursday I did come to see you. In any case I am in such a state that even justifiable reproaches would be too much for me.

13

My dear Max

You are lucky you are not at home; you are getting out of several little kindnesses you might have liked to have done for me. I am lucky, because I can all the more easily and firmly beg you to forgive me, and to make my excuses to the world if I can't manage to get to Baum's before nine o'clock. We have some relations staying with us. What is more, on

Monday at five o'clock I am coming to see you for a moment. If I am disturbing you in any work, please refuse to see me.

Your Franz

14

Dear Max

You know I have a job, so a New Year has begun, and my worries, granted that up till now they went on foot, now follow suit and go on their hands. I should very much like to see you at 2.30 near the statue of the Madonna in the Square, punctually. Please, make it possible!

Your Franz K.

15

Dear Max

Written in the street, as we shall always write to each other from now on, because the shoves you get from people passing by gives life to the writing.

I am in front of a photograph of Paula K. Yesterday I saw her in the flesh several times. She stood for a while, and for a while she walked all white along Hyberner street with a young man who was wearing unpressed trousers. Just to get hold of something solid: her teeth are all over the place in her mouth, on the right cheek only she has a dimple, her complexion is fairly moldy, covered with ashes, not with powder at all; obviously her complexion takes a rest by day. I am coming on Thursday. Do me a favor and work hard.

Franz

If one tried to quote verbal utterances of Kafka's, to complete these occasional written utterances in which it is just the fact that they are occasional that lights up and makes clear the genius that is in them, one could go on forever. But let me quote a few examples. He was coming to see me one afternoon—I was still living with my parents then—and his coming in woke up my father. Instead of apologizing, he said, in an indescribably gentle way, raising a hand as if to calm him and walking softly on tiptoe through the room,

"Please look on me as a dream." Once he went to the Berlin aquarium with a lady, who told me the story later with emotion. Suddenly he began to speak to the fish in their illuminated tanks, "Now at last I can look at you in peace, I don't eat you any more." It was the time that he turned strict vegetarian. If you have never heard Kafka saying things of this sort with his own lips, it is difficult to imagine how simply and easily, without any affectation, without the least sentimentality—which was something almost completely foreign to him—he brought them out. Among my notes I find something else that Kafka said about vegetarianism. He compared vegetarians with the early Christians, persecuted everywhere, everywhere laughed at, and frequenting dirty haunts. "What is meant by its nature for the highest and the best, spreads among the lowly people." In the same notes, which I made while Kafka was still alive, I find: "Theosophy is nothing but a surrogate for literature" (literature in our use of the word at that time, was used in Flaubert's sense of the word—meant real literature). "Insurance [1] is like the religions of primitive peoples who believe they can ward off evil by all kinds of manipulations." "Karl Kraus confines the Jewish writers into his own hell, guards them well, and keeps them under stern discipline. The only thing he forgets is that his proper place is in the same hell with them." He told me that his "loveliest dream" was that he "was sitting in a boat, and flying along an empty river-bed." Talking about his headaches, a frightful tension in the temples, he said, "It's the sort of feeling a pane of glass must have in the spot where it cracks." Talking about a fir tree lightly covered with snow, when he was taking a walk with me, in Schelesen in the winter, he said, "They haven't yet had a headache so long as I have"; at the time his deep black hair had gone gray at the temples. Talking about a play he had written—probably "The Watchman of the Tomb"—when we very much wanted to hear it, he said, "The only thing about the play that is not dilettantish, is that I shall *not* read it to you." (From Oskar Baum's "Memories of Franz Kafka," in *Witiko*, 1929, Part 3.)

[1] The reference is to Kafka's daily work.

At the beginning of 1911, I made this note: On Sundays Kafka goes for walks by himself, without any objective, without thinking. He says, "Every day I wish myself off the earth." "There is nothing wrong with me except myself." He has done no work. In the afternoons he sleeps or looks at the papers in the Arts and Crafts Museum. In company, he is cheerful, full of humor, as a critic, unsurpassable for his witty observations; with his conversation it is the same; it could and should all be written down. When asked what after all was responsible for his sad condition, and why he couldn't write, he said, "I have hundreds of wrong feelings— dreadful ones—the right ones won't come out—or if they do, only in rags; absolutely weak." I protest (in reply) that when one is writing one sometimes has to work one's way through one's first worthless ideas in order to come to the nobler thoughts that lie beneath them. He answers, "That's all right for you, but not for me—that would mean giving these wrong feelings the upper hand." Here is another conversation I noted down that I had with him on February 28, 1920. He: "We are nihilistic thoughts that came into God's head." I quoted in support the doctrine of the Gnostics concerning the Demiurge, the evil creator of the world, the doctrine of the world as a sin of God's. "No," said Kafka, "I believe we are not such a radical relapse of God's, only one of his bad moods. He had a bad day." "So there would be hope outside our world?" He smiled, "Plenty of hope—for God—no end of hope—only not for us."

But it was not only when it was a question of themes of such greatness that Kafka revealed his powerful intuitive command of imagery, but at all times—that was just the re- markable thing about him. What seems peculiar to us in his remarks was, for him, the natural and absolutely unavoid- able shape of life and thought. He couldn't speak or write in any other way than this. It *was* natural, it can be found again partly even now in the way in which his sisters express them- selves. Quite peculiar to him were his dream-poetical and his paradox-humoristic turns of expression. Talking of a man who worked in the same office, he said, half in recognition, half in mockery, "He doesn't mind how long his office hours are"—and then went on reflectively, "But one might perhaps persuade him to." As we were coming home once after one of our nights of roving about, in the early hours of the morning, and the first awakening sounds of town life were making themselves heard—milk carts, etc.—he stopped and listened and said, "The crickets of the metropolis." Once when he was taking up some of my time, and asking me to do something for him, he said, "You forgive me for this, for I can't forgive myself for it." One of his very last words has this same tinge of paradox. When Dr. Klopstock, who was treating him, refused to give him any morphine, he said to him, "Kill me, otherwise you are a murderer." When he had his first attack of blood-spitting, which heralded his tuberculosis, he exclaimed—and he used these words to describe his disease as a way out, which was even not unwelcome, from the difficulties he was then faced with on the question of the marriage he had been planning—"My head has made an appointment with my lungs behind my back."

However revealing the citation of details may be, it cannot give the sum total of the effect that Kafka's personality produced. It was not the wit he displayed but the deep sureness on which it was based, and the peacefulness there was in his physical movements, that was the real thing that made itself felt in his vicinity. I shall once again call my Garta to the rescue and quote: "In his presence one felt directly that what is great must prove to be as great, even when every appearance speaks against it—that the noble kernel of the world remains untouched by all the abuses and perversions that exist. He didn't say this, it is only very rarely that he speaks about things like that, and when he does it is only hesitatingly, in fleeting images that often sound almost like jokes. But his whole behavior, down to the smallest detail, even if you only watch the way he brushes his hair, is based on the belief that there is, as a premise taken for granted without discussion, a mode of life which is right, thorough, clean, and unshakably natural. It is there. But to find it, to arrive at it—that is the difficulty. Deny this enormous diffi-
76

culty—that he is far from doing. On the contrary: he sees all the confusion and all that is in a nasty way comic in the world more intensively than any other man. He knows one can't take a step without getting into complications, without stumbling. And yet there is this deep confidence that the inner excellence will mature."

CHAPTER III

TO EARN ONE'S LIVING OR LIVE
ONE'S LIFE?

ON JULY 18, 1906, Kafka obtained his doctorate in jurisprudence at the Imperial and Royal Karl-Ferdinand German
University of Prague.

He did the usual so-called year in the courts, i.e. the un-
paid practice in the law courts which those lawyers who intend to be called to the bar have to go through. Kafka never
had any intention of following a legal career—he used this
year only as a breathing space after the strain of the examinations, and also as a breathing space in which to look round
for a properly paid job. For it was taken as settled that he
wouldn't be a burden on his parents' pockets a day longer
than was necessary. That his father would never have understood anyhow, and would have regarded as the worst of im-
positions. As I have said, the question whether this exceptionally gifted son (but did his parents have any clear idea
of his gift, had it manifested itself at all?) should not be
granted some exceptional liberty, such as a few years' study
in foreign countries, for example, was not raised. The financial prospects of the family were favorable enough at that
time. But Franz would have needed push to have won such
a favor for himself. And what was there that Franz lacked
more than push? His energy was directed inwards only and,
anyhow, manifested itself as stubbornness, a passive tenacity.
Herein perhaps lay the fatal weakness of his life. He suffered
and kept silent. At the same time one must also not forget
that the special nature of his gift, in fact, and not only in the
minds of his parents, precluded its being turned to any practical value. Furthermore, to turn it to any such practical
value was utterly and completely incompatible with the purity of Franz's idea of art. "Writing is a form of prayer," the
diary affirms. Indeed, when it came to the point of choosing
a profession, Franz postulated his job should have nothing
78

to do with literature. That he would have regarded as a debasing of literary creation. Breadwinning and the art of writing must be kept absolutely apart, a "mixture" of the two, such as journalism, for example, represents, Kafka rejected—although at the same time he never laid down dogmas, but merely withdrew, as it were, with a smile, explaining that "I just can't do it." He influenced me and my choice of a profession for years with these views of his and, like himself, out of respect for art, I went through agonies, in the most hideous, prosaic, dry, profession of the law and didn't find the road to theatrical and musical criticism until years later. Today I regard Kafka's severity on this point as a noble error, and regret the hundreds of joyless hours I let slip by in a mood almost of despair, wasting God's high creation, time, in offices just like those in which Kafka now set out on his martyr's way.

What we both strove after with burning ardor was a post with a "single shift"—that is, office from early morning till two or three in the afternoon—now I can write this "or" so easily as though to us at the time it didn't seem as if the whole health of our souls depended on this *one* hour—and none in the afternoon. Jobs with commercial firms, which meant being in the office mornings and afternoons, didn't leave any continuous stretch of the day over for literary work, walks, reading, the theater, and so on. And even when one came home after three, by the time one had eaten, recovered a little from the soul-destroying work, and was ready to switch over into the state of freedom one had been looking forward to—there was already very little of the day left. The desired office hours till two o'clock only were offered by extremely few offices, however, being almost exclusively in Government offices which even then, under the old Austrian Empire, were open to Jews only if they had influence in very high quarters. I don't want here to go into the story of all our disappointed hopes of suitable jobs which haunted our conversation at that time. It will suffice to say that Kafka, after a short prelude in the most strenuous of commercial offices (the "Assicurazioni Generali"), finally achieved the longed-for job in July 1908, in a semi-Government office, the

"Workers' Accident Insurance Institute for the Kingdom of Bohemia, in Prague."

In both posts Franz had men over him who were well disposed towards him. Nevertheless it soon became evident that he couldn't get on with it, in spite of all his experiments in dividing up his time in such a way as to allow him to indulge unrestrictedly in his passion—writing. For that he needed a succession of many hours, to permit the great impetus which his creative power gave him to soar to its proper climax and then die down again. But this was impossible for Kafka in one short afternoon with the prospect of the next barren day in the insurance institute always in front of him—for me, who had to go through the analogous experience shortly afterwards, it was only half possible by the application of extreme energy and concentration. So hard times began for both of us. Significant of what we suffered is the poem I wrote during one of the holiday tours we made together, and which I dedicated to my friend. Kafka tried sleeping in the afternoon and writing at night. That always went all right for a certain length of time, but he was not getting his proper sleep— Franz suffered from poor sleep, and an unusual sensitivity to noise anyhow—conditions of exhaustion set in, and so he had to call upon his last reserves of strength to get through his work in the office. A lot was expected of him there, among other things jobs that he described—and this is the strongest word of disapproval I have ever heard from him—as "disgusting," as for example a kind of press campaign against not unjustified attacks to which social insurance was then exposed. This explains an entry in the diary, "A sophistical article written for and against the institute." (What irony that he didn't after all completely escape journalism!) Here is the poem I mentioned above:

LAKE LUGANO

To Franz Kafka

With their delicate wings outspread,
Dragonflies glittered above our legs
Dangling in the water as we sat on the sun-baked wall,
To them we might seem like rocks.

80

High above us wound the road
Bright with lime-dust scorched clean and white.
And from the vineyard rich grapes did greet us
And coolth descended caressing like a gentle woman.

Our bodies bore the warm tan of the generous sun.
But our souls, dear Friend, knew no peace or richness
And shook with thoughts and words, dark distant but searing,
Despite the beauty that cradled us
We knew that near days would bend us and bleach us
With the same relentless burden.

The years that I spent as an official in the post office, and during which I wrote, among other things, in the afternoons and evening, my *Tycho Brahe*, remain so dimly in my memory that I can hardly see a single detail any more. It has all been forcibly crammed into the maw of the subconscious. Perhaps it may yet emerge once again. What remains is a direct sympathy for the almost unrealizable suffering that weighs on the working classes—that weighs on all who have to do work that does not interest them. Suffering that has been raised to a degree that one can only describe as fantastic by the "Taylor System" and the "conveyor belt." How can such suffering be borne at all? Perhaps we are all only dreaming that it is borne—this almost unimaginable suffering—because in reality it surpasses the limits of human powers of resistance, and of what is unfortunately the same thing in this case, of the possibilities of human degradation. The attitude towards social problems which wants to see a fair distribution of the burden of labor meets with my full approval—but my own experience points to a quite different problem that lies much deeper, to the question of the happiness of labor, joy in one's work, in one's own handicraft. Perhaps I shall have more to say on that point later.

A few days ago, after an interval of many years, I was once again on the premises of the Workers' Accident Insurance in Poříč street, at the scene of Franz Kafka's daily work. How often I had been to see him there, walked up and down with him in one of the bleak, echoing corridors. This time I spoke to one of the head officials who once worked with Kafka.

Franz Kafka, so the gentleman told me, was popular with everyone; he hadn't a single enemy. His devotion to duty was exemplary; his work was very highly thought of. The gentleman emphasized that Franz Kafka attacked every question from the opposite end of that from which everyone else generally did. (A very apposite remark on the part of the gentleman, who, be it noted, did not know that Kafka had since become world famous.) Another thing he emphasized was a certain naïveté in Kafka's make-up. He was "our office baby." He told me a story that is very characteristic of Kafka. "One day he came into my office just as I was eating a slice of bread and butter. 'How *can* you swallow that fat?' he said. 'A lemon is the best food.'"

His department in the Workers' Accident Insurance Institute was the study of the prevention of accidents and the appeals in respect of the classification of trades under the various degrees of risk.

He himself never considered his professional work was first-class. His superiors, however, thought very highly of it. He used to talk of the specialized knowledge and the "cleverness" of his boss—Marschner—with an admiration that bordered on enthusiasm.

His social conscience was greatly stirred when he saw workers crippled through neglect of safety precautions. "How modest these men are," he once said to me, opening his eyes wide. "They come to us and beg. Instead of storming the institute and smashing it to little pieces, they come and beg."

The annual report of the accident institute for the year 1909 contains an article I give below which Kafka wrote as a clerk of the office. Naturally, Kafka is not mentioned by name in the report itself. But I remember exactly Kafka bringing me the annual report that year, and telling me this article was his work. His boss had corrected his draft, but Kafka's style can be seen unmistakably in passages here and there even in this technical work. The high official who was kind enough to see me also pointed out the passage, as well as another one in the annual report for 1910, and told me they were Franz Kafka's work.

Here is an extract from this document which is interesting in more respects than one:

"Our illustrations show the difference between square spindles and cylindrical spindles as it affects the technique for the prevention of accidents. The cutters of the square spindle are connected by means of screws direct to the spindle and rotate with exposed cutting edges at speeds of 380 to 400 revolutions per minute. The dangers to the operator, presented by the large space between the cutter spindle and the surface of the table, are obvious. Such spindles were used either because the danger was not recognized, which may incidentally have increased the danger, or with the knowledge of the presence of a permanent danger which could not be avoided. Although an extremely cautious operator could take care not to allow any joint of his fingers to project from the timber when guiding it over the cutter head, the main danger defied all caution. The hand of even the most cautious operator was bound to be drawn into the cutter space if it slipped, particularly when, as often happened, the timber was hurled back (by the cutter block) while the operator was pressing the article to be planed against the table with one hand and feeding it to the cutter spindle with the other. This lifting and recoiling of the timber could not be anticipated nor prevented as it may have been due to gnarls or knots in the timber, to an insufficiently high cutting-speed, to warped cutters, or to uneven pressure of the operator's hands on the article. In such accidents usually several joints, and even whole fingers, were severed. Not only every precaution but also all protecting devices seemed to fail in the face of this danger, as they either proved to be totally inadequate or, whereas they reduced the danger on the one hand (automatic covering of the cutter slot by a protecting slide, or by reducing the width of the cutter space), they increased it on the other by not allowing the chippings sufficient space to leave the machine, which resulted in choked

83

cutter spaces and in injured fingers when the operator attempted to clear the slot of chippings.

"By turning back the spindle according to Schrader's patent and flattening it in a gentle slope right up to the cutters, clogging up of the cutter block will be avoided, whereby easy feeding of the timber to the cutter spindle and sufficient space for the chippings to leave the machine will also be effected.

"The most important point in this connection, however, from the point of view of the prevention of accidents is that only the cutting edges of the cutters should be permitted to project, and that these cutters, forming as it were an integral part of the spindle, can be very thin without danger of fracture."

It is clear that Kafka derived a great amount of his knowledge of the world and of life, as well as his skeptical pessimism, from his experiences in the office, from coming into contact with workmen suffering under injustice, and from having to deal with the long-drawn-out process of official work, and from the stagnating life of files. Whole chapters of the novels *The Trial* and *The Castle* derive their outer covers, their realistic wrappings, from the atmosphere Kafka breathed in the Workers' Accident Institute. Compare too the sketch "New Lamps," and an entry in the diary dated July 2, 1913: "Wept over the account of the trial of twenty-three-year-old Marie Abraham, who, through want and hunger, strangled her almost nine-months' old child with a tie which she was using as a garter and which she unwound for the purpose. A thoroughly typical story." Compare also the following scheme for reform, which is almost unique in Kafka's work, drawn up towards the end of his life, the plan of a workers' collective, voluntary of course, almost monastic.

GUILD OF WORKMEN WITHOUT POSSESSIONS

"*Duties.*—(1) To own or accept no money, no valuables. The following the only possessions allowed: the simplest clothing (details to be settled), materials necessary for work, books, food enough for one's own needs. Everything else be-

84

longs to the poor. (2) To earn one's keep only by work. To shrink from no work for which one has the strength without damage to one's health. Either to choose one's work oneself, or if that is not possible, to submit to the orders of the work committee, which is under the orders of the government. (3) To work for no other reward than one's keep (to be settled according to the district, for two days). (4) The most temperate life. To eat only what is absolutely necessary, for example, as minimum recompense, which is in a certain sense also maximum recompense; bread, water, dates. The food of the poorest, the lodgings of the poorest. (5) To treat the relationship with one's employer as one of trust, never to demand the intervention of a law court. Any work taken on to be finished under all circumstances, except when serious considerations of health prevent it.

"*Rights.*—(1) Maximum period of work, six hours; for manual labor, four to five. (2) In the case of illness, and when a man is too old to work, acceptance in a state home for old people, hospitals.

"The working life to be a matter of conscience and faith in one's fellow-man.

"Property a man brings with him to be given to the state for building hospitals and homes.

"For the present at least, exclusion of married men and women.

"Advice—heavy responsibility—to be given by the government.

"Where a man can help, in forsaken districts, workhouses, as teachers. . . .[1]

"Limit, 500 men.

"One year's novitiate."

Not that Kafka ever took any active part in political movements. But his reflective interest was claimed by any efforts that aimed at improving the lot of man. That is why he zealously attended Czech mass meetings and debates. I have

[1] At the beginning of the third sentence from the end there is a line in which I cannot make out the shorthand signs.

often heard him describe the characteristics of great popular speakers like Soukup, Klofáč, Kramář in detail, and generally very critically. It wasn't until after his death that I found out by accident, while I was collecting the material about the Czech anarchic-revolutionary movement of before the war (1914) for my novel *Stefan Rott*, that Kafka was personally known to one of the survivors of this movement, old Kacha. On the basis of his authentic reports, confirmed also by other sources, I was able to write these lines in my novel: "With another group of Czechs seated at the table in this big inn room sat another German guest, who looked very thin, and very young, although he was apparently over thirty. He didn't utter a word the whole evening, only looked on attentively with his great gray gleaming eyes, which stood out in strange contrast to his brown face under his thick coal-black hair." It was Franz Kafka the writer. He often came and attended this gathering quite peacefully. Kacha liked him, and called him a "klidas," that is, a "close-mouth," if one may be allowed an attempt at creating something like Prague-Czech slang. The gathering in question was the famous "Klub Mladých," the "Young People's Club," to which the Czech writers Gelner, Toman, Šrámek, Stanislav Neumann, Mareš, and Hašek also belonged.

Naturally Kafka's office life was not always overshadowed entirely by completely dark overtones. He had the ability to make firm friends with his colleagues and subordinates, even with some of them who were very simple or very confused. For example, I find among my papers an extraordinary memorandum written by one of these men that he brought to me. It begins with the words "*Nos exules filii Evae,*" and at the end it has a note on it in Franz's handwriting, "From an experience of the fifty-year-old author, which he hints at in the beginning, grew this further program, ecstatically conceived, according to which a uniting of Polish Jews (Dalila— the present Jewish mother) with the Slavs (Ursus—the present Slav man) shall effect the salvation of both, and the creation of Samson, who will create a new religion." Franz brought the author of this curious memorandum along and

86

introduced him to me, and then we went all three of us to one of the performances given by the Polish Jewish theater company, about which I shall write more later.

In one of his letters, putting me off, his office work is described in the following humorous fashion which anticipates a Charlie Chaplin film. "If you only knew how much I have to do! In my four district headquarters—apart from all my other work—people fall, as if they were drunk, off scaffolds and into machines, all the planks tip up, there are landslides everywhere, all the ladders slip, everything one puts up falls down and what one puts down one falls over oneself. All these young girls in china factories who incessantly hurl themselves downstairs with mountains of crockery give one a headache. By Monday I hope to be over the worst. . . ."

In his diary he wrote down in detail the experiences of a young bookkeeper. But he found the dignity of those who sit on high hard to bear. One day he came to me in the greatest excitement. He told me he had just done the silliest thing—which might cost him the wonderful job he had managed to ferret out with so much trouble—and which he valued for his parents' sake. What had happened was he had been appointed drafting clerk. A high personage on the Board of the institute had summoned the new drafting clerks to his presence and given them a talk which was so solemn, and so full of fatherly sanctimoniousness, that he (Franz) had suddenly burst out laughing, and couldn't stop. I helped the inconsolable Franz to write a letter of apology to the high official, who luckily turned out to be a considerate person, not without a sense of humor. It is altogether remarkable how Franz, as if in compensation for his inner repressions, hit upon people who were well disposed towards him, who helped him on, or at least did not knowingly get too much in his way—whereas other people, who have achieved their own inner balance in life, have to scuffle almost the whole time with obstructionists. Thus everything is reduced to some kind of order—that is, it is all arranged for nobody to have an easy time of it.

The happy and encouraging episodes in his profession

87

must, however, be considered as rare exceptions in the course of a burden that daily grew heavier because it was daily felt to be less and less bearable. The diary says such shattering things on the subject of office work preventing him from writing, that there is nothing more one can say on the subject. But there is one utterance of his which must be underlined, coming as it does from one who was otherwise so modest, that he had to force a piece of writing for his office out of himself, as if he were tearing a piece of flesh out of his own body, and who then in "great fear" sets forth "that everything in me is ready for creative work, and such work would be a heaven-sent solution of my problems and a real coming-to-life, while here in the office for the sake of such a miserable bit of an official document I must rob a body which is capable of such happiness of a piece of its flesh." There are, of course, in the still unpublished parts of the diary other passages in the same vein. And they rise to a really mighty climax when the time comes for him to take up formally a share in a factory in the interests of his family, and later to be constrained to show, if only occasionally, a practical interest in this undertaking. That he finds unbearable. He knows, in fact, what tremendous creative powers there are in him, which are clamoring to be unleashed and which are pent up by responsibilities of this kind. His complaint sounds very similar to that letter from Paris in which Mozart wrote the following refusal to his father who was urging him to start taking on pupils. "You must not think it is laziness—no!—but because it is utterly against my genius, against my way of life. . . . You know that I am, as one might say, stuck fast in music—that I am busied with it all day long—that I love to speculate—to study—to think things over. But now here I am prevented from doing so by this way of living (i.e. the lessons). I shall, it is true, have a few hours free, only—these few hours I shall need to rest in, rather than to work in." Unfortunately there will always be Philistines who are of the opinion that it is enough if genius has "a few hours free"—they don't understand that all the available hours barely suffice to guarantee to an even tolerably uninterrupted ebb and flow of inspiration

88

and repose its right and proper far-flung arc of oscillation.

To those who are of the opinion that Kafka in all seriousness considered his literary work bad or indifferent, and that
this was the reason for his refusing to publish anything, it
will come as rather a surprise to find him making the following entries in his diary concerning his "capacities," and "how
they are irritated by the pernicious daily drudgery," with
exactly the same confidence with which Mozart speaks of *his*
"genius" in the above letter. It is truly ridiculous also to suppose that genius—clear-sighted, form-bestowing genius—
should be in doubt about the powers which are most pe-
culiarly its own. To the outer world Kafka did, it is true,
display a certain amount of self-depreciation—in comparison
with that which he strove after, with religious enlighten-
ment, which was what finally concerned him most, he felt
himself petty—but that did not in the least prevent his esti-
mating at its true worth the divine grace that had been con-
ferred upon him and how perverse it was that it should meet
with temporal obstructionism. He writes:

"11/15/1911. Last night it was already with a certain pre-
sentiment that I took the spread off my bed, lay down, and
again became conscious of all my capacities, just as if I were
holding them in my hand; they tightened my chest; they set
my head on fire; for a while, to comfort myself for not getting
up and working, I said over and over to myself, 'It can't be
good for you; it can't be good for you,' and tried, with an almost visible effort to pull sleep over my head. I kept on thinking of a cap with a brim which I was pulling hard down over
my forehead, to protect myself. How much I lost yesterday;
how my blood pulsed through my tight-packed head, capable
of anything, and only held back by forces which are indispensable for just keeping alive, and are being thrown
away here!

"Certain it is that everything that I have conceived beforehand, although with a clear apprehension of every word,
or even only approximately but in definite words, when I sit
at my desk, when I try to set it on paper, seems dry, perverse,
stiff, embarrassing to the whole neighborhood, timid, but

above all full of gaps, although I have forgotten no jot of my original conception. The explanation lies, of course, largely in the fact that I conceive good things only when I am not tied to paper, at the time of inspiration, which I dread rather than long for, and that then the richness is so great that I must renounce it, and so just follow blindly my luck, and take things out of the flood, in handfuls, so that what I have acquired, when I come to write it down in reflection, is nothing to compare with the richness in which it lived, is incapable of summoning this richness up and is therefore bad and disturbing because it only entices one in vain."

"12/28/1911. What agony the factory costs me! Why did I not protest when they made me promise to work there in the afternoons! Of course no one makes me do it by force, but my father does by reproaches and K. by silence and my guilty conscience. I know nothing about the factory, and this morning when I was being shown over the factory I stood around helpless and like a whipped schoolboy. I swear I shall never be able to get to the bottom of all the details of the workings of the factory. And if, after asking endless questions and being a nuisance to all concerned, I were to do so, what would the result be? I should not know any practical use to put this knowledge to; I am built only for cooking up something that looks all right, to which the sound common sense of my boss [1] adds salt and makes it look like a really good piece of work. But through this useless expenditure of energy on the factory, on the other hand, I would rob myself of the possibility of using the few hours of the afternoon for myself, which could only lead to the complete destruction of my existence, which is getting more and more circumscribed as it is."

"6/21/1912. The tremendous world I have in my head! But how can I release it and release myself without tearing myself apart? And it is a thousand times better to tear myself apart than to keep it in check or buried in me. That is what I am here for, of that I am quite clear."

"The tremendous world I have in my head!" The diary is

[1] i.e. in the Workers' Accident Insurance.

90

alive with plans, sketches, and beginnings—only the very smallest part of them carried out. Mozart resisted, and stood up to his father. Kafka kept silence. But I have a letter of his in which he makes the evil of his being caught up in his daily work completely apprehensible. It is here, and not in his relations with his father, that, in my opinion, lie the roots of his later absorption into the world of sorrows that finally led to his illness and death. And only in so far as his exaggerated feeling of his tie with his father held him firm in the bonds of his profession did it contribute to the disaster—but the disaster was essentially caused by the fact that a man so tremendously richly gifted, with such a rich creative urge, was forced just at the time when his youthful strength was unfolding itself, to work day in and day out to the point of exhaustion, doing things which inwardly didn't interest him in the least. This is what he says in his letter to me:

After some good writing in the night from Sunday to Monday—I could have gone on writing all through the night, and all day, and all night and all day, and finally flown away —and today I am sure I could have written well, too—one page, really only the last dying breath of yesterday's ten, is even finished. I must stop for the following reason: Mr. X, the factory owner, early this morning went away on business, which I, in my fond absent-mindedness, hardly noticed, and will be off for ten or fourteen days. While he is away the factory is really left in control of the works manager alone, and no employer, least of all one so anxious as my father, will doubt that the most utter fraud is now being perpetrated in the factory. I myself in fact believe it too, although not so much for the sake of the money, but because of my ignorance and pangs of conscience. But after all, even an impartial person, so far as I can imagine such a person, couldn't have very much doubt that my father's fears are justified, even though I must not forget that I myself, at bottom, cannot comprehend why a German works manager from Germany, even during the absence of Mr. X, whose superior he is by far in every technical and organizing question, should not be able to keep everything running in the same good order as usual; for after all, we are men, not thieves. . . .

When I was trying to tell you some time ago that nothing from outside can disturb me when I am writing (which was said, of course, not as a boast, but to comfort myself), I was only just thinking how my mother whimpers to me almost every evening, that I should after all take a look at the factory now and again just to keep father's mind easy, and how father has said the same thing, on his side, in a far nastier way with looks and in other indirect ways. All this whimpering at me and reproaching me wouldn't, for the most part, amount to stupidity were it not that—and that, one can't deny it for all the world, is where the stupidity of all this talk lies—I can't bear such a control even in my brightest moments.

But it's not a question of that for the next fortnight, when all that is necessary is that any pair of eyes, even mine, should wander about over the factory. I can't make the slightest objection to this demand being made of me, of all people, because everybody thinks that I am chiefly responsible for founding the factory—though I must have taken this responsibility on in a dream, it seems to me at least—and moreover, there is no one here besides me who can go to the factory, because my father and mother, of whose going one couldn't dream, anyhow, are now in the middle of their busiest season (business seems to be going better in the new shop, too) and today, for example, mother didn't even come home for lunch.

So when mother once more began the same old story this evening, and, apart from the reference to making my father unhappy and ill by my behavior, produced the further reason of Mr. X's business journey and the complete desertion of the factory, a wave of bitterness—I don't know if it was only gall —passed through my whole body, I saw perfectly that I had only the alternatives of either waiting until everyone had gone to bed and then jumping out of the window, or of going every day to the factory and sitting in X's office every day for the next fourteen days. The former would have given me the opportunity of rejecting all responsibility both for interrupting my writing and for deserting the factory, the latter would have interrupted my writing without any doubt—I can't just rub fourteen nights' sleep out of my eyes—and would leave me, if I had enough strength of will and hope, the prospect of perhaps being able to begin again where I stopped today, fourteen days later.

So I didn't jump out through the window, and also the temptation to make this letter a letter of farewell (my motives for writing it lie in quite a different direction) is not very strong. I stood at the window a long time, and pressed my face against the glass, and I more than once felt like frightening the toll collector on the bridge by my fall. But I felt too firm a hold on myself the whole time for the decision to dash myself to pieces on the pavement to be able to depress me to the necessary level. It also seemed to me that by staying alive I should interrupt my writing less—even if one does nothing, nothing, but talk of interruptions—than by dying, and that between the beginning of my novel and its continuation after a fortnight, I might somehow in the factory, in full view of my satisfied parents, move and have my being in the heart of my novel.

My dearest Max, I am putting the whole case before you, not because I want you to judge it, for you are not in a position to have any judgment on it, but since I had firmly decided to jump from my window without writing a letter of farewell—after all one has the right to be tired just before the end—now that I am going to walk back into my room again as its occupant, I wanted to celebrate it by writing you a long letter of meeting again, and here it is.

And now a last kiss and good night, so that tomorrow I can do what they want of me, and be the boss of the factory.

When I read the letter, I was gripped by cold horror. I wrote freely and openly to Franz's mother, and pointed out to her the danger of suicide in which her son stood. Of course, I asked her not to mention my intervention to Franz. The answer which I received on October 7, 1912, is full of touching mother love. She begins, "I have just received your letter, and you can see from the way my writing shakes how much it has upset me. I, who would give my heart's blood for any of my children, to make them all happy, am helpless in this case. But nevertheless I shall do everything in my power to see my son happy." The mother then outlines a scheme for a white lie. She wanted to pretend to the father, who had to be kept from any shock because of his illness, that Franz was going to the factory every day, and in the meantime look around for another partner. "I shall speak to Franz this very day, without mentioning your letter, and tell him he needn't go to the factory tomorrow any more. I hope he will listen to me and calm himself. I beg you, too, dear Doctor, to calm him and thank you ever so much for the way you love Franz."

One's verdict on the affair depends upon what relation it bore to Franz's writing, and the importance one gives to that.

"Writing as a form of prayer" is, as I have said, the most revealing entry in the diary. From the account that Franz has left, unfortunately only in a fragmentary form, of his interview with the anthroposophist Dr. Rudolf Steiner, it is clear that while he was working Franz experienced conditions that "very clearly resemble the conditions of second sight" which Dr. Steiner has described. He compares his creative work with a "new occult doctrine, a kind of Cabala." Literary work was his "sole desire," his "sole profession," he says in the draft of a letter to his presumptive father-in-law, which is not only remarkable in itself but also significant in more directions than one. And on August 6, 1914, he writes in his diary: "My preoccupation with portraying my dreamlike inner life has relegated everything else to a secondary position; other interests have shrunk in a most dreadful fashion, and never cease to shrink. Nothing else can ever make me happy. But it is impossible to calculate how much strength I have for this portrayal. It may already have vanished forever; it may come back to me once again, but the circumstances under which I live are not favorable to it. So I vacillate, fly incessantly to the peak of the mountain, but cannot rest on the height for a moment." "I have a mandate," he explained in another passage, and at first it would appear that it was a question of a purely literary mandate, were it not

94

that fundamentally one feels right from the start that it is a religious question that lies at the back of the literary one—a religious question after the peculiar quality of Kafka's religion, which was a religion of the life fulfilled, of work, good work, that fulfils life significantly, of co-ordination in the right and proper life of national and human community.

"To be alone brings nothing but punishment"—this sentence from the diary is a *leitmotiv* that occurs again and again with Kafka, and finds its strongest positive expression just in the last piece he wrote, in the story called "Josephine the Songstress—or The Mice-Nation." On January 6, 1914, after reading Dilthey's "Experience and Imagination," he wrote down, "Loving one's fellow-man, having the highest respect for everything in its perfected forms, standing back calmly on the most suitable observation platform." The letters to Oskar Pollak ("It's better to bite Life than to bite one's tongue") repeatedly bring out the motive of active participation.

And at the end of 1913 we find the following formulation: "The uniformity of mankind, which every man, even the best of mixers and the most adaptable of men at one time or another begins to doubt, even if only sentimentally, on the other hand reveals itself, too, to every man, or at least appears to reveal itself in the complete community of the development of mankind as a whole, and as individuals, which we come across again and again. And this even in the most isolationist feelings of individuals." Is this written by the same man in whose work descriptions of the most utter human distances and loneliness occur over and over again, such as in all the animal stories (the soul of the animal cannot be got at by a human being), such as the ideology of the mole in *The Giant Mole,* or the still unpublished fragment from August 1914 which begins with the sentence, "At one time in my life I had a job with a small railroad in the heart of Russia," and which then goes on, "The wider the loneliness that surrounded me, the better pleased I was"? Two opposite tendencies fought for supremacy in Kafka: the longing for loneliness, and the will to be sociable. But you don't under-

95

stand Kafka properly until you realize that the tendency to loneliness (which undeniably existed in him) he disapproved of, and it was life in the social community and significant work that meant the highest goal and ideal for him—the life into which K., the hero of the *Castle* novel, tries in vain to thrust himself.

So, too, all the many pictures of a bachelor's life which play so great a part in his work are absolutely to be apprehended as the image in reverse of what is right and what is to be striven for. It is true that Kafka needed loneliness for his literary work, he needed a high degree of self-absorption, such as could sometimes be disturbed by a conversation—as his diary tells us—such as even communicating it to a friend could endanger. But he examined himself minutely. In 1911 he makes this discovery about himself: "In periods of transition such as I have undergone the last few weeks, and of which the present moment is yet even more marked, I am often seized with a sad but calm astonishment at my lack of feeling. I am separated from everything by a space to whose limits I can't even force my way out." And in March 1912, "who will confirm for me the truth or probability of the fact that solely as a result of my literary bent I am without interest in anything else, and heartless."

O, all too conscientious friend! Your literary work itself was after all for you only the symbol of a life well lived, but it was at the same time something much more too; it was the thing itself, it was your life, it was the right and proper use of the powers you were born with. It was that which you demanded of yourself and of all mankind: not to misuse the good powers one has been given, not to let them decay, but to make every use of them to fulfil the "Mandate," and in this way to enter into the "Law," thrusting aside the wicked man at the gate who tries to keep one from entering in. It is difficult, all the same. The temptations are many. "Once you have followed the false alarm of the night-bell—you can never put it right again." "Nobody, nobody can point you the way to India. Even then [in the time of Alexander] the gates of India were inaccessible, but the King's sword pointed the way. Today the gates have been conveyed elsewhere, to a more distant, a higher place; nobody points the way; many carry swords; but only to flourish them, and the gaze that would follow them is confused." (From the collection *The Country Doctor*.) And yet the "incorruptible," "indestructible" in us remained. We look for it "far from the battle of Alexander," we read and turn over the "pages of our old books," wait for the arrival of the "imperial emissary." It is just as the Rabbi Tarfon in his *Sayings of the Fathers* taught us with exactly the same elastic tension between pessimism and optimism, "It is not granted you to complete the task—and yet you may not give it up."

His literary work was not the be-all and end-all for Kafka, however much many passages in his diary, if taken literally, might seem to say so. His business was a little different from that of Flaubert, for whom art really meant the essence and the proper meaning of existence, which was almost always (almost, please!) looked on skeptically and with hostility by Flaubert. But look at Kafka in contrast: "Our art consists of being dazzled by the Truth. The light which rests on the distorted mask as it shrinks from it is true, nothing else is." Art is a reflection of religious experience. But with Kafka art is a way to God, not only in this sense—he who shrinks back also sees the way, indeed it is the way from which he shrinks back —but also in the positive sense explained above—as a midwife for a man's powers, as a governess teaching the fulfilment of life according to one's natural abilities. Thus Kafka affirmed on August 15, 1914: "I have been writing for a few days, may it continue! So completely protected and wrapped up in my work as I was two years ago,[1] I am not now, but all the same I have got the feeling that my regular, empty, mad, bachelor life has some justification. I can once more hold a conversation with myself, and am not gazing into such a complete blankness. This is the only way in which I can ever get better."

Thus art serves the religious principle of giving a meaning

[1] In 1912 Kafka wrote "The Verdict," "The Stoker," and *The Metamorphosis*.

to life. As work, as an unfolding of good creative abilities given by God, it has the same rights as other work which men do, which is significant and constructive and leads the writer out of the desert of idleness back into the circle of the active communal existence. All the same, writing, of however high a standard, was not enough according to Kafka's lights. Other things were needed to become a fully qualified citizen of this earth, e.g. founding a family. I shall never forget the deep emotion with which Kafka read to me the last paragraph of *Souvenirs intimes* by Flaubert's niece, Caroline Commanville. The passage describes how Flaubert sacrificed to his idol "La Littérature," everything—love, tenderness—everything, and the author asks if he never towards the end of his life regretted this departure from the "route commune." She is inclined to believe he did. A few excited words that Flaubert once said to her on one of their last walks together led her to think so. They had been to see a woman friend of theirs, and found her in the midst of her charming children. As they were walking back home along the Seine, Flaubert said, " 'Ils sont dans le vrai' . . . [Commanville explains] en faisant allusion à cet intérieur de famille honnête et bon. 'Oui,' se répétait-il à lui-même gravement, 'ils sont dans le vrai' . . ." Kafka often quoted this sentence. Art alone then had not been enough for him on which to build a proper life. But it was an indispensable part of the foundation of it, it was at the same time the beginning, the innermost circle, upon the health of which other circles depended. One can understand from this the deep tragedy that lay in the fact that circumstances prevented him from taking this first step towards a fulfilled, which is to say in his sense a good, religious life, from properly saying the prayer which he felt he was capable of saying. Had he been allowed to let his artistic capabilities have their full run, undoubtedly many other things would have gone better for him later on. As it didn't happen, the harmful effect of having a profession forced upon him in which he found no pleasure, gradually worked down into the metaphysical depths.

That is obviously not to say that, had one first step succeeded, Kafka would have solved all the other problems of his life smoothly. But without the first step, failure was certain. Only that can be recognized, and no more. It seems indeed that many of Kafka's problems bordered at least very closely on the absolutely insoluble. Nevertheless—given a maximum of physical and spiritual inviolacy (a maximum which was precluded in advance by the slavery of his profession) we should—of that I am convinced—have experienced in Kafka's later development things which go far beyond our present stock of ideas.

CHAPTER IV

UP TO THE PUBLICATION
OF "CONTEMPLATION'

THE brief summer holidays which freed us from the thrall of
our office work for two or three weeks, gained a double significance for us through this association. To be free for a few
whole days, to be able to meet the world and fresh people
without bothering and with open minds—we enjoyed this
happiness with the unbroken strength of youth. We went on
our holidays together, and looked forward to them for
months beforehand, made our preparations for them with a
care that we ourselves laughed at more than anyone, but
which lit up the gray workday like a ray of sunshine. The
day we could leave came at last! Never in my life have I been
so equably cheerful as during weeks of holiday spent with
Kafka. We turned into happy children, we hit upon the
queerest, loveliest jokes—it was a great happiness to live in
Kafka's neighborhood and to enjoy at first hand his lively
thoughts as they bubbled forth—even his hypochondria was
still entertaining and full of ideas.

Moreover, it was not only the long summer holidays that
we spent together, but all the year round there were lots of
excursions in Prague's immediate and farther neighborhood.
Many a summer we took long walking tours every Sunday. At
Easter and Whitsuntide we stayed away two or three days,
and at other times, too, we often left the town as early as
Saturday afternoon. Felix Weltsch was generally a third in
the party. We hiked (so I find out from my diary, alongside
the adjective "indescribably beautiful") seven or eight hours
a day; it was our sport. Bathing in brooks and rivers was part
of it. We used to swim, we used to sun ourselves, we got
hardened. One day the young Franz Werfel, still a schoolboy
then, was taken along with us to Senohrab, and introduced
to our uninhibited nature-life. He got horribly sunburnt in
100

doing so. The poems of his which he read aloud to us on the reedy banks of the Sazawa moved us to enthusiasm. I shall quote here one of the many original letters I have in which Kafka used to propose excursions like this.

My dear Max
Don't rush into a great outlay of cash on an express letter to say you can't be at the Franz Joseph Station at 6.05, because you must be, since the train we are going to take to Wran leaves at 6.05. At 7.45 we shall walk the first step towards Davle, where we shall eat a goulash at Lederer's. At 12 o'clock we shall lunch at Stěchowitz, from two till a quarter to four we shall walk through the woods to the rapids on which we shall row about a bit. At seven we shall take a steamer back to Prague. Don't think any more about it, but be at the station at a quarter to six. Apart from that, you may after all write a special-delivery letter to say you would like to go to Dobřichowitz or somewhere else.

We spent countless happy hours on the boards of the bathing establishments of Prague, in rowboats on the Vltava, in doing climbing stunts on the mill weirs, many an echo of which you can find in my novel *Stefan Rott*. I admired Franz's swimming and rowing. He was particularly clever at handling a so-called "man-drowner." He was always less clumsy, bolder than myself, and had a special trick of leaving one to one's fate in breakneck situations with an almost cruel smile which seemed to say something like "Help yourself." How I adored that smile, in which, after all, there lay also so much confidence and encouragement. Franz was inexhaustible in finding out new lines of sport, or so it seemed to me. In this too his personality expressed itself, this too he did, as he did everything, with complete abandon.

Our first summer holiday together began September 4, 1909, and took us to Riva. Kafka, my brother Otto, and I spent many hours of contemplation in the little bathing place under the Ponale road, at the "Bagni della Madonnina." When I came back to Riva after the war, I no longer found

101

the lovely sunny gray boards, and no longer saw the gleaming lizards gliding over the garden paths that had led the way down from the dusty road full of cars to the cool place of the spa. Unforgettable, modest little establishment, under the towering walls of cliffs, I have dedicated an obituary to you and the happiness we found in your bay—here we ourselves were guests of peace, of the classic simplicity of the South. Never since has the South revealed herself to us so kindly and so exalted at the same time. Kafka, too, in later years was drawn once more to visit Riva; but he lived there alone, in 1913, after his first great unhappy love affair, in the Hartungen sanatorium on the other side of the lake.

In 1909 we were all still doing very well And even the discussions we had with Dallago, the poet and apostle of nature, who came to visit the same bathing resort as ourselves, failed to disturb our comfort. The traveling experiences of my brother, who was much more useful in practical things than I, and whom Kafka very much admired, helped us out of many a difficulty. My brother had, so to speak, "discovered" Riva for us, had been there already the year before, and now took us the easiest way to everything that was beautiful and of interest. One photograph is of Franz under the colonnades of Castell Toblino, another shows him with my brother sitting on his haunches on a slab of marble in the green wilderness on the shore of the lake.

Into the idyll of the Madonnina Spa burst the newspaper story—of course we were reading nothing at the time except the Italian local papers from Riva—that the first flying meet was to take place at Brescia. We had never yet seen a flying machine, so we decided with great enthusiasm, although funds were low, to go to Brescia. Kafka was keener than anybody on making the trip—and this is I think a good place once again emphatically to point out how false the view is that considers Kafka was at home in an ivory tower, a world of fantasies far removed from life, and imagines him as an ascetic consumed by nothing other than religious speculations. He was entirely different: he was interested in everything new, topical, technical, as for example, in the beginnings of the film; he never proudly withdrew himself, even in the case of abuses and excrescences of modern development, he went down to their roots with patience and inexhaustible curiosity, preserved his hopes in man's common sense, never, in proud "distinction," never, in the attitude of Stefan George, rejected contact with the inferior, organized world around him. Only what was dirty, immoral, seemed to have no attraction for him. He had the wonderful gift of finding it just boring. Thus, for example, I could never persuade him to read more than a line or two of Casanova—whom I then rated more highly than his deserts perhaps, but whom I still find significant and worth reading.

Brescia was overcrowded. As we had to be very careful of our money, we finally spent the night in a room which we thought must be a den of robbers, and in the middle of the floor of which—even today I ask myself if it can't be a trick of my memory perhaps—was a large circular hole, through which one could look down into the taproom which lay underneath. We thought Sparafucile was bound to join us at any moment. But the next day, in the sunlight on the aerodrome, we laughed the unpleasant hours of the night to smithereens. On our way back, when we spent a night at Desenzano, I must admit we were driven into the streets by the bugs that lurked behind hundreds of pictures of saints, and we sat shivering on the benches on the quay by the lake side waiting for the morning. Yes, that is how we traveled in those days; we knew nothing of first-class hotels, and yet were heedlessly jolly. It was, one must admit, a time which had its great advantages. Riva was Austrian, Brescia Italian. There was occasionally some talk of tension; there were rumors about the underground fortresses of Monte Brione near Riva, but fundamentally nobody took it seriously; war was an unreal idea, something like the philosopher's stone and, when we crossed the frontier on our walks, we didn't even notice it.

The first flights we saw made a great impression on us. I told Franz he must immediately take notes of everything he observed, and gather them together into an article. By the idea of making it a sporting competition between him and me, I made it attractive to him. I was going to write an article, too, and we should decide who had succeeded in making the best remarks. Playful, not to say childish aims of this nature seldom failed in their effect on Kafka. For example, it gave him tremendous pleasure when we made this excursion and took great pains to hide our first reactions from each other, and to betray nothing of what we felt about the things we saw. Only at the end one might see who had hit the mark.

But behind all this solicitation I had a secret plan. At the time Kafka's literary work was lying fallow; for months he had not produced anything, and he often complained to me that his talent was obviously seeping away, that it had completely and utterly gone from him. Indeed he sometimes lived for months in a kind of lethargy, in utter despair; in my diary I find note after note on his sadness. *Le cœur triste, l'esprit gai*—this description fits him excellently and explains how it was that, even when he himself was in the most depressed state, he never, except perhaps in the hour of extreme intimacy, had a depressing, but rather a stimulating effect on those with whom he went about. But how deeply he suffered, I knew even then from many a confession, and so I wanted to give him a concrete example of how one must pull oneself together, wanted to prove to him that his fears of literary barrenness were without foundation, that it only needed a certain amount of will, a certain amount of concentration, to bring his gift into working order again.

My plan succeeded. The article "The Aeroplanes at Brescia" Franz wrote with joy, finished it, and then had it published, very much cut, at the end of September 1909, in *Bohemia*. I had handed it to Paul Wiegler, at that time editor of *Bohemia*—and later succeeded in persuading Franz to let me publish it without cuts next to my own essay on the same theme in my book "On the Beauty of Ugly Pictures." In this book I introduced Franz's essay with the following remarks:

"It is really an extremely far-fetched, and at the same time also banal idea that only *one* author should get a hearing in
104

one book. And if we two friends, inseparable in our thoughts on this journey and in other things, have always stood so near to each other in a foreign land, shall we not dare do so in this book in our own home? And what if these two variations on the same theme would not have come into being the one without the other, although the two authors kept their ideas secret from one another with comic and purposely exaggerated fear, or even, in the heat of rivalry, attacked the third fellow-traveler, my brother Otto, for advice? What if these variations, then, belong to one another, complete one another, make one another clearer, beautify one another? And what if we wish it? And what if nothing can be done about it anyway?" I have the galley proofs of the two essays in front of me. I was proud to have effected the first publication of Kafka in book form in this way. But, alas, it never got further than good will. In the end the book turned out to be far too long, and at the wish of the publisher, along with several other essays, these two had also to be cut out of the final set-up of the book. Kafka's essay is now published as an appendix to this book.

The article as such was not, of course, the end I had in view, it was to serve only as an incitement to bring Franz's pleasure in creation into flow again. This success I achieved. Albeit always against the strong resistance the stubborn author put up against me. At times I stood over him like a rod, drove him and forced him, not directly naturally, but again and again by new means and new tricks; at any rate I didn't let his gift break down again. There were times when he thanked me for doing so. But often I was a burden to him with my prodding and he wished it to the devil, as his diary informs one. I felt that, too, but it didn't matter to me. What mattered to me was the thing itself, the helping of a friend even against the wish of the friend.

I claim that it is thanks to me that this diary ever came into being; even Franz's quartos grew directly out of our little notes on our journeyings, were in fact in a certain sense sequels to them. A conscious and already cultivated tendency of Kafka's to render such an account of his experiences found

105

fresh nourishment in the reportage of the journeys we did together, and was now systematically developed. That is exactly what I had wished for. The diaries have a significance for Kafka which is not only autobiographical and an aid to the mastery of his soul; in between remarks of a personal content stand the pieces which he then later took for his first book, "Contemplation." In fact many of these pieces selected by himself are, in their substance, indistinguishable from the entries in the diary; we don't know why the author considered one worth publishing and kept back the other.

In the context of the diary [1] there are also many fragments of short stories which have got thus or thus far; they pile up, until suddenly out of the throng the first finished story of considerable length, "The Verdict," shoots out like a jet of flame. With it, during the night of September 22–23, 1912, the writer succeeded in breaking through to the form that suits him, and a powerful genius of the art of story telling, unique in his genre, finally found his freedom.

In October of 1910, we went to Paris for our holidays. There were Kafka, Felix Weltsch, my brother, and I. Our circle of friends had grown, a development which ha l already begun some years previously. I brought Kafka along to Felix Weltsch and Oskar Baum. The clear-sighted philosopher ("Grace and Freedom," and "The Risks of the Via Media," are his most important books, and there is also the—

[1] Here are some beautiful passages from entries in the diary: "One advantage of keeping a diary is that one becomes conscious, with comforting clarity, of the changes one is constantly undergoing, which one also, in general, believes, guesses at and admits, but which one unconsciously denies, when it comes to extracting hope or peace out of any such admission. In a diary one finds the proofs that one has oneself lived, looked around, written down observations, under circumstances which today appear unbearable; that, in fact, this right hand went through the same movements as it does today, when we are of course wiser about the conditions at that time, since we have the possibility of having a bird's-eye view of them, but are therefore all the more obliged to recognize the fearlessness of our strivings at that time, which persisted despite all our lack of knowledge." Another extract reads: "On the way back home after saying goodbye, regret for my falseness, and pain at its inevitability. Intention: to begin a notebook of my own on my relations with Max. What one doesn't write down flickers before one's eyes, and optical accidents determine the result."

philosophical—treatise, "Perception and Concept," which was written in collaboration with me)—as well as the writer—who in addition to the list of works quoted elsewhere has just written the impressive historical novel, "The People Who Slept Hard"—felt drawn towards Kafka. Our foursome was also unique in that between the pairs of friends there existed an intimate friendship, in whose harmony no jarring note was ever felt. The four of us came together regularly, and this for many years gave our lives a firm rhythm.

Oskar Baum, the writer, describes how he first met Kafka in the following words: "Our first meeting still remains quite clear in my memory. It was Max Brod who brought it about. He brought Franz Kafka along to my place and read to us, that autumn afternoon in 1904, his short story, 'Excursions into the Dark Red,' which he had just finished. We were little more than twenty at the time. I can still remember many of the things we said during the enthusiastic exchange of opinions in which the problems of the story involved us, and which was carried on with the extremely controlled economy of words which was then the fashion with us. Kafka, for instance, among other things, said, 'When there is no necessity to digress from the action through tricks of style, the temptation to do so is strongest.'

"Kafka's first gesture as he came into my room left a deep impression on me. He knew he was in the presence of a blind man. And yet, as Brod was introducing him, he bowed silently to me. It was, you might think, a senseless formality in my case, since I couldn't see it. His hair, which was smoothed down, touched my forehead for a moment as he bowed, probably because the bow that I made at the same time was a little too violent. I was moved in a way that for the moment I could see no clear reason for. Here was one of the first people in the world who had made it clear that my deficiency was something that concerned nobody but myself —not by making allowances or being considerate, not by the faintest change in his bearing. That was what he was like. He stood so far from the accepted utility formulas, that he affected one in this way. His severe, cool reserve was so superior in depth of humanity to the ordinary run of kindness —which I otherwise recognize when I am first introduced to people in a pointless increase in warmth of words, or tone of voice, or shake of the hand.

"This co-ordination of every involuntary movement, of each everyday word with his whole personal outlook on life made his behavior, his outward appearance, unusually full of life, despite the abstract battles that continuously dominated his mind. When he read aloud—and that was his particular passion—the emphasis on each separate word was completely subordinated, although every syllable was perfectly distinct—with his tongue sometimes working at a speed which almost made one giddy—to a musical breadth of phrasing, with enormously long breaths, and mightily swelling crescendos of the dynamic levels—just as you find them in his prose, where you occasionally find that a complete separate piece like "The Circus Equestrienne" has arisen in the form of one marvelously constructed sentence."

I don't wish, however, to create the impression that Kafka was to be met only in the innermost circle of the "Prague Four." On the contrary, it was much more in accordance with his nature to try and meet everyone who seemed to share his feelings, or at any rate, at least as long as his health lasted, not to refuse to. Among the men who consorted with Kafka are Martin Buber, Franz Werfel, Otto Pick, Ernst Weiss, Willy Haas, Rudolf Fuchs, in later years the elocutionist Ludwig Hardt, Wolfenstein, and many others. Perhaps a few of them will still take up the tale, and complete the picture of the life of Kafka (cf. Appendixes III and IV).

Our holiday in Paris was a failure owing to a small carbuncle that Franz developed, and a few terrifying experiences at the hands of French doctors. After a few days he went back home to Prague. Kafka was always very sensitive on the question of any risk to his health. Every imperfection of the body tormented him, even, for example, scurf or constipation, or a toe that was not quite properly formed. He distrusted drugs and doctors. He demanded that Nature

108

herself should restore the balance, and despised all "unnatural" medicines.

This tendency was strengthened in 1911, when, on a journey—probably on behalf of the office—to Warnsdorf, he met the industrialist Schnitzer, who preached the "nature cure." I find the following entries on the subject in my notes dated May 1911. "Kafka came back to Prague on Friday, but didn't come to see me or Baum. Finally, the following Thursday, I rang him up in a temper." He was "so weak, felt so rotten; his stomach was out of order; he wasn't going out at all, he was so miserable." On Friday afternoon he came to see me and told me a lot of wonderful things about the garden city of Warnsdorf, about a "magician," a believer in natural healing, a rich industrialist, who had examined him, had looked only at his throat in profile, from the front, and had then talked to him about poisons in his spinal marrow and almost up to his brain already, which had developed through living on the wrong lines. To cure them he recommended sleeping with the windows open, sun-bathing, working in the garden, joining in the activities of a club for natural healing and subscribing to a magazine published either by the club or by the industrialist himself. He speaks against doctors, medicines, and injections. He explains the Bible from a vegetarian standpoint: Moses led the Jews through the desert so that they might become vegetarians in these forty years. Manna as a meatless diet. The dead quails. The longing for the "fleshpots of Egypt." Even more clearly, in the New Testament Jesus addressed bread with the words, "This is my body." Franz's attitude to the "natural health methods" and reform movements of a similar nature was one of very intense interest, nicely tempered by making good-natured fun of the follies and fads which go along with these movements. Fundamentally he saw in the efforts to create a new healthy man, and to use the mysterious and freely proffered healing powers of nature something extremely positive which agreed with many of his own instincts and convictions, and which he widely put into practice too. He slept with the window open all the year round. When you went to his place to see him, the cool fresh air there was a thing that struck you. He always wore light clothing, even in winter, went for long periods without eating meat and drank no alcohol. When he became ill he infinitely preferred being looked after in a private house (in Zürau), in a primitive country district, to any sanatorium, and only went to sanatoriums when he was finally forced to do so.

In 1910 there was another important meeting. For May 1 of this year I find this entry in my diary: "Café Savoy. Theatrical company from Lemberg. Very important for J. F."—the novel I was planning at the time. For May 4: "Went with Kafka to the Savoy this evening. Marvelous!" Franz's notes about this Polish Jewish troupe of actors who acted folk drama in Yiddish, and sang in Yiddish, don't begin until the following year, but from then on they fill many pages of the copybooks, and the greatest actors have seldom been written about with such love and such penetrating understanding, not only with regard to their art, but also to their private lives, as Kafka devoted to describing Mr. and Mrs. Klug, Mr. and Mrs. Tschissik, Mr. Pipes, and above all, the young Isak Löwy.

I was the prime mover in this case. That was just the beautiful thing about our friendship, that I learned from Kafka in many points, as I have already explained, but in other questions Kafka followed my lead. Generally, I must admit, in these cases, he guided the first impulse which he received from me into a depth and a breadth I had never before suspected. I, for example, was a frequent member of the audience at the performances in the Café Savoy, and learned a lot there towards appreciating Jewish folklore. But Franz, after the first time I took him there, entered into the atmosphere completely. It was the same intense and creatively fruitful dogged determination with which he himself did everything. A curious kind of shy love and veneration bound him to one of the actresses, who is hardly likely to have noticed anything of it,[1] and he treated the actor Löwy as a

[1] In his literary plans he writes in his diary, "Love of an Actress," and several dreams about the theater.

110

friend, often took him back home with him—to the intense annoyance of his father, who never could get on with any of Franz's friends—made this passionate person tell him all about his life, his surroundings and his development, and gained deep insight into the customs and spiritual crises of the Polish-Russian Jews. His diary makes it clear what he got from Löwy; in this way, too, Kafka was brought to the study of Jewish history (Graetz) and the study of the history of Yiddish literature—in the French edition of Pines' book.[1] Long portions of the quarto copybooks contain extracts from the latter book, followed by discussions, rich in ideas, on the structure and peculiarity of the literatures of small nations. In this way many a sidelight is thrown on the way in which Kafka followed up the development of Czech literature in every detail. The many-sidedness of Kafka's interests is shown by the fact that the extracts from Pines are followed by extracts just as full from Biedermann's *Conversations with Goethe*. (It should be mentioned here that in later volumes of the diary Kafka's entries include excerpts from "The Memoirs of Countess Thürheim," "which have been my joy for the last few days," from "Memoirs of General Marcellin de Marbot," and from Paul Holzhausen's "The Germans in Russia in 1812." Kafka preferred reading biographies and autobiographies to anything else. The diaries of Grillparzer and Hebbel, the letters of Fontane, were among his favorite books, and he knew them much better than he knew these writers' fiction.)

Perhaps the following postcard may give some idea of the enthusiasm and joy with which Kafka threw himself into this world of the Polish Jewish folk-energy which was so new to us:

Dear Max

We are in luck! They are doing *Sulamith* by Goldfaden.

---

[1] *Histoire de la littérature Judéo-Allemande*, Paris, 1911, which was later published in German too. In his diary Kafka writes he is reading this history of literature "with such a thoroughness, speed, and pleasure as I have never done other books of this kind."

With pleasure I am wasting a card to write you what you have read already. I only hope you have written it to me too.

Franz began to write a kind of autobiography of Isak Löwy, using the material the latter gave him, and giving a survey of the Yiddish theater. The beginning of the book has survived. Short as it is, it gives a good picture of the kind of conversations the two used to hold, and in which I often took part, and of the circle of interests which was busying Kafka at the time, and which was able to show us the question of Jewry from a more living and colorful side than the abstract theories of Zionism could. It was the time when I first came into contact with Zionists and the Zionist outlook, and I passed their influence on to my friend, influences which came from the Prague club "Bar-Kochba," and particularly from the wonderful Hugo Bergmann. At first Kəfka's attitude was one of rejection. l, too, was not at first in agreement with everything that was preached to me on this side—often in a form all too fine and polished—and in the beginning used to go to the tiny, not very inviting Café Savoy on Ziegen square, where they gave the generally despised melodrama as a direct protest against Zionistic academics. I zealously championed the thesis that however near to unconscious humor and trash they might come, from the performances of these actors more could be learned about the essence of Judaism than from the philosophic deductions of Jews of the West who were, it is true, striving to get to the people, but who were at heart already estranged from them.

It was not until much later by the laborious accumulation of knowledge that I learned how interdependent East and West, Zion and Diaspora are. Kafka held out against these views much longer than I did, in fact. Later when I had become a convinced Zionist and was vainly trying to convert Kafka to recognizing the necessity of the Zionist policy— while we were rowing on the Moldava—we often came to an argument and once to the only quarrel we ever had, a short and passing one. In my diary for January 18, 1913, for example, I find entered the record of a conversation with
112

Buber, Werfel, Kafka, Pick, Baum, and myself, which was obviously on this theme, and on August 23, 1913, there is this entry: "Afternoon with Kafka. Bathing, rowing. Conversation about feelings of community. Kafka says he has none, because his strength just about suffices for himself alone. Argument in the boat. My change of heart on this point. He shows me Kierkegaard, and Beethoven's letters." In December there is the little note that we had quarreled. But on December 24 it was all right again: "Kafka talked about social questions. In the Town Park."

From then on Kafka gradually came distinctly nearer my Zionist standpoint, and in the eventful days of 1918, 1919— the founding of the Jewish National Committee, and of the Jewish School, he stood by me with advice, interest, encouragement, and loving agreement, his recognition of my work was my greatest support—finally, by studying Hebrew deeply, he left me far behind in this field too.

But I am anticipating. Let us go back again for a moment to the poor Yiddish troupe from which we both of us received the impulse which set us on to reach later stages of development which seem so far removed from it. Kafka was unwearying in the service of these artists who were always in need. According to his diary, he drew up a circular to all the Zionist clubs in Bohemia to make a tour possible for this company; he had it duplicated himself, too. In this affair he revealed how much energy and activity slept pent up in him, before earning-his-living and marriage plans, etc. had quite crippled him. On February 18, 1912, he organized an evening of recitations for Löwy in the banquet hall of the Jewish council chamber, and the whole burden of getting everything ready and the technical arrangements rested on him. He bore it with a groan, and yet with grace, not without pride. The speech with which Kafka opened the evening has been preserved in my wife's notes. It begins:

"Before the Polish Jews begin their lines, I want to tell you, ladies and gentlemen, how very much more Yiddish you understand than you think you do. I am not really afraid of the effect that is waiting for each one of you this evening, but I

113

do want it to be given free play as soon as it has deserved it. But this can't happen if some of you . . ."

That the Russian friend in "The Verdict" bears traces of the actor Löwy is clear. And how deeply the heart is moved by this beautiful sentence in the diary: "The pity we feel for these actors who are so good, and earn nothing, and apart from that receive nothing like enough gratitude and praise, is really nothing but pity for the sad fate of so many noble efforts, and above all of our own." From Prague, after breaking with his company, Löwy turned to Budapest. Among the papers Kafka left behind I find Löwy's letter from Vienna dated 10/28/13. It runs, with its characteristic original spelling and grammar: "Think you, how deep am I sunk that even with you I have lost touch. . . . And how I miss your letters? I have now been torne [*sic*] away from everything for a long time, no friends any more, no parents, no family . . . and the dearest of all, Dr. Kafka, also lost. . . . Of this loss I never dreamed. . . . You were after all the only one what was so good to me . . . the only one what spoke to my soul, the only one what half understood me. And you I must also lose, I'm sorry. . . . You mustn't write to me, I'm sorry. You mustn't be good to me. Please don't think I'm 'mad,' I am normal, cold as death." . . . Further on in the letter is the sad sentence: "What have I to wait for? Another shot of morphine." Franz's draft of an answer either to this or some other letter lies next to it.

Dear Löwy

I was much more pleased you remembered me than one might guess from the fact that I have taken so long in answering. I am in great confusion, and work, without myself or anyone else getting much out of it.

Anyhow, here is some good news for you. I've got engaged, and think I've done something good and necessary in doing so, even if the world is of course so full of doubts that nothing is safe from them.

That you are still in trouble, and can't find a way out is very sad. That you are staying so long in Hungary is strange, but probably has its bad reasons. I imagine we were both much more hopeful when we walked about Prague in the evenings. Then I thought you must make good somehow, and at one stroke too. Anyhow, I am not giving up hope for you at all, let me tell you. You despair easily, but are easily happy, too; remember *that* in your despair. Only look after your health in preparation for better days. What you have gone through seems bad enough, don't make it worse by damaging your health.

I'd like to hear more about you and your friends. Aren't you going to Karlsbad this time? All my best wishes.

Franz K.

I don't know whether this letter reached Löwy and what has happened to him. I wonder if he is still alive.

1911. End of August. Rejoicings, holidays! The journey to Zürich. Then Flüelen, then Lugano. Everywhere the thing that we are keenest on is bathing in the lake. They were days of sunshine and every glorious thing in the world. Our friendship was growing more and more intimate at this time; the working year that had just ended had brought us again many a dizzy height, including moments of sympathetic solicitude. Thus I find in my notes on March 13: "Kafka rang up, because the light in his room was going on and off." I showed my love for my friend, too, by setting to music his poem, "Little soul—thou leaping dancest," to a simple melody accompanied by variations on the piano. Here let me remark that Kafka, as if to compensate for the remarkable gift he had of musical speech, had no talent for pure music. I have frequently noticed that many an author whose verse or prose bears all the characteristics of good music in its rhythm and dynamic, at the same time expends all his musical energy on speech, so that no specific capacity is left for the world of musical sounds. Kafka played no instrument. He once told me he couldn't tell the difference between *The Merry Widow* and *Tristan and Isolde*. There is this amount of truth in these words, that he never took much trouble to get to know the higher music. And yet he was not without a natural feeling for

115

rhythm and tune. I often heard him sing Löwe's ballad, "Count Eberstein," to himself—it was his favorite piece.

I often used to drag him along to concerts until I gave it up, when I found his reactions to them were of a purely visual character. "Listening to music, by its nature, sets a wall around me," he writes in his diary after a Brahms concert, "and the only lasting musical effect is that, shut in in this way, I am anything but free." There follow descriptions of the singers, the public, some clergymen in a box; not a word about the music. All the more receptive was Franz to plays and recitations. How many evenings we spent together in theaters, cabarets—and also in wine bars with pretty girls! For the idea that Kafka was a kind of stylite or anchorite is completely wrong. He asked not too little from life, but rather too much, perfection in fact, or nothing—and the result of that, of course, was that in later years he steered clear of dalliance, looked at the erotic side of life only from the most serious angle, and never told a dirty story or even stood for one being told in his presence. That is to say, he never protested against one; it simply would not have occurred to anyone to tell one in his presence. But in those young days this strict way of thinking had not yet developed so markedly. I remember his passion for a barmaid called Hansi, of whom he once said that whole cavalry regiments had ridden on her body. Franz was very unhappy while this affair lasted. You can see that, too, in a photograph taken of him together with Hansi, but in which he looks as if he would like to run away the next moment. An entry in my diary runs: "Trocadero wine bar. There he [Franz] is in love with a Germania from the German postage stamps, *chambre séparée*. But he is so extraordinarily shy. When he says, 'I'll pay your rent for you,' he laughs as if he meant it ironically." Many of his letters refer to this and similar contacts. These ambiguous and, one may say, even in his opinion, in fact most of all in his opinion, unclean affairs with women have left many traces in his three great novels and in other parts of his writings. I shall quote here another postcard, from Spitzberg in the Bohemian Forest, and three letters, which bear witness to his

116

craving and unsatisfied feelings as far as the world of women is concerned. (The book Franz mentions is my novel, "Norne-pygge Castle," 1908.)

(Postcard)

My dear Max

I am sitting under the roof of the veranda. In front of me it is about to begin to rain. I'm protecting my feet by lifting them up from the cold brick floor and putting them on a rung of the table, and I am exposing only my hands as long as I am writing. And I am writing to tell you I am very happy, and that I should be glad if you were here, because there are things in the woods that one could lie in the moss for years and think about. Adieu, I shall be back soon.

Your Franz

(Notepaper headed "Assicurazioni Generali.")
6/9/1908

Dear Max

Thank you. I am sure you forgive unhappy me for not having thanked you before, when you hear that Sunday morning and early afternoon I was trying for a job in vain, dreadfully in vain, of course, solely on account of my physical appearance, and the rest of the afternoon I was sitting with my grandfather, although from time to time affected by the idle hours; and then in the evening let me admit I was on the sofa near the bed of my dear H., while she twisted and turned her boy's body under her red blanket. In the evening with the rest of them at the exhibition, in the night in a wine bar, home at half-past five. That was where I first looked at your book, for which I thank you again. I have read only a little, the parts I knew already. What an uproar, a kind of controlled uproar!

Your Franz

My dear Max

It's half-past twelve in the night, that is to say, an unusual time for writing letters, even on a night as hot as this. The

117

moths won't even come to the light. After my light happy days in the Bohemian Forest—the butterflies there fly as high as the swallows do at home—I have now been in Prague four days, and so helpless. Nobody can stand me, and I can stand nobody, but the second is only a result of the first; only your book, which I am now reading straight through, does me good. It is a long time since I was so deep in misery without any explanation for it. As long as I go on reading it I hold tight on to it, even if it is in nowise intended to bring help to the unhappy; but if I don't do this, I have so urgently to go and look for someone who will only just give me a friendly pat that yesterday I went to a hotel with a whore. She is too old to feel melancholy any more; but she is sad, even though she doesn't wonder at it, that one is not so loving with a whore as one is with a mistress. I didn't bring her any comfort, because she didn't bring me any.

Dearest Max

Not because it is in itself anything that must be said without delay, but because it is after all an answer to your question, for which our way yesterday (not really "yesterday" because it's quarter-past two in the morning) was not long enough any more for me to find the right answer. You said she loves me. Why did you say that? Was it a joke, or the seriousness of over-sleepiness! She loves me, and it doesn't even occur to her to ask me whom I was with in Stěchowitz, what I am doing these days, why I can't go for a picnic on a weekday, and so on. Perhaps in the bar there wasn't time enough, but when we went on the excursion there was time and everything else you want, and yet any answer was good enough for her. But one can plausibly refute anything; yet in the following case one can't even attempt a refutation. In D. I was terribly afraid of running into W., and told her so, and then she immediately got afraid on my behalf of meeting W. That gives us a simple geometrical figure. Her attitude to me is the greatest friendliness, as incapable of developing as anything you can think of, and as far from the highest, as from the lowest love, because it's something quite

118

different. Myself I naturally don't need to obtrude into the figure at all, if it is to remain clear. Now I have really earned my sleep.

Your Franz

It is obvious that we often had a lot of other things, too, to tell each other about our first experiences with women, and on a few of these occasions Franz would sometimes remember a relationship he had with a French governess, which happened a long way back. He used to talk, too, about a woman he once met in Zuckmantel. And I found a puzzling postcard from Zuckmantel in my possession, from very early days: my address is written on it by Franz. The writing under the view of a walk through the forest is that of an entirely unknown woman. "This *is* a forest, in this forest one can be happy. So come along here, then!" The signature is in shorthand, absolutely indecipherable. It is to this episode and another later one in Riva, in 1913—about the latter Franz preserved an inviolable silence, he had vowed to the girl he would do so—that this entry in the diary of the year 1916 refers: "I had never yet been intimate with a woman apart from the time in Zuckmantel. And then again with the Swiss girl in Riva. The first was a woman, and I was inexperienced; the second was a child, and I was completely and utterly bewildered."

In Lugano we lived happily in the open air. Franz was a master of that joy in nature that bestows life and as in a dream marries earth to heaven. (Read again the lines he wrote me when he came back from the Bohemian Forest. "The butterflies there fly as high as the swallows do at home.") At the Hotel Belvedere au Lac (Lugano) and the bathing-place near by, as well as on our long walks, we enjoyed our good idle days, in the evening on the terrace of the hotel. We kept our diaries fervently; but this time not keeping it secret from each other, but in communion. Out of this came the plan for a novel in collaboration, "Richard and Samuel," in which we had a little good-natured laugh at each other. With Kafka, when he was happy, nothing was carried out without a touch of mischief, which was always, however, combined with a great amount of affection. At that time we worked out, besides, from our habit of keeping diaries, a whole theory of how to enjoy life, or at least travel. I remember going on a steamer on Lake Lucerne and pitying those tourists who took "only" cameras with them, and obviously had no idea of the higher art of recalling one's travels through the medium of diaries.

And there was yet another plan which came out of that short but so endlessly significant journey—which took us to Milan too, and from there, diverted through a cholera scare, to Stresa and Paris—a plan that bordered on lunacy but which was worked out by the two of us with determination and continual new jests. We hit upon the idea of creating a new type of guidebook. The series was to be called "On the Cheap." There were to be titles like "On the Cheap through Switzerland," "On the Cheap in Paris," etc. Franz was untiring and took a childish pleasure in compiling, down to the finest details, the principles of this type that was to make millionaires of us and above all take us out of the hideous routine of office work. I then wrote in all seriousness and put our plans for "The Reform of Guidebooks" up to publishers. Negotiations always broke down on the point that we refused to deliver up our precious secret without an enormous advance.

Franz took special delight and displayed a high degree of virtuosity in balancing in this way on the line between seriousness and the comic. It was often impossible to tell whether he meant what he said seriously or as a joke: he himself didn't always know, I am sure, but simply surrendered himself to the creative imagination of a great teller of fairy stories. Just so, with me too, he played this game of our new Baedeker—our "On the Cheap," which we could see already posted up on the walls of the Paris métro alongside Byrrh and the other most widely advertised apéritifs. Well, "On the Cheap" was above all to save tourists from having to choose, so that it needed imperative routes, only *one* hotel in each town, only *one* means of travel, the one that gave the best value for money. There was to be an organization to check our information frequently. "Exact amount of tips," Kafka writes in the memorandum we wrote together. And a note saying, "Neither tourists that want to go too fast or too slow, but a certain in-between class. Departures from plan are easier to arrange because they can be linked on to something precise." "On the Cheap" was also to devote a separate chapter to each of the following questions: what to do on a rainy day; travel souvenirs; what to wear; free concerts; where and how does one get free tickets for the theater, like a native of the place; in picture galleries see only a few important pictures, but study these thoroughly. We got particular fun out of an "On the Cheap" guide to conversation, which worked out on this principle: "It is impossible to learn a foreign language properly. We therefore prefer to teach it you badly straightway. This gives you less trouble, and is quite enough for making yourself understood. It is a kind of Esperanto, bad French or bad English, invented by us. In addition, we give dialects and the language of signs in current use locally." All the plans we developed with so much fun and friendship and at which we laughed ourselves sick, contained of course an undercurrent of irony, which was directed against our own shortcomings—we neither of us had any talent for languages—and against the economies we were unfortunately compelled by circumstances to make.

To cast a faint shadow on those days, which perhaps shine all too brightly in my memory, I shall be conscientious and quote another passage from my diary: "What a thought, that Plato several times tried to put his teachings into practice (Sicily). What on earth can have been going on in him and round about him? The very sound of reasonableness which one associates with the name of Plato doesn't fit in with this undoubtedly lunatic reality. And must not his contemporaries lawfully have looked upon such a man, who after all was wrong on so many points, as a fool and a nuisance? Posterity suffers less, or not at all, from his extremes, and so the 'Ideal' in him shines clearly forth—but we forget that these extremes and this ideal are part and parcel of one another. If

121

I may be absolutely honest, didn't I find Kafka a nuisance now and then? For instance, in Lugano, when he refused to take any laxative, faithful to his nature principles, but ruined the days for me with his moanings? At the same time Kafka was an exception among geniuses, he was so indescribably gentle and considerate. He went to personal trouble to damp down until they were completely unfelt the dissonances which had their root in the principle of genius. They were also really hardly noticeable, nothing but rudiments of them, e.g. unpunctuality."

For the journey to Weimar in the following year, 1912, we were especially well prepared by our love of Goethe, and the study we had been making of Goethe's works for years. To hear Kafka talk about Goethe with awe was something quite out of the ordinary, it was like hearing a little child talk about an ancestor who lived in happier, purer days and in direct contact with the Divine. And now again let me sound the little note of mischief at once: Kafka sometimes emphasized that he was amazed that some authors are so incautious as to quote Goethe—a sentence from Goethe, after all, cannot fail to stand out all too dazzlingly from the rest of the prose of any author. To the unusual reverence Kafka felt for Goethe the following passage from his diary bears witness. "Goethe by the power of his writings probably retards the development of the German language. Even if prose has often traveled away from him in the intervening period, yet it has always, as it is doing just at this moment, finally returned to him with increased longing, and has even taken to itself archaic turns of speech which are to be found in Goethe, but otherwise have nothing to do with him, in order to enjoy the completest picture of their unbounded dependence on him." I am putting alongside it another passage on one of Lessing's characters which will at least suggest the outline of the whole complexity of Kafka's position with regard to the German classics. On Tellheim in *Minna von Barnhelm,* he quotes Dilthey: "He has that free movement of the life of the soul which, as the circumstances of life change,

takes us by surprise again and again by showing us quite
new aspects that only the creations of true poets possess."

In this mood of reverential gratitude we paid our first and
last visit to Weimar. Kafka's diary covering this most important journey I have now published. To complete the picture I
shall here repeat the appropriate passages from my *Kingdom
of Love,* making only one correction. That is, that we two
poor lower-grade civil servants had not one whole month,
but only a little over one week to spare for Weimar.

"They go for their summer holidays together. Only to Weimar, just one month in Weimar; from the very first they had
been one in their reverence for the primeval force of Goethe,
and both of them were quite uninfluenced by the fashionable
pooh-poohing of his greatness. In this case there was no need
for any mutual influence, the only result was perhaps a
strengthening of their feelings. Moreover, they have no wish
to do any such thing as study Weimar, but they live there
just as in any summer resort, bathe every day in the town
swimming-pool, in the evening eat dishful after dishful of
good strawberries in a restaurant in the Town Square; above
all, they intend to have a good rest. But as with everything
that touches Garta, this stay in Weimar also takes on a special shape—at the same time without Garta's wishing it, only
from the fundamental characteristics of his nature, a special
honesty and accuracy (not of the head but of the heart).
You see, a tiny, ever so tender relationship springs up between him and the lovely daughter of the caretaker at
Goethe's house in the Frauenplan. To call it a love affair
would be saying too much; it is nothing but a shy, teasing,
perhaps also gently painful, pleasure in seeing each other on
the part of the two young people. The result of it is that
Garta, and Christof with him, are asked in to the caretaker's
flat, that they can go in and out of Goethe's flat as though
they were at home; that they have the entry into the garden,
which is otherwise out of bounds, and can wander about in
Goethe's rooms outside visiting hours, that is to say, undisturbed by the trampling of tourists. They feel as if they belonged even, in the most distant, ancient Roman sense, to

123

Goethe's 'family.' Like a ghost, something of Goethe's music echoes through their merry meetings with the caretaker's daughter, on these summer evenings crowned with green and ringed with roses in his garden with its ancient ivy-covered walls. He is there, the kingly old man; he is invisibly there! Of all the sights of Weimar, even of those which have to do with Goethe, they see very little else. Garta's experiences are always full of gaps; it is only single things he grasps always, but these with loving penetration to their very depth, but there is never any question of completeness. This also could easily be turned into stereotyped praise: the intensive life that does not wish to record impressions. But Garta does not consider it an advantage, but only as a personal weakness, as a defect, that his capacities are insufficient for a complete comprehension, and when he finds a man who has this complete grasp of experience, or thinks he can presuppose in him a forceful striving to achieve it, he admires him beyond measure. From many things he said one can see that he took Christof for a first-class man of this kind—perhaps not altogether correctly. Anyway, they supplement one another in the most salutary fashion. It hurts them a little when they have to part after the days they spent together in Weimar—Christof to go home, Richard to go back again to a home for nature treatment in the Harz Mountains. They go together by train a little way. At the junction where their lines part, Christof in a sudden wave of affection embraces his friend and kisses him—just this once—lightly on the cheek. When they both get home, not a day passes without their speaking at least for a fleeting moment. Many weeks they spend, afternoon after afternoon, at the good old Prague 'Zivil' swimming-baths, lying on the burning boards under the autumn chestnut trees, or in the Vltava which has already grown cooler. Worries about work, families, first meetings with girls—everything they confide in one another."

The journey to Weimar was also important for the reason that it took us through Leipzig, where I brought Franz together with Ernst Rowohlt and Kurt Wolff, who were then running the publishing house of Rowohlt. For I had long

124

cherished the burning desire to see a book of my friend's in print.

Franz's attitude towards this wish of mine was very divided. He wanted to—and again he didn't want to. At times his disinclination won the day, particularly at the time when, having returned to Prague, he had to set to work and choose those short pieces of prose which he considered were ready to be printed out of the wealth of his manuscripts, that is to say, the diaries, and give them the final polishing up—which took place not without a lot of hesitation, looking-up of dictionaries, and despair at his uncertainty of the rules of spelling and punctuation. The publishers had already expressed their readiness—these were happy days!—after seeing the specimens I had taken with me to Leipzig. It was only up to Franz to submit a definite manuscript. And that was just the point at which he began to kick good and proper, and discovered that everything he had written was bad, and that piecing together these "worthless" old fragments prevented him from getting on and producing better work. But I wouldn't let up any more. Kafka's diary is a witness to the resistance he put up against me, but it didn't help him in the least. The book had to be finished, and finished it was. When the amount of material chosen by Franz as worthy of publication turned out to be incredibly small, the publishers decided to have the "Contemplation"—that was the title of the book—set in unusually large type. The first edition, now very rare, consisted of eight hundred numbered copies, and the ninety-nine pages with their gigantic lettering resemble ancient votive tablets. And thereby, by one of those rare accidents which according to Schopenhauer have nothing accidental left in them, the innermost character of this great prose was after all unsurpassably brought out.

Thus Franz's resistance was overcome, and turned to a healthy purpose by good forces which in those legendary days at least maintained an equilibrium with the bad forces of the world. Here I must insert the remark that Kafka had led me a similar dance the year before. I insisted on carrying out the plan we had made in Lugano to write "Richard and

Samuel." We began; the work soon came to a standstill. I wouldn't give in, however, until at least a respectable slice of the book had been written. A part of it then appeared in the *Herderblätter* published by Willy Haas. The continuation was to show that the course of friendship was exposed to the same ups and downs and complications as that of true love. The two friends were to get really angry with one another on the journey, their incompatibilities were to come into the open, and only the danger of cholera they shared in sultry, torrid Milan—where I moved Franz almost to tears by begging him not to let me be buried without putting a bullet into me, should I die there away from home—was to fan the ashes of their old feeling for each other to its highest glory. "The journey ends in the two friends putting their forces together to produce a new work of art with a character of its own," says the preface to the published chapter. The two friends were not, of course, drawn true to nature, above all not Samuel, who was intended to be practical, rich, and independent—yet we got a great deal of fun out of using for Richard preferably Kafka's characteristics and notes on the journey, and mine for Samuel—although we sometimes followed the opposite procedure. But Franz struggled against this work, too, and yet it is a good thing that I held his nose to the grindstone for a while at least. He got used to regular work, overcame internal inhibitions, forcibly tore himself away from a period of sterility—it is just in the period in which we were writing "Richard and Samuel" that his own diary begins to flow more richly—he even occasionally, as an exception, found some pleasure in the work on "Richard and Samuel," and the discipline he subjected himself to opened up to him the idea that "the transformation of emotion into character" which Schiller postulated was beginning to take place in himself. Thus the quantity and quality of his production grew until the final break-through was achieved in the night of September 22–23, 1912, when he wrote down the whole of "The Verdict" at one sitting. In moving words Kafka describes this night in his diary—I believe that this self-revelation will forever remain an important document for

126

the understanding of what a true artist is. "This is the only way to write, only in a coherence like this, with such a complete flinging open of body and soul." By saying this Franz at the same time, without complaining, utters the severest criticism of the pestilential necessity he found himself under of earning his daily bread.

The redeeming moment that brought about this sudden break-through was a visit paid to us by a girl from Berlin, Miss F. B.—his relations with her were the guiding principle in Franz's life for five years. With the words, "When I went to see Brod on August 13, she was sitting at the table," the diary begins the story of this fateful meeting, and then follows the sentence, "As I was taking my seat, I took a good look at her for the first time, and by the time I had sat down, I had already formed an unshakable opinion." This meeting is also noted down in my diary for August 13, and in connection with the note on the meeting in my parents' house there follows: "Café City. Kafka brings the finished book and it pleases me immensely. Miss B. Then I read 'Contemplation' once again. Divine. Wednesday, August 14, sent 'Contemplation' to Rowohlt."

The year 1912 is a decisive one in Kafka's life. And two important events took place on this same one day, August 13. I have preserved a little note that Franz sent me by messenger the following morning. It shows, among other things, that it would be wrong to picture me only in the role of the one urging publication, and Kafka only in that of the one striving against it. The letter runs, "Good morning, dear Max. While I was arranging the pieces yesterday, I was completely under the influence of the girl, as a result it is quite possible that some stupidity has crept in, some sequence that may strike one as comic only in secret. Please see if this is so, and let me add my thanks for that, to all the great thanks I owe you." There follow two small directions for changes to be made.

When I came back on September 29 from Portorose where I had been working with my friend Felix Weltsch on the book "Perception and Concept," Franz came to the station to

127

meet us, and began at once telling us about the short story "The Verdict" which he had just finished, and which he willingly gave me for my annual *Arcadia*. In this it duly appeared —in the only year in which the publication itself appeared, 1913—with a dedication to his fiancée.

Immediately after "The Verdict," Franz set to work on the first chapter of his novel, which he had most probably begun before, but which was only now getting into its stride. It was "The Man Who Disappeared," or *Amerika*. I shall quote my diary notes from this period. September 29: "Kafka is in ecstasy, writes whole nights through. A novel, set in America." October 1: "Kafka in unbelievable ecstasy." October 2: "Kafka is still greatly inspired. One chapter finished. I am happy about it." October 3: "Kafka is doing well." On October 6 he read me "The Verdict" and "The Stoker," the first chapter of his novel *Amerika*. Immediately after that on October 8 took place the correspondence between his mother and myself (concerning his contemplated suicide). On October 14 the great Vienna novelist, Otto Stoessl, for whom Kafka and I had special admiration, was staying with me, and we went for walks together, all three, in the streets of the Mala Strana of Prague. But on October 28 there is already the foreboding entry that Franz has written a twenty-two-page letter to Miss F., and is troubled by worries about the future. That was the beginning of the tragedy of their relations. (Franz's own diary reveals a gap from October 1912 till February 1913, which is why I am quoting my own diary just for this period.) On November 3 I find: "Went to Baum's where Kafka read us the second chapter of his novel. He is completely in love with F., and happy. This novel of his—an enchantment." And as early as November 24 of this unusually rich end-of-year, Kafka read to us at Baum's, "his glorious short story about a noxious insect"—i.e. *The Metamorphosis*. Thus between the end of September and the end of November 1912, that is to say, within two months, three of Kafka's chief works came into being, or at least, as far as the novel is concerned, had reached the decisive stage.

On "The Verdict," this stormy tale of how the good and
128

dutiful son is, in spite of all that, found refractory and diabolical by his father, and condemned to "death by drowning," whereupon he throws himself into the river with the cry, "Dear parents, after all I have always loved you"—on this story which at first sight seems quite clear from the psychoanalytical point of view, but which, when you take a second and third look at it becomes more and more veiled in its meaning, Franz himself has left three commentaries. One was in a conversation with me. He told me, in fact, and to the best of my recollection, more or less in so many words, "Do you know what the last sentence means? When I wrote it, I had in mind a violent ejaculation." (*Note.*—It followed the description of the suicide, and ran, "At this moment passed over the bridge a truly unending stream of traffic.") The other two explanatory hints are to be found in the diary, and were written while the story was being printed:

"2/11/1913. I am taking advantage of the proof-reading of 'The Verdict' to jot down, as far as I can remember them now, all the relationships that became clear to me during the course of the story. This is necessary, because the story came out of me like a real human birth, covered with dirt and slime, and I am the only person that has the hand that can reach the body itself, and that cares to do so. The friend is the link between father and son, he is the greatest thing they have in common. Sitting alone at his window, Georg takes a sensual pleasure in rooting about in this common possession, believes he has his father in himself and, but for a fleeting, sad hesitation, considers that everything is peaceful. The development of the story now shows how out of this common thing, the friend, the father comes to the foreground, and sets himself up as Georg's opposite, strengthened by other lesser common possessions, such as by the mother's love and devotion, by the loyal memory of her, and by the customers whom, it is true, the father originally cultivated for the sake of his business. Georg has nothing, the fiancée who lives in the story only through her relations with the friend, i.e. with the common possession, and who just because there has not yet been even a marriage, cannot enter into the blood-

129

bond that is drawn round the father and the son, is easily driven away by the father. The whole of what they have in common is built up on the father, Georg finds nothing in it but what is foreign, what has come to be taken for granted, something he has never sufficiently looked after, something exposed to Russian revolutions, and it is merely because he himself has nothing else left save the sight of his father, that the verdict that shuts his father off from him completely has such a powerful effect on him.

"Georg has the same number of letters as Franz. In Bendemann, the 'mann' is there only to strengthen the syllable 'Bende' [bonds] in case of any unforeseen possibilities in the story. But Bende has the same number of letters as Kafka, and the vowel 'e' is repeated in the same positions as the vowel 'a' in Kafka.

"Frieda has exactly the same number of letters as F. and begins with the same letter; Brandenfeld begins with the same letter as B. and, through 'feld,' has a certain connection of meaning too. Possibly, too, the idea of Berlin was not without influence, and the Brandenburg province may have had something to do with it.

"February 12: While writing my description of the friend abroad, I thought of St. a great deal. When I ran into him by accident three months after this story, he told me he had got engaged about three months before.

"After I had read my story out to them at Weltsch's yesterday, the old man Weltsch went out of the room, and when he came back after a little while praised particularly the descriptive passages in the story. Pointing with his hand, he said, 'I see this father in front of me'; and as he said so, he was looking exclusively at the empty chair in which he had been sitting while I was reading it.

"The sister said, 'It's our house.' I was astonished at their getting the setting of the story so wrong, and said 'Well, then the father must have lived in the lavatory.'"

In January 1913 "Contemplation" appeared. The book is dedicated "To M. B." and in the copy that Franz gave me these lines have been written in under the inscription: "Just as
130

it now stands here in print, for my dearest Max—Franz K."
One year later I was able to return thanks by dedicating my
novel *Tycho Brahe's Redemption* to him.

I wrote about his first book and about his literary work
in general in the only long essay on him that appeared during Franz's lifetime, in the *Neue Rundschau,* November
1921, and among other things said, "Where shall I begin?—
It doesn't matter where. For among the peculiarities of this
phenomenon is that one can approach it from any angle
and reach the same conclusion.

"This already shows how true, how unshakably genuine,
how pure it is. For a lie offers a different aspect from every
angle, and what is impure is iridescent. But in the case of
Franz Kafka, and let it be said in his case alone in the
whole literary circle of the 'moderns,' there is no irides-
cence, no changes of view, no scene-shifting. Here is truth,
and nothing but the truth.

"Take his language, for example. The cheap means, coin-
ing new words, compounds, playing chess with the clauses,
he despised. 'Despised' is perhaps not the right word. They
are inaccessible to him, just as the impure is inaccessible to
the pure, is forbidden to it. His language is clear as crystal,
and on the surface one can, as it were, detect no other aim
than that of properly and clearly suiting the subject. And
yet underlying the serene mirror of this well of pure language are dreams and visions of unfathomable depth. One
peers into it and is enchanted by its beauty and individuality. But one cannot say, least of all at the first glance can
one say, wherein lies the peculiar quality of this simple sentence construction which is after all nothing except right,
healthy, and simple. Read a few sentences of Kafka aloud,
and your tongue and your· breath will feel a sweetness
never experienced before. The cadences, the breaks, seem
to follow mysterious laws; the little pauses between phrases
have an architecture of their own, a melody is heard that
has its roots in other material than that of this earth. It is
perfection, simply perfection, that perfection of pure form
that brought Flaubert to tears in front of the ruins of the

131

walls of the Acropolis. But it is perfection on the move, on the march, at the double, even. I am thinking of things like 'Children on the Post Road,' which was the introductory story in his first book, 'Contemplation,' this classically beautiful prose that nevertheless derives so completely from the cottage. There you have fire, the completely restless fire and blood of a tense childhood, full of forebodings; but the walls of fire obey the baton of an invisible conductor; they are not ragged sheets of flame but a palace, whose every stone is a roaring blaze. Perfection—and just for that reason not *outré* and not extravagant. One turns somersaults only so long as one has not reached the utmost limit, the line that embraces the universe. The all-embracing does not need to turn somersaults. But don't things get dull at this level? This is the heart of Kafka's importance as an artist. I said before, he is perfection on the move, on the road. Hence the all-embracing consorts without effort with the minutest, yes, the most scurrilous detail. Oceanus with the comic tricks of the trade of office life, the sweetness of redemption with a new lawyer, who is, however, really the war-horse Bucephalus, or with a worried country doctor, or a little commercial traveler, or with the pink tinsel of a little equestrienne. Hence these great sentences full of artistry, and this simplicity of style, which is yet shot through with ideas in every phrase, in every word. Hence the inconspicuousness of the metaphors which nevertheless—it is only some time after that one notices it with surprise—say something new. Hence calm, perspective, freedom, as if above the clouds—and yet good natural tears and the compassionate heart. If the angels made jokes in heaven it would have to be in Franz Kafka's language. This language is fire, but it leaves no soot behind. It has the sublimity of endless space, and at the same time it palpitates with every palpitation of things created.

"That the pure dare not touch the impure is its strength, but also, at the same time, its weakness. Its strength, because it means the perception, the full perception of the distance between it itself and the absolute. But this distance is something negative, is weakness. And so the strength of the pure
132

can only express itself by insisting that it will not try to lie away its distance from the absolute, but rather exaggerate it directly, as though through a spy-glass that magnifies a thousandfold. But that just to do this is strength, it may and dare not admit, if it wishes to maintain its position. Thus there results a double foundation and, as there always is where there is a double foundation, humor. Yes, even in the midst of the terror of such self-will, such persistence in the most dangerous of all attitudes—for it is a question of life ànd death in this case—there plays a loving smile. It is a new kind of smile that distinguishes Kafka's work, a smile close to the ultimate things—a metaphysical smile so to speak—indeed sometimes when he used to read out one of his tales for us friends of his, it rose above a smile and we laughed aloud. But we were soon quiet again. It is no laughter befitting human beings. Only angels may laugh in this way, angels that we certainly cannot picture in the likeness of Raphael's cherubs—no, angels, seraphim with three great pairs of wings, demonic beings between man and God.

"In a quite special way, then, strength and weakness, rise and fall, interpenetrate in Kafka's writings. At first sight it is weakness that meets the eye—something that on the surface puts one in mind of decadence, and satanism, of the love of decay, death and horror that breaks out in Poe, in Villiers de l'Isle Adam, and other later writers. But this first sight is entirely misleading. A short story like Kafka's *In the Penal Colony* has nothing whatever in common with Poe, although scenes of horror occur in it along the same thematic line. A comparison of the style, if nothing else, should teach one that, or at least give one to think. What has the brightly colored narrative of Kafka, with its sure line, like a drawing by Ingres, in common with the vibrating prose, sometimes indeed violently set in vibration, of these specialists in making one's flesh creep? They are specialists in the deep-sea exploration of hells, having a more or less scientific interest in their explorations; a little religious end-resolution, a kind of 'moral of the tale,' is stuck on more or less out of embarrassment. Writers, certainly great writers even, and honestly confounded—but don't you hear throughout a note of being 'proud of confusion'? But in Kafka's case after all it is the deep earnestness of a religious man that fills the scene. He shows no curiosity about the abysses. It is *against his will* that he sees them. He does not lust after decay. He falls into decay, although he follows the narrow path, sees and loves determination and coherence, and there is nothing he loves so much as the blue unclouded heaven above him. But this heaven begins to pucker like the forehead of a scowling father. And as much more terrible and more shudderingly gruesome the fear for keeping heaven unclouded is than making a study of a tolerable couple of hell's abnormities and turning them into capital, so much more powerful is the shattering effect of Kafka's polished work of art than the sensations to be got from those sketch-books of 'interesting' pathology of the 'uncanny' type.

"That is exactly why his books—*The Metamorphosis* or 'The Verdict,' etc.—give the reader such a shudder. Because all around them, and really in the midst of them, too, the whole of the free world is revealed. But they are not 'on principle meant to horrify'—but rather on a principle that is the opposite of 'horror-making'—on a principle that is perhaps idyllic or heroic, in any case honest, healthy, positive, inclined to everything that desires to live, everything gentle and good, the blooming girlish body that shines over the corpse of the hero at the end of *The Metamorphosis*, farm labor, everything natural, simple and fresh with a child's freshness, full of striving after joy, happiness, decency, physical and spiritual strength, on the principle then on which a well-meaning God worked when He created the world—but 'not for us.' Against the background of a good Divine Will this 'only not for us' has a doubly terrifying effect, as a confession of sin of the utmost possible force. It is not life that Kafka rejects. He does not strive with God, only with himself. Hence the dreadful severity with which he goes to law. All through his writings there are judges' chairs, sentences are executed. *The Metamorphosis*—the man who is not perfect, Kafka degrades to an animal, to an insect. Or, what is still more horrible ('A Report to an Academy'), he lets the animal be raised to the level of a human being, but to what a level of humanity, to a masquerade at which mankind is unmasked. But even that is not enough! Mankind must sink deeper still—it is a question only of 'all or nothing'—and if a man cannot raise himself to God's level, if the Father has found him guilty, if entire union with the fundamental morality, entry into the 'Law,' is forbidden him by a hefty doorkeeper, or rather when the man has not the courage to thrust this doorkeeper on one side, when the 'imperial messenger' of the dying sun-prince never comes to you—very well, then change yourself into some useless object that is neither animate nor inanimate, into a reel of cotton, which as 'something in the care of the heavenly householder' wanders upstairs and downstairs without stopping. 'What's your name, then?' —'Odradek'—and a whole range of Slav words is set ringing, which all mean renegade, renegade from one's race, 'rod,' renegade from the council, 'rada,' the divine decision of the creation, 'rat.' 'And your address?' 'No fixed abode.' From this you can understand that Kafka writes, alongside the general tragedy of mankind, in particular the sufferings of his own unhappy people, homeless, haunted Jewry, the mass without form, without body, as no one else has ever done. He writes it, without the word 'Jew' appearing in any one of his books."

In May 1913, appeared "The Stoker," the first chapter of the novel *Amerika* which was not published until after his death. This time Franz put the whole thing through without any assistance or urging on my part. I shall quote a letter of a later date, which shows the unusual relations that existed between Franz Kafka and his publisher Kurt Wolff, and which do the author and the publisher equal personal honor. It may also lay claim to be praised for having in itself the charm of rarity. Kurt Wolff writes, November 3, 1921:

Dear and honored Mr. Kafka
Fourteen days ago I happened by accident to meet, in

Leipzig, Ludwig Hardt, who came from Prague, and traveled in his company from Leipzig to Berlin. On this journey we made together, Ludwig Hardt told me about the recitations he had given in Prague, and about the special pleasure it had given him to be in your company.

Talking to Ludwig Hardt gives me an opportunity of giving you another proof that I am still alive. Our correspondence is rare and frugal. None of the authors with whom we are connected comes to us with wishes or questions so seldom as you do, and with none of them do we have the feeling that the outward fate of their published books is a matter of such indifference as it is with you. In this case it would seem to be the right thing for the publisher to write and tell the author from time to time that this lack of interest on the author's part in the fate of his books does not lead the publisher astray, and make him lose his faith and trust in the special quality of what he has published. From the bottom of my heart may I assure you that I personally have so strong a feeling for you and your work as I only have in the case of perhaps two or at most three of the writers whom we represent, and whom we are permitted to bring before the public.

You must not consider the outward results achieved by your books as a measure of the work we put into selling them. You and we know that it is generally just the best and most valuable things that do not find their echo immediately, but only much later, and we still have faith in German reading circles that they will one day have the receptive capacity that these books deserve.

It would be an especially great pleasure for me if you would care to make it practically possible for us to demonstrate tangibly the unshaken confidence that unites us with you and your work, by entrusting us with further manuscripts for publication. Every manuscript that you can bring yourself to send us will be welcome, and will be published in book form with love and care. If, in the course of time you could once send us, together with collections of short prose pieces, a long connected story or novel—I know, after all, from yourself and from Max Brod how many manuscripts of this kind

136

are nearly finished, or perhaps quite finished—we should welcome it with special gratitude. It must also be taken into consideration that the public for a connected, comprehensive prose work is naturally much greater than that for a collection of short prose pieces. That is a banal and senseless attitude on the part of the reader, but there it is. The stir which a longer prose work would make would at least enable us to achieve incomparably greater sales than we have so far done, and the success of a book of this kind would also make possible a livelier trade in those already published.

Please, dear Mr. Kafka, give us the pleasure of letting us know if and what we may hope for in the near future.

I hope your health is again passable, and greet you with unchanged feelings, as your honestly and heartily devoted

Kurt Wolff

Despite encouragement of this kind Franz could not bring himself to finish even one of his three long novels. Of the way he planned to finish the novel *Amerika*—which I am dealing with here, because the first two chapters of it were written still in the period which falls before the publication of "Contemplation"—I remember that it was to be the sole work of Kafka that was to end on an optimistic note, with wide-ranging prospects of life. On the other hand Franz seems at other times to have pictured a different, tragic end for his hero, Karl Rossman. This we see from a note in his diary, dated September 29, 1915, in which he compares his two novels "The Man Who Disappeared" (*Amerika*) and *The Trial,* of which the hero is called K. "Rossman and K., the innocent and the guilty, finally without distinction destroyed by legal sentence, the innocent man with a lighter hand, more pushed to the side than hurled to the ground."

The novel *Amerika* is kept with a lighter hand, in brighter colors, and with more joy in hopes than the two later long books. On this book, too, there is to be found a short commentary, a self-portrayal in the diary. I quote the following lines also because in them is clearly revealed the great discretion with which Kafka combines admiration for Dickens

137

with keen criticism of him. Just through a direct insight of this kind one gets perhaps an inkling of the wealth and the surety of judgment one met with in the company of a man who, with all his devotion to the unfathomable, remained sober and aloof from excursions into the temptations of cheap mysticism, who never allowed himself to be so blinded by the good qualities of a man or a writer as to fail to see the bad side, and for whom, on the other hand, openly displayed vices and failings in any phenomenon never distracted his attention from a just appreciation of the virtues it possessed at the same time. As clearly, truly, and complicatedly as he here evaluates Dickens, Kafka looked at the whole world.

The page in the diary runs: "Dickens' *Copperfield*. 'The Stoker' a sheer imitation of Dickens, the novel I have planned even more so. The story of the trunk, the happiness-spreading and charming hero, the menial tasks, the loved one on the country estate, the dirty houses, and so on. Above all, the method. It was my intention, I now see, to write a Dickens novel, only enriched by the sharper lights I have taken from my period, and the duller ones which I dug out of myself. Dickens' wealth and carelessly powerful sweep, but in consequence passages of horrible powerlessness, in which the only thing he does is to muddle up together what he has already achieved. Barbaric is the effect of the senseless whole, a barbarism which I, thanks to my weaknesses and taught by my epigonism, have at least avoided. There is heartlessness behind this manner overflowing with emotion, these rude, rough characterizations which are artificially in-jected into every person, and without which Dickens would be unable to scramble up his stories even for a fleeting mo-ment."

CHAPTER V

THE ENGAGEMENT

FRANZ KAFKA had the highest conception of marriage. In the "Letter to My Father," he writes about it in these terms: "To get married, to found a family, to accept all the children that arrive, to maintain them in this uncertain world, and even to lead them a little on their way is, in my opinion, the utmost that a man can ever succeed in doing. That so many people succeed with apparent ease in doing it is no proof to the contrary, because, in the first place, not many really succeed; and secondly, these 'not many' don't generally 'do' it, but it just 'happens' to them. This is not that utmost that I mean, it is true, but it is nevertheless a very good thing and worthy of all respect—particularly as 'doing' and 'happening' cannot be separated absolutely one from the other. And finally there is no question at all of this utmost, but only of some kind of distant, but respectable approach to it; after all, it is not necessary to fly right into the middle of the sun, but just to crawl to some clean spot on the earth on which the sun sometimes shines and where one can warm oneself a little."

Similarly in a story like "Eleven Sons" this high esteem for the family, one may even say for the patriarchal way of life, such as Franz so admired as the natural attitude of his father, stands out clearly. The enormous joy of a father who tells everybody in the house that a grandson has been born to him, is described in the diary with that mixture of astonishment, deep approval, and light, critical mockery which characterizes the relations between son and father in "The Verdict." The prose piece "Eleven Sons," which has already challenged several forced explanations of its meaning is, in my opinion, to be understood as a wishful picture of fatherhood, of founding a family, which can be held up against the father's example as something of equal value, that is to say, something just as magnificent and patriarchal, some-

139

thing bordering on the mystic in all the simplicity of its life. This explanation is not contradicted by the fact that Franz once said to me, "The eleven sons are quite simply eleven stories I am working on this very moment." After all, stories were his children. In his writing he was accomplishing, on a remote territory, but independently, something which was analogous to his father's creative power—I am following Franz's conception of this point, not my own—and which could be set alongside it. The ideal that hovered before his eyes when once he was reading "with suppressed sobs" a book on the war of 1870–71 was "to be a father, and talk quietly with one's son. But then one may not have a little toy hammer in place of a heart."

After all that, one may well understand how the meeting with the girl who for the first time awakened in him the desire to get married stirred him to the very depths of his being. He got to know F. in August 1912. As early as November 9, 1912, we find in the papers he left behind him the draft of a letter; I do not know whether the letter corresponding to it was ever posted, but it at least reflects sharply enough his first mood of fear and retreat.

Dearest Fräulein

You mustn't write to me any more, and I, too, shall not write to you any more. I could not help but make you unhappy by my writing, and I myself am past all help. To admit that to myself, I didn't really need to count the chimes each hour all last night, I was fully aware of it in fact before my first letter, and if in spite of that I tried to cling to you, I should deserve to be cursed for it anyway, if I were not cursed for it already. If you want your letters back I shall of course send you them, much as I should like to keep them. But if you do really want them after all, write me a postcard with nothing on it as a sign that you do. Quickly forget the ghost that is me and live in happiness and peace as you did before.

Despite this letter, or draft of a letter, the correspondence
140

between Prague and Berlin went back and forth with great liveliness. Things hung in the balance for a long time. The girl began to have doubts, Franz seemed to her—and one cannot hold it against her—uncanny and impossible to fit into the ordinary course of affairs. She wanted to break it off. That made him redouble his efforts to keep her. When no news came he was miserable. When news came he tormented himself with doubts. How was he going to manage to live in a menage of two? At the same time he experienced then an epoch of the highest literary productivity. Immediately after "The Verdict," in addition to the works which were published later, he began a story, the chief character of which was called Gustav Bleukelt, the tale of "a simple man of regular habits," who dies at the age of thirty-five. "Kept myself from writing by force," he writes twice following in his diary. And, "the rush of blood to the head and this useless drifting past! What harmful things." At Baum's he read "The Verdict" to us and had tears in his eyes. "The indubitability of the story is confirmed." Those are strong words of self-conviction, rare enough in the case of Franz. In May 1913 he attempted to counterbalance his mounting emotions by garden work. On July 1 he was seized by "the wish for solitude undisturbed by thought. To have only myself to face. Perhaps I shall find it in Riva." But on July 3 again we find, "the extension and heightening of existence through marriage. Text for a sermon. But I can guess it almost." On July 21 he draws up for himself a list of all the points "for and against my marriage." The deeply affecting document closes with the appeal in large letters: "Miserable me!" and "What misery." It lists the following points:

"1. Inability to bear living alone, not any inability to live, quite the contrary; it is even unlikely that I understand how to live together with someone; but to bear the onslaught of my own life, the onset of time and old age, the vague pressure of the itch to write, my sleeplessness, the near approach of madness—I am unable to bear all this alone. Perhaps I should fit in naturally. My connection with F. will lend my existence greater powers of resistance.

141

"2. Everything immediately starts me thinking. Every joke in the comic papers; every memory of Flaubert and Grillparzer; the sight of the nightshirts laid out on my parents' twin beds made for the night; Max's marriage. Yesterday N. N. said, 'All the married men (among our friends) are happy, I don't understand it'—when he said this, it also started me thinking and I became frightened again.

"3. I must be alone a great deal. All that I have accomplished is the result of being alone.

"4. Everything that is not connected with literature I hate; it bores me to carry on conversations (even when they are concerned with literature); it bores me to pay calls, the joys and sorrows of my relatives bore me to the very soul. Conversation takes the importance, the seriousness and the truth out of everything, I think.

"5. Fear of being tied to anyone, of overflowing into another personality. Then I shall never be alone any more.

"6. In front of my sisters, this was especially so in my earlier days, I was often a quite different person than with other people. I laid myself open, was fearless, strong, unexpected, carried away, as I otherwise am only when I am writing. If I could only be these things before all the world through the intermediation of my wife! But wouldn't it in that case be at the expense of my writing? Only not that! Not that!

"7. Single, I might perhaps one day really give up my job. Married, it would never be possible."

On August 13 he made the note, "Perhaps it is now all over, and my letter of yesterday [i.e. to F.] may be the last. That would undoubtedly be the right thing. What I am suffering, what she will suffer—it's nothing to compare with the mutual suffering that would result. I shall slowly pull myself together; she will get married, it is the only way out for mortals. We two cannot blast a road through the rocks for our two selves, it is enough that we have wept and tormented ourselves for a whole year trying to do so. She will see that from my last letters. If she doesn't, then I shall certainly have to marry her because I am too weak to stand up against what
142

she thinks about our mutual happiness, and quite unable not to put into practice, as far as in me lies, what she considers possible."

But the affair developed along different lines. On August 14: "The opposite has happened. Three letters came. The last I couldn't resist. I love her, as far as I am capable of that, but my love is buried almost to suffocation under fear and self-reproaches." On August 18, during a long walk, he told me he had proposed to F. I had gone and fetched him at the nursery garden in Troja, and then he had given me some very worldly-wise, positive advice to help me to get rid of the worries which were piling up on me at that time. Finally, with less assuredness this time, he began to talk about his own affairs. I made this entry about our conversation in my diary: "Franz on the subject of his marriage. He has proposed. His unhappiness. Everything or nothing. His justification, pure emotion, without analysis, without the possibility or need for analysis. A complicated situation, which engages my deepest attention. He talks of Radeschowitz [1] where the married women are bursting with sexuality, with children, the unborn too, who rule everything. He counsels complete retirement from the world." The same mood of despair expresses itself in entries in his own diary. For example, on August 15: "Tormented in bed towards the morning. The only solution I can see is to jump through the window. Mother came to my bed and asked if I had sent the letter [2] off, and if I had stuck to the same wording. I said the wording was the same, only still sharper. I said she didn't understand me in any case, and not only in this affair. Later she asked me if I was going to write to Uncle Alfred—he deserved to be written to. I asked her how he deserved it. He has wired, he has written, he means so well by you. 'Those are only outward things,' I said, 'he is a complete stranger to me, he misunderstands me utterly, and has no idea of what I want and need, I have nothing to do with him.' 'Well then, nobody understands you,' said mother. 'I suppose I am also a stranger

[1] A summer house near Prague.
[2] To F.'s parents.

143

to you, and so is your father. We all wish nothing but your harm.' 'Certainly, you are all strangers to me, it's only blood that connects us, but that doesn't express itself. You don't wish me any harm, of course.'

"From this and a few other observations of myself, I am led to the conclusion that in my ever-increasing inward determination and confidence there lie possibilities that I could after all stand the test of marriage, and even guide it towards a development favorable to my vocation. It is however a belief I have clutched at, in a certain sense, standing on the window ledge.

"I shall shut myself up away from everything until I have lost all recollection. I shall set myself at enmity with everybody, speak to nobody."

He was reading a Kierkegaard anthology, "The Book of the Judge." The similarity between Kierkegaard's fate and his own becomes clear to him.

In September 1913 he took refuge in Riva, at the Hartungen nursing home. "The very idea of a honeymoon fills me with horror," he writes to me. He experiences the curious episode with the Swiss girl. It remains obscure. "Everything struggles against its being set on paper. Were I sure that her command not to say anything about it had any influence on this—I have obeyed her command strictly, almost without effort—I should be satisfied." Then later the words, "Too late! The sweetness of mourning and of love. To be smiled at by her in a boat. That was the most beautiful thing of all. Always the longing to die and yet keeping oneself alive, that alone is love."

In November "an ambassador from F." appeared in Prague, a girl friend who later played a role in this relationship which is not quite transparent. In the most tactless way I was plaguing him just at this time with my project for an "Education in Communality," in Zionism. It is the only small cloud on our friendship, which I have already mentioned. "The day before yesterday in the evening with Max. He becomes more and more of a stranger; he was often that to me, now I am becoming it to him too." And a little later comes the

144

outcry—later recanted by word and deed—"What have I in common with Jews? I have almost nothing in common with myself, and should hide myself quietly in a corner satisfied with the fact that I can breathe." His diary swarms with dreams, beginnings of short stories, sketches. Everything seems to be caught up in a tremendous fermentation. And among them we find this important note, which makes clear one root of his spiritual housekeeping and economy, directing him away from the over-indulgence in self-analysis, which was also sapping his marriage plans, towards the realm of story-telling and of fiction: "Hatred of active self-observation, explanations of one's state of mind, such as: Yesterday I was so, and the reason was such; today I am so, and the reason is such. It is not true, the reason was not such, and the reason is not such, and therefore also not so, and so. Conduct yourself with calm, without being hasty, and live as you must, and do not chase round after your own tail like a dog."

In the following year, 1914, a crisis broke out in his relations with F. She wanted to have nothing to do with him. On the fifth of April he entered in his diary, "If it were only possible to go to Berlin, to become independent, to live from day to day, even to go hungry, but to let one's whole strength gush forth, instead of conserving it here, or rather turning oneself away towards nothingness! If only F. wanted it, if she would stand by me!" He wanted to live in Berlin as a journalist, as a freelance. At the end of May or the beginning of June—I cannot make our dates agree—the official engagement took place in Berlin. A flat was taken in Prague. The engagement, which took place under the most unfavorable auspices ("I was bound like a criminal, etc."), was followed, at the end of July, by the break, which also took place in Berlin. "The court of law in a hotel," he writes about it. It was, so he told me, the hotel "Askanischen Hof" near the Anhalter station. Present at the decisive talk was not only F. but also her girl friend. Then the scene with his parents. "Solitary tears on my mother's part. I told the whole story. Father understood it rightly from every side. Came in fact from Malmö for my sake. Traveled overnight. Sat in his shirt-

145

sleeves. They admit I am in the right, there is nothing, or at least not much that can be said against me. Diabolical in all innocence."

I believe I am not going wrong when I look in those terrible upheavals, during which Kafka was always troubling his own conscience with questions ("To have to bear and to be the cause of such suffering," he laments in his diary), for the origin of two new long works which were written after the breaking-off of the engagement. In September he read aloud to me the first chapter of the novel *The Trial*, and in November, *In the Penal Colony*. They are documents of literary self-punishment, imaginative rites of atonement. What K., the hero of *The Trial*, had done is never said. By ordinary civil standards he is undoubtedly innocent. There is "nothing, or at least not much that can be said against him." And yet he is "diabolical in all his innocence." Somehow or other he has not lived up to the laws of the good life. He is called to account by a mysterious court, and finally the sentence on him is carried out. "On the eve of his thirty-first birthday," says the last chapter. As a matter of fact Kafka, when he began his novel, was thirty-one. There is a girl who appears in the book several times, Fräulein Bürstner—in his manuscript Kafka generally writes this character's name abbreviated to Fr. B., or F. B., and then the connection is surely quite clear. At the end, K. is still trying to keep the bailiffs off. "Then in front of them, from a little alley that lay deep in the shadows, up a short flight of steps, Fräulein Bürstner came out into the square. It was not quite certain that it was she, the resemblance was certainly great. Whether it was really Fräulein Bürstner or not, however, did not matter to K.; the important thing was that he suddenly realized the futility of resistance." It is really of no importance whether the apparition is Fräulein Bürstner or is only like her. The whole failure of his attempt to get married, indeed, was important for the life of Kafka, as will soon become clear, as a pattern, and not individually—independent of the person of his fiancée—or rather as a pattern that, as the last year of his life shows, could be broken through by the personality of a woman of unusual character.

About a journey he made to the Danish seaside place on the Baltic, Marienlyst, in the company of a writer whom he esteemed very highly, Ernst Weiss (who seems to have played a certain part, by his advice, in the happenings in Berlin), he drafted a revealing letter to his parents, revealing also because it shows that there were periods when Kafka had counted on the possibility of earning a living by his literary work. In this letter, among other things, he writes:

I have not finished with Berlin, however, in so far as I believe that the whole business, for your good and for mine (for they are certainly one and the same thing) prevents me from going on living as I have done. Look, really serious pain I have probably never caused you till now, unless it were that this breaking-off of my engagement is one, at this distance I can't judge it as such. But really lasting pleasure I have given you still less, and that, believe me, solely for the reason that I couldn't give myself this pleasure continuously. Why that is so, just you, Father, although you cannot recognize the real thing I want, will understand the easiest! You sometimes relate how badly things went with you when you were making your first beginnings. Don't you think it is a good training for self-respect and satisfaction? Don't you think—anyway you have already told me so in so many words—that I have had things too easy? So far I have grown up in complete dependence and outward well-being. Don't you think that that was not at all a good thing for a nature like mine, kind and loving as it was on the part of all who saw to it that it was so? Of course there are men who know how to ensure their independence anywhere, but I am not one of them. You must admit that there are also people who never lose their dependence, but to put it to the test as to whether I don't perhaps belong to that class, seems to me an attempt which must be made. Even the objection that I am too old for such an attempt doesn't hold water. I am younger than would appear. The only good result of dependence is that it keeps one young. That of course only in the case that it comes to an end.

In the office I shall never be able to achieve this improvement. Not anywhere at all in Prague. Here everything is ar-

147

ranged to keep me, a man that fundamentally asks for dependence, in that state. Everything is so nicely laid to my hand. The office I find very burdensome and often unbearable, but at bottom, all the same, easy. In this easy way I earn more than I need. What for? Whom for? I shall go up in the scale of salaries. To what purpose? If this work doesn't suit me and doesn't even bring me independence as a reward, why should I not throw it up? I have nothing to risk, and everything to gain if I hand in my resignation and go away from Prague. I risk nothing, because my life in Prague leads to nothing good. Sometimes you say for fun I am like Uncle R. But my way of life will not lead me so far apart from his if I stay in Prague. I shall presumably have more money, more interests, and less faith than he has; I shall be correspondingly more dissatisfied, because other differences there will hardly be. Away from Prague I can gain everything, that is to say, become an independent man at peace with himself, who is employing all his faculties, and as a reward for good and genuine work gets the feeling of really being alive, and of lasting contentment. A man like this—this will not be the smallest gain—will also behave better towards you. You will have a son whose every single action you will not perhaps approve of, but in whom, as a whole, you will be well pleased, because you will be obliged to say, 'He does his best.' This feeling you have not now, and rightly.

The way to carry out my plan I imagine is this: I have 5,000 crowns. That enables me to live somewhere in Germany, in Berlin or in Munich, for two years, if needs must, without earning anything. These two years will enable me to go on with my literary work, and to produce from out of myself that which I cannot produce in the same clarity, wealth and coherence in Prague, what between inner lethargy and outer disturbances. This literary work will enable me, after these two years, to live, however modestly, on what I earn myself. But let it be as modest as you like, it will be incomparably better than the life which I am now leading in Prague, and that which awaits me there in future. You will object that I am mistaken in my abilities and in the possibility of making a living out of these abilities. That's certainly not out of the question. Only the answer to that is that I am thirty-one, and mistakes of that kind cannot be taken into account at that age, otherwise it would make any accounting impossible. A further answer to it is that I have already written a certain amount, little though it be, which has half succeeded in meeting with recognition, but the objection is finally answered by the fact that I am not in the least lazy, and have fairly few pretensions, and therefore, even if this hope should fail, can find other ways of earning my living, and in any case should not make any claims on you; for that would anyhow, both in its effects on me, as well as on you, make things still worse than my present life in Prague is, in fact it would be completely unbearable.

My position therefore seems clear enough to me, and I am anxious to hear what you will have to say about it. For even if I am convinced that this is the only right way, and that if I miss putting this plan into action I shall miss something of decisive importance, yet it is naturally very important for me to know what you have to say to it all.

With best love,
Your Franz

But these plans were not to mature. The Great War broke out. A period began against the background of which all we had ever suffered hitherto retired by comparison into a land of fairy tales round which played a rosy glow of childhood.

Undaunted by all the excitement, Franz worked at three manuscripts simultaneously, *The Trial, In the Penal Colony,* "The Railroad in Russia." In October he took a week's leave, "to push the novel on a bit." He prolonged his leave by a further week. "Fourteen days, good work in parts, complete understanding of my position." A letter arrived from F.'s girl friend, which attempted to mediate between them. The relationship with F. had been dropped for two months by this time, although a correspondence was still kept up during this period with F.'s sister. To the answer to F.'s friend's letter, a copy of which he kept for himself, and in which he writes, "I

149

don't wish to mention what your letter coincided with," he adds the note, "Suicide, letter to Max with a lot of requests." And somewhat later, "Have been turning over the pages of my diary. Have got some kind of idea of the organization of such a life."

It is astonishing that his creative powers did not fail in the midst of all these visitations. But on the contrary, they were just at their height at that period. On December 13 he finished his "Exegesis of the Legend"; that was how he himself described the chapter which I have published as the ninth—next to last—in *The Trial*—and writes about it in his diary, "Contentment and a feeling of happiness, which I feel particularly in face of the Legend." [1] Already on December 19 he writes, "Yesterday I wrote The Village Schoolmaster almost without knowing what I was doing." He is referring to the story of *The Giant Mole*. In the Christmas holidays he took a little trip with my wife and me to Kuttenberg, to look at the architectural monuments there, and to have a short rest—it was only four days—from the terrors and privations of the war which were already making themselves very much felt in the city. In a hotel in Kolin he read aloud to us the unfinished last chapter of his American novel, which inspired us with the brightest enthusiasm. (This trip was preceded by a trip to Hellerau with Otto Pick in the summer of the same year.) On the last day of December 1914, contrary to his usual custom, he made a review of his work: "Have been working since August, in general not little and not bad, but neither from the first nor the second point of view to the limit of my capacities, particularly as my capacities, judging by all the prospects—sleeplessness, headaches, weak heart—will not last very much longer. Written, unfinished: The Trial, Memories of the Kalda Railroad, The Village Schoolmaster, The Assistant Public Prosecutor, and short beginnings. Finished, only In the Penal Colony, and one chapter of The Man Who Disappeared, both during my fortnight's holiday. I don't know why I am making this survey, it's not in my line at all."

[1] "Before the Law."

The relationship with F. was far from being finished and done with. In the last months of 1914 it experienced a painful rebirth. It goes against the grain for me to go into details, it is enough, apart from the extensive correspondence—there are extant perhaps several hundred letters from Franz to F. —to mention the main stages, a meeting at Bodenbach, January 1915, and in Marienbad, July 1916, and to make clear the constant and increasingly important connection between this great experience and Kafka's creative work and religious development. His mood is one of despair. In his diary he writes: "Am I to lodge my complaint here, in order to find salvation here? It won't come from this copybook, it will come when I am in bed, and will lay me on my back, so that I lie beautiful and light and bluish white; no other salvation will come." Or, "I think it is impossible we should ever become one, but don't dare to say it either to her, or, at the decisive moment, to myself." Or, "The hardship of living together. Under the compulsion of strangeness, pity, cowardice, vanity, and only deep down in the ground a thin trickle of a brook worthy to be called love, not to be found when you look for it, but suddenly shining forth in the twinkling of an eye." Or one of these comparative lists which are much more likely to make a decision much harder than to prepare the way for one.

August 20, 1916.

To remain chaste.	To get married.
Bachelor.	Married man.
I remain chaste.	Chaste?
I preserve all my powers in coherence.	You will remain without your coherence; you will become an idiot, will follow every wind, but will never get any forwarder. I draw from the blood circulation of human life all the power that is available for me.
Responsible only for myself.	The more infatuated with yourself. (Grillparzer, Flaubert.)
No worries, concentration on work.	As I grow in strength I shall stand more. But there is a certain kernel of truth in this.

151

At the same time there is no lack of assertions in which he pictures to himself a marriage with F. as something completely possible and desirable. Thus he writes to me from Marienbad, "But now I have seen the look of trust on a woman's face, and could not shut myself against it. Many a thing gets torn up that I wanted to preserve forever (it isn't single details, but wholes), and from this tear there comes out, I know it, enough misery for more than one man's life; but it is not something one has summoned up, but something laid upon one. I have no right to defend myself against it, because to receive just that look again, I should do that which happens voluntarily, with my own hand, were it not to happen." And, "Now it is all different and all right. Our compact is, in brief: Get married shortly after the war is over; take two or three rooms in a Berlin suburb; leave each one only his own economic worries; F. will go on working as before, and I, well I, that I can't yet say. But if nevertheless you look at the menage carefully, you get the picture of two rooms, in Karlshorst, shall we say; in one F. gets up early, runs off to work and falls dead tired into her bed in the evening; in the other there is a sofa, on which I lie and feed myself on milk and honey. 'There he lies and takes his ease, the man whom morals do not tease,' as the saying goes. Nevertheless—now there is peace there, certainty, and therefore the possibility of living." *P.S.*—"Looking back on them, strong words, hardly to be held down forever by a weak pen."

In a certain sense F. remained still later, even after the final farewell, an ideal figure for Franz. Thus he writes to me from a sanatorium, when I wrote and told him about my lectures in Berlin: "Wasn't F. at your lectures? To have been in Berlin and not to have seen F., it seems to me, privately, all wrong, although of course it would have been exactly the same had I been there. For F.—a happy mother of two children—I have the love an unfortunate commander has for a town he could never take, and which has nevertheless somehow become great." Elsewhere he writes, "I loved a girl who loved me too, but I had to leave her . . . and so on."

152

For five years Kafka's strivings to wrest a marriage with F. from himself and the opposing circumstances were the prevailing motive in his life, the thorn in his creative work and in his harassed religious questionings. He read a lot of Strindberg at this period—also the Bible, Dostoievski, Pascal, Herzen, and Kropotkin. On Herzen's "London Fog," he passed the following judgment: "I had no idea what it was all about, and yet the complete, unknown man emerged, purposeful, self-torturing, in control of himself and then again falling to pieces." Werfel used to read his poems aloud for him, from a drama called "Esther, Empress of Persia," for example. He took a lively interest in all the positive activities of his friends, as for instance in the courses of lectures Felix Weltsch was giving; he always cheered them up, praised, criticized, encouraged, allowed none—except himself—to yield to despair, interested himself in my work in the school for refugee children from Galicia, often came to my lessons, made friends with the family of one of my little girl pupils. An understanding of the tenderest kind developed between him and the eldest daughter of this family. He also took part in debates between Jews from the East and Jews from the West—in silence, observing. At that time I used to spend a lot of time, together with my cabalistic friend Georg Langer at the house of a miracle-working rabbi, a refugee from Galicia who lived in dark, unfriendly, crowded rooms in the Prague suburb Žižkov. Unusual circumstances of life had brought me near to a kind of religious fanaticism. It is worthy of note that Franz, whom I took with me to a "Third Meal" at the close of the Sabbath, with its whispering and hasidic chants, remained, I must admit, very cool. He was undoubtedly moved by the age-old sounds of an ancient folk life, but on the way home he said, "If you look at it properly, it was just as if we had been among a tribe of African savages. Sheerest superstition." There was nothing insulting, but certainly a sober rejection in these words. I understood him very well. Franz had his own personal mysticism, he couldn't take over from others a ready-made

153

ritual.[1] He was often alone, and enjoyed being alone. The "most beautiful place in Prague" was the description he gave of the Chotek gardens, where he used to go again and again for lonely walks. "The birds were singing, the castle with its gallery, the ancient trees, with last year's leaves still hanging on them, the semi-darkness."

He also made some energetic attempts at this time to escape from the spell of the family circle, to become independent. For some time he didn't live with his people but in a room of his own. The first he took was in Bílek street, February 1915, the second in Langen street, Dlouhá, in the house "At the Sign of the Golden Pike," where in April 1915 he gave me unutterable pleasure and compelled my admiration by reading me the fifth and sixth chapters of *The Trial*. In February he wrote *Investigations of a Dog*. He passes a very severe judgment on this story in the diary: "I have just been reading the beginning. It is ugly and gives one a headache. For all the truth it contains, it is bad, pedantic, mechanical, a fish just able to gasp on a sandbank. I am writing '*Bouvard and Pécuchet*' [2] at a very early age. If the two elements most clearly stamped on The Stoker and In the Penal Colony don't unite, I am finished. But is there any prospect at hand of such a union?" By the two elements he means most probably the realistic-hopeful and the idealistic-severe tendencies in his writings.

One journey that Franz made with his sister to Vienna, Budapest, and Nagy-Mihály to see his brother-in-law, who had been called up, brought him very near the front. Then Franz received his "calling-up papers," but was exempted as being employed in an indispensable Government office. Later, when he could see no way out of his difficulties any longer, he tried to have his exemption canceled and go into the army. His illness brought this plan to nothing.

The award of the Fontane prize in October 1915 was a temporary consolation in the midst of these sorrows, and was

[1] Yet the impression was strong and had its after-effects. The beginning of a Golem story seems to go back to this episode.
[2] i.e., a work displaying every sign of an old man's opus.

accepted with a certain amount of satisfaction. If I am not mistaken, this is how it all happened; that it was Sternheim who was really awarded the prize, but handed it down to the "young writer" for his short story, "The Stoker," which had already been published in 1913. Poor consolation. For in the diary you find wild pen-and-ink drawings, complaints without end about sleeplessness and headaches, the beginning of the meditation on the fall of man, lines like: "The ragings of God against the human family"; "Only the Old Testament sees—say nothing about it yet"; "Take me, take me, network that I am of madness and pain"; and also the fragments from which I have reconstructed the poem, "In the troubled heart a clock strikes." He reproaches himself in his conduct towards F. with "the office clerk's vices of weakness, meanness, indecision, counting the cost, caution." And again, "the soul of a clerk, childishness, a will broken by my father." "Improve it, work at it, it lies directly to your hand. That means then, don't spare yourself (at the cost moreover of the human life of F. whom you love), because you can't spare yourself; this apparent sparing of yourself has now already almost ruined you. It is not only the question of sparing yourself as far as F., marriage, children, responsibility, etc., are concerned, but sparing yourself as far as the office in which you are stuck is concerned." And in his agony the following prayer is wrung from him, "Have mercy on me, I am sinful in every corner of my being. But I had not entirely despicable talents, little, tender capabilities, dissipated them, ill-advised person that I was, am now ready at the last gasp, at a time when outwardly everything might take a turn for the good for me. Don't thrust me among the lost souls."

Unmistakably two kinds of causes working together effected Kafka's engagement tragedy, exactly as they did the tragedy of his employment: those of a metaphysical, and those of an economic, nature. As far as the latter are concerned, the fact cannot be overlooked that Franz's financial position was, in fact, extremely unfavorable if he followed the dictates of his pride, and refused to call on his parents' aid, and was not prepared to do violence to his gift of writing.

155

Perhaps one can imagine a social and political order in which such a unique narrative talent and such a literary genius would not be damned to scribbling legal documents, and when he thinks of the marriage he wishes to make and the responsibility towards wife and children bound up with it, would not see himself faced with the abyss and flaming despair. "You belong to me," he once wrote to F. (according to a copy of the letter in the diary), "I have taken you to myself. I can't believe that in any fairy story any woman was more often and more desperately fought for, than you were in me." Certainly Kafka would have had a hard time of it even in an ideal social order; the metaphysical, erotic roots of his pain, the irremovable misery would then have come out more clearly. But in his soul the corresponding antidotes would have been found. Anyhow, as a result of our as yet still very primitively organized community, he foundered on obstacles which were removable (I call them in another passage "ignoble"), and therefore the great struggle in the metaphysical sense never found expression at the right level.

In the winter of 1916–17, Franz lived in Alchemists' street. Legends are already growing up around the place where he stayed, and foreigners who come to Prague are shown the tiny little house and the room that "the author" used to live in—they are almost identical. The house consists of only the one room, together with a tiny kitchen and a loft. But Franz didn't choose this quarter at all from any mystic or romantic inclination, or at least any such inclination was not the deciding factor, except perhaps subconsciously, in the form of an old love for old Prague; in the foreground was Franz's need for a quiet place to work in. His extraordinarily keen sensitivity to noise, with which he even occasionally infected me, by suggestion—when we traveled together, for example —made the choice difficult. In Alchemists' street Franz felt comparatively happy, and was extremely grateful to his youngest sister who had discovered this refuge for him—as she did another later in Zürau. On February 11, 1917, a Sunday, I wrote, "With Kafka in Alchemists' street. He read aloud beautifully. The monastic cell of a real writer." A letter

156

to F., the copy of which has been preserved in the posthumous papers, gives an account of this lodging, in which was conceived *The Bucket Rider*—the sole thing of beauty that came out of the coal shortage, with its quietly sad gaiety, its ironic treatment of human weaknesses, as though looking at them from above, its singing quality—and of Franz's next lodging in the Schönborn Mansions. At the same time the seriousness with which Franz approached the preparations for his marriage can be seen from this letter. It is a fact that in the following summer a flat was taken for the young couple, furniture was bought, and Franz had already begun the conventional round of calls on relatives and acquaintances and even went to Hungary, to Arad, with F., to pay a visit to her sister. Franz and the conventions! It was a pitiful sight. At the same time he certainly made every effort to conform to the conventions that were held to be seemly. Another partner might, it is true, have freed him from this compulsion with a good hearty laugh. At the same time it is doubtful, too, whether Franz would have accepted or wanted this freedom. Comically enough the pair of them paid even me a formal call, on July 9, 1917—the sight of the two, both rather embarrassed, above all Franz, wearing an unaccustomed high stiff collar, had something moving in it, and at the same time something horrible. (On July 23 after this there was quite a large party at my place, at which were present in addition to Kafka, Adolf Schreiber, the musician, Werfel, Otto Gross and his wife. Gross unfolded a plan for a newspaper which very much interested Kafka—this is the last note I have on him before the catastrophe.) The letter to F. that deals with questions of the flat and the wedding follows below (the beginning refers to the flat in Dlouhá—the stay in Munich was the occasion for a reading, at which Kafka read, besides works of his own, also some poems from my "Promised Land," and with his usual conscientiousness insisted afterwards on handing over a share of his fee to me).

Dearest
Well, here is the history of my flat. A tremendous theme.

I am terrified I shall not be able to master it. Too big for me. I shall be able to relate only a thousandth of it, of that thousandth only one-thousandth will come back to me when I begin writing, and only one-thousandth of that shall I be able to make clear to you, and so on. Nevertheless, it must be done, I want to have your advice. So read carefully and advise me well: how much sorrow I have had for two years you know; little in comparison with the contemporary sorrow of the world, but sufficient for me. A comfortable, friendly room on a corner, two windows, a door leading on to a balcony. A view over lots of roofs and churches. Tolerable people, because after a little practice there was no need for me to see them any more. A noisy street, heavy lorries at dawn, to which however I had already almost got accustomed. A room, however, that I couldn't live in. It is true it lies at the end of a very long entrance hall, and to outward appearance is sufficiently shut off, but the house is a concrete one; I hear, or rather heard, until well past ten in the evening the sighing of my neighbors, the talking of the people on the floor below, now and then a clatter from the kitchen. Moreover, just above the thin ceiling is the loft, and one cannot count the number of times, late in the afternoon, when I am just settling down to work, some servant girl hanging out her washing digs her heel so to speak innocently into my skull. Now and then, too, someone would play the piano, and in summer, from the semi-circle of the other houses that cluster around, there would be singing, a violin, and a gramophone. Even an approximation to complete peace then, not before eleven at night. Well then, impossibility of finding peace, complete homelessness, breeding-grounds for every kind of madness, ever increasing weakness and hopelessness. How much more there is to say on this subject! But let us get on! In summer I once went flat-hunting with Ottla, I didn't any more believe in the possibility of real peace, but all the same I went in search of it. We looked at a few places on the Mala Strana, all the time I was thinking, if only there were some place in a quiet attic corner in one of the old palaces, where one could at last stretch oneself out in peace. Nothing; we found nothing that would do. For a joke we asked in one of the little alleys. Yes, there would be a little house to let in November. Ottla, who is also, only in her own way, looking for peace, fell in love with the idea of taking the house. I with my native weakness advised her against it. That I could be there too, that hardly entered my head. So small, so dirty, so uninhabitable, with every conceivable inconvenience. But she insisted on it, and after the huge family that had inhabited it had moved out, had it painted, bought a few pieces of cane furniture (I know of nothing more comfortable in the way of chairs than a cane one), kept it, and keeps it, a secret from the family. At about that time I came back from Munich full of fresh courage, went into a flat agency, where almost the first thing they offered me was a flat in one of the most beautiful of the palaces. Two rooms and a hall, one half of which had been fitted up as a bathroom. Six hundred crowns a year. It was like a dream come true. I went to see it. The rooms were lofty and beautiful, red and gold, like something in Versailles. Four windows looking on to an entirely hidden quiet courtyard, one window looking over the garden. The garden! When you come to the gate of the castle, you can hardly believe your eyes. Through the lofty semi-circle of the second door which is flanked by caryatids standing on stone steps, beautifully divided in a zig-zag to the great garden, you see a broad balustrade rising gradually and in sweeping curves to a gloriette. Well, the flat has one small fault. The former lessee, a young man living apart from his wife, had made his home in the flat, with his manservant, for a few months only, was then unexpectedly transferred (he is a civil servant), had to leave Prague, but had invested so much money in the flat in this short space of time that he was unwilling to give it up just like that. So he was hanging on to it and looking for someone who would at least in part cover his outlay—putting in electric light, fitting up a bathroom, building cupboards, putting in a telephone, and laying down a big carpet. I was not the man he was looking for. He wanted 650 crowns for it—certainly little enough. It was too much for me, also the

159

over-lofty, chilly rooms were too magnificent for me; finally I had no furniture after all, and there were other, smaller considerations to be taken into account as well. Now in the same castle, however, there was another flat to let, direct from the agent, on the second floor, the ceilings somewhat lower, looking on to the street, the Hradschin close up in front of the window. The furniture was more friendly, more human, modest; a countess who had been here on a visit, probably a person with more modest pretensions, had lived in it; it was still arranged as she had had it, with a maidenly air about it, its furniture consisting of a few old pieces thrown together. But there was some doubt as to whether the flat could be got. That threw me into despair at the time. And in this state I moved into Ottla's house, which just happened to be ready at the time. There was a lot wrong with it in the beginning. I haven't the time to go into the whole story. Now it suits me down to the ground. To sum up its advantages: the lovely way up to it, the quiet there—from my sole neighbor I am separated by only a very thin wall—but the neighbor is quiet enough, and generally stays there until midnight; and then the benefit of the walk home: I have to make up my mind to stop. I then have the walk that cools my head. And the life there: it is something special to have one's own house, to shut in the face of the world the door not of your room, not of your flat, but of your own house; to step out through the door of your lodgings straight into the snow of a quiet alley. All that for twenty crowns a month, provided with everything I need by my sister, "done" by the little flower-girl (Ottla's pupil) for as little as is necessary, everything lovely and in order. And just at this moment it turns out that the flat in the castle is at my disposal after all. The manager, whom I once did a favor, is very kindly disposed towards me. I get the flat on the street I told you about for 600—without the furniture on which I had counted, it is true. There are two rooms and a hall. There is electric light there, but no bathroom, certainly, not even a bath; but I don't need one. Now in brief, the advantages of my present lodgings as compared with the flat in the castle: 1. The ad-
160

vantage of letting things be as they are; 2. I am content now; after all, why create for myself the possibility of regrets; 3. Losing a house of one's own; 4. Losing my nightly walk that is an aid to sleep; 5. I should have to borrow furniture from the sister who is living with us now; for the one room, which is enormously big, I should have really only a bed. The cost of moving; 6. Now I live ten minutes nearer the office. The flat in the castle faces west, I fancy; my room gets the morning sun. On the other hand, the advantages of the flat in the castle: 1. The advantage of change in general and change in particular; 2. The advantage of a quiet lodging of one's own; 3. In the flat I have now to work in, I am after all not entirely independent; really I am taking it away from Ottla; kind and self-sacrificing as she is towards me, one day when she is in a bad mood she will let me know it without wanting to. It's true she will certainly be sorry if I stop coming to the little house; at bottom she is quite satisfied if she can be there occasionally in the afternoon and on Sundays till six o'clock; 4. I shan't have my walk home, it is true; going out at night will also be difficult, because the gate cannot be opened from the outside, but to balance that I can very well take a little walk at night in the part of the park which is otherwise reserved for the gentry. 5. After the war I shall try at any rate to get a year's leave, if I can, but that will surely not be possible now—if I get any leave at all. Well in that case we two would have the most wonderful place to live in that I can imagine in Prague, all ready for you, only for a comparatively short time it's true, during which you would have to go without a kitchen of your own, and even without a bathroom. But anyhow it would be to my taste, and you could have a thorough rest for two or three months. The indescribable park, perhaps in spring, in summer (the gentry are away), or in autumn. But if I don't make sure of the flat now, immediately, either by moving in, or—mad extravagance that is far beyond the capacity of a civil servant to grasp—by paying the rent only, 150 crowns a quarter, I shall hardly be able to get it later. To confess the truth, I have taken it already; but the agent will certainly release me from my undertaking with pleasure, particularly as the whole affair, I can well understand, has not the tiniest fraction of the importance for him that it has for me. How little I have told you! But give me your opinion, and soon.

His coughing blood, which began in August for the first time, Franz described as being psychic in origin. That is how I find it noted down without possibility of doubt in my diary in his own words. "August 24, 1917. Steps taken in the matter of Kafka's illness. He insists it is psychic, just like something to save him from marriage. He calls it his final defeat. And yet he has been sleeping well since. Has he found release? Tormented soul!" It is possible that the flat in the Schönborn Palace, which couldn't be heated, hastened the breaking out of the illness, and that therefore his father, who warned him against "extravagances" of this kind, and who always expressed his deep disapproval of them, once more appeared after all to be right in a certain sense. This aspect of his illness which Kafka probably never took into consideration might be taken straight out of one of his own short stories, from which, however, the only thing that emerges clearly is the close connection between his life and his creative function. If you go deeper, however, the illness was after all the result of years of stress, efforts to unfold his literary gifts to the full despite all the hindrances of his profession, and his marriage plans, and of the bodily weakness bound up with all that, combined with "hygienic" treatment that only a much stronger body could have supported.

It took till September 4 before I could finally persuade Franz to call in a doctor. In such matters he was quite unbelievably pig-headed; it took a great deal of patience and perseverance to handle him properly. My description of the decisive, wretched day runs:

"September 4. In the afternoon went with Kafka to Professor Friedl Pick. It has taken all that time to carry it through.

"Catarrh in the lungs diagnosed. Must have three months' leave. There is a danger of T.B. My God! Nothing so horrible can happen. Then the Sophie Island. Swimming-pool with Franz. He feels himself released and beaten at the same time. There is a part in him which resists, and considers marriage as a distraction from the one direction of his gaze—towards the absolute. Another part fights for marriage as in accordance with nature. This struggle has worn him out. He considers his illness as a punishment, because he has often wished for a violent solution. But this solution is too drastic for him. He quotes against God, from the *Meistersinger,* 'I should have taken him for more of a gentleman.' "

Then: "December 10. Went with Kafka to see Professor Pick again. His revelation that he had been learning Hebrew, forty-five lessons in Rath's handbook; never said anything to me about it. So he was trying me out when he asked me some time ago, with every appearance of innocence, how do you count in Hebrew. This making a big secret of everything. There is something very great about it, but also something evil."

To go to a sanatorium for T.B. patients—Franz fought against the idea with all his might. It was not until he was older that he had to give in. You might find a certain self-contradiction in the fact that he refused to go and stay in any sanatorium now that it was advisable for him to do so, whereas in previous years he had gone for a rest to sanatoriums like Erlenbach near Zürich, Jungborn in the Harz Mountains, Hartungen in Riva. But these had been centers of "nature healing methods," where Franz spent days, or even weeks, so to speak, profitably pandering to the "living-according-to-nature" which he loved and also made fun of, but which at the very bottom, he welcomed so hopefully. The threat of institutions run according to orthodox medical principles was quite another thing; and it was only to be expected from Franz's way of looking at things that he should resist such demands upon him as long as possible. Chance came to his aid this time. Franz's youngest sister took over the management of a small estate that belonged to her brother-in-law at Zürau (Post Flöhau, near Saaz). It was decided and finally agreed upon by all sides that Franz should

163

spend his convalescent leave there. This leave was prolonged several times, once or twice Franz tried to take up his office work again but succeeded only for short spaces of time. At last it became inevitable that he should be retired. From his surroundings at Zürau, where Franz was for the first time brought into close contact with country life, farming, German peasants, grew the novel *The Castle*.

On September 12 I wrote in my diary, "Said goodbye to Kafka. It hurts me. I have not been without him for such a long time for years. He now thinks he can't marry F. because of his illness. Despairing letter from her, although she knows nothing about it yet. Two people come from the shop with handcarts to take his luggage. He says, 'They are coming for the coffin.' "

Now I got very many letters from him; they are too precious to be given piecemeal. I must hope I shall one day be able to publish them complete. They throw light on Kafka's studies of Kierkegaard, which grew deeper and deeper, and on his religious and ethical development. Other letters from Zürau—to Baum and Weltsch—have already appeared in my collected edition of Kafka. They give the picture, growing clearer and clearer, of a man who feels himself at home in the most primitive of country districts, and never wishes to return to the town. Characteristic of his mood and of the fundamental material of the novel *The Castle* are pages in the diary like these: "Was at Farmer Lüftner's. The great long room. The whole thing quite theatrical. There he is with his 'Ho ho!' and his 'Ha ha,' and banging on the table, and waving his arms and shrugging his shoulders and raising his glass of beer like somebody out of *Wallenstein*. Sitting next to him is his wife, an old woman whom he married when he was her serving-lad ten years before. His passion is to be out with a gun; he neglects his farm. Two gigantic horses in the stable, Homeric forms, in a fleeting ray of sunshine that came through the stable window." Slowly Franz got better. Only when a letter came from F. he wouldn't eat for half a day, and didn't open the letter. I myself, caught up in terrible soul-storms, as well as in a heap of work, unfortunately

164

never went to see Franz in Zürau. I met him only at the rail-
way station of Michelob, where he traveled down to meet
me, when I was giving a lecture somewhere near the place.
Moreover, he used to come to Prague for a day or two from
time to time, to settle things that could not be put off. Oskar
Baum spent a week with him as his guest at Zürau; the "village was then under deep snow," Baum writes in his *Memoirs*. "In the long nights we talked right through till the
morning, I got to know more about him than in the ten previous years, and the five that followed."

In September still, that is to say, soon after the diagnosis
of the serious illness, F. came to see him. The diary reports:
"F. was here; traveled thirty hours to see me. I should have
stopped her. As I imagine it to myself she is suffering the utmost unhappiness essentially through my fault. I myself
can't control myself; I am quite unfeeling, and just as helpless, keep thinking of the disturbance of a few of my comforts, and the only thing I do by way of compromise, is to
do a little play-acting. In small details, she is wrong, wrong
in defending the rights she pretends to or perhaps really has,
but on the whole she is an innocent woman condemned to
be severely tortured; I have committed the fault for which
she is being tortured, and even work the rack. The day ends
with her departure (the carriage, with her and O. in it, goes
round the pond, while I take a short cut straight across which
brings me near her once more) and a headache (the left-over
of my play-acting)."

At the beginning of November I recorded a conversation
with Franz. It had to do with my conflict with myself, but
throws light on his own too.

"HE: That's the way it is always. The fault lies just in the
fact that we think things over.

"I: Well, should one do things without thinking them
over?

"HE: That is, of course, not a law. But it is written: Thou
shalt not be able to think things over. You can't do it by
force. Thinking things over is the advice of the serpent. But it
is also good and human. Without it one is lost."

165

At the end of December Franz came to Prague, met F. here, who, as the manageress of a big Berlin firm—tact, efficiency, generosity are among her excellent qualities—had to use her Christmas holidays to come and have the last talk with him. The tragic drama was nearing its end. On the evening of December 25, Franz and F. were the guests of my wife and myself. "Both unhappy, don't talk." On December 26 I wrote, "Kafka came at half-past seven in the morning, wants me to give him my morning. Café Paris. But it isn't to get advice that he wants me for, his firmness of purpose is admirable. Yesterday he told F. everything quite clearly. We spoke about everything but that. Kafka on Tolstoy's *Resurrection:* 'You cannot write about salvation, you can only live it.' In the afternoon, an excursion with Baum and Weltsch. So three married couples, alongside Kafka and F. Kafka unhappy. He said to me, 'What I have to do, I can do only alone. Become clear about the ultimate things. The Western Jew is not clear about them, and therefore has no right to marry. There are no marriages for them. Unless he is the kind that is not interested in such things—business men for example.'"

The next morning Franz came to my office to see me. To rest for one moment, he said. He had just been to the station to see F. off. His face was pale, hard, and severe. But suddenly he began to cry. It was the only time I saw him cry. I shall never forget the scene, it is one of the most terrible I have ever experienced. I was not sitting alone in my office; right close up to my desk was the desk of a colleague—we worked in the legal section of the general post office. This particular section was housed on the top floor of a block of flats, not in the main office building of the G.P.O. The way in which the office had succeeded in turning a friendly four-room flat, with kitchen and bathroom into proper dusty, ugly, impersonal office premises, into something bad-temperedly unreal, had something uncanny about it. Private visitors such as I sometimes had, I generally received—and this too with a guilty conscience—in the kitchen, which had been half pulled down and turned into a lumber room for

166

legal documents. But Kafka had come straight into the room I worked in, to see me, in the middle of all the office work, sat near my desk on a small chair which stood there ready for bearers of petitions, pensioners, and debtors. And in this place he was crying, in this place he said between his sobs: "Is it not terrible that such a thing must happen?" The tears were streaming down his cheeks. I have never except this once seen him upset quite without control of himself.

A few days later he returned to Zürau. He showed me another very unhappy letter from F. His attitude towards her, however, was quite firm, he had given up not only her, but *any* possibility of married bliss. The pain he inflicted on himself gave him the strength to conquer his natural weakness even where others were concerned, and not to turn back when he had once realized the inevitability of the bitter decision.

Some fifteen months later I received the news that F. had got married. I broke the news gently to Franz. He was moved, full of the most sincere good wishes for the new marriage, wishes that then to his great joy were duly fulfilled. "It is a good thing that some things which are insoluble seem to find a solution after all," was how I summed up the story for myself, knowing full well that on Franz's side at least it was far from the case that a road to salvation had been thrown open by the disappearance of this one overshadowing problem.

CHAPTER VI

RELIGIOUS DEVELOPMENT

KAFKA'S failure to find a way out was, from now on, chiefly due to his illness which, rising out of the crises of his soul, or at least harmfully stimulated by them, had developed into an evil that had its own independent, injurious, nay devastating, effect, and to which Franz finally succumbed. Franz bore his sufferings heroically, generally even with cheerful equanimity. Only once, in his later years, did I ever hear him complain about pain. I went to see him after he had had a severe bout of fever. He was lying in bed; while he was speaking he pulled a face: "It takes such a long time before one is crushed up quite small, and squeezed through this last narrow hole." As he was saying this he was clenching his hand as if he were crumpling a handkerchief up in it.

Until the summer of 1918, Franz stayed, with short interruptions, in Zürau. Then he came to Prague, worked for some time again in the Civil Service, but devoted his afternoons to gardening at the Pomologic Institute in Troja, a suburb of Prague. I often used to go and call for him there, and take him for long walks. We had two chief topics—the war, and learning Hebrew. At that time, too, I was asking his advice on a literary affair. Kafka's sense of justice, his love of the truth, his simple honesty that never had the least pose about it were unsurpassable. "One must limit oneself to what one is absolutely master of" is one of his sayings that I have preserved from those days. Sometimes, I must admit, this led in his case to a state in which he curled up painfully in himself. He wanted to withdraw from everything, finally even to give up meeting me.

On July 1, 1918, I have a note on his views: "Country as opposed to town. And yet he feels better in Prague, because in Zürau he was lying about doing nothing. Here he studies Hebrew and gardening. The positive things in his life. Wants to keep these quite pure—they are the 'country things.' Would like to withdraw from everything else."

"July 3. Sleepless night because of Kafka. Feel I am deserted, but respect his decision. There has never been any quarrel. His fine way of seeing what is positive in everybody—even in his opponents—what they are right in, what they can do nothing else about—Hans Blüher, for example—often comforted me, gave me a basis. His confidence that a pure intention, an objective piece of work is never meaningless, that nothing good can ever go lost—on that I leaned for support." This "obituary," however, is immediately followed by the correction, "A few days later he came along to me. Then often on the Sophie Island, the swimming-baths with him. Troja, too."

The following extract from one of his letters gives an account of the severity with which he conducted his own life and judged everything at this period. I had passed on to him a request from an actress who wanted to give a reading from his books in Frankfort. He wrote back to me, from Zürau, "I am not sending anything to Frankfort; I don't feel it is a matter that I should bother about. If I send anything I shall be doing it out of vanity; if I don't send anything, it will also be out of vanity, but not out of vanity alone, that is to say, out of something better. The pieces I could send mean really nothing to me, I respect only the moment in which I wrote them; and now an actress, who can find something much more effective with which to show herself off, is to drag them out of the abyss into which they are sooner or later to fall, and give them a moment of glory for one evening? That would be senseless trouble."

But he didn't always dismiss all his literary work so contemptuously. He began to arrange the stories which were to be put together to form the volume *The Country Doctor*. This time he even insisted on having them published. That can be seen from the following lines—also addressed to me from Zürau: "Thanks for speaking to Wolff's for me. Since I have decided to dedicate the book to my father, I lay great importance on its coming out soon. Not as though I could reconcile my father by doing so, the roots of this enmity are ineradicable in this case; but I should, all the same, have at least traveled along the map with my finger even if I haven't emigrated to Palestine."

One sees from these few lines how strongly Kafka's yearning to be made a proper member of the family, for peace with his father, links up with incorporation into the people's way of life (Palestine) that is after nature's plan and morally right; and in fact these motives, which are nothing else than a making concrete of Kafka's fundamental problem—how is a properly fulfilled life for everybody, the whole of mankind, to be realized?—make themselves felt with ever increasing force in the last years of Kafka's life.

What I emphasize, and what I believe distinguishes my exposition of Kafka from all the others—e.g. Schoeps, Vietta, and Stumpf—is the fact that I consider that the positive side of him, his love of life, of the earth earthy, and his religion in the sense of a properly fulfilled life, is his decisive message, and not self-abnegation, turning his back on life, despair—the "tragic position."

The three quotations which I have placed at the head of this monograph speak a clear language. I beg you to read them again before going on with the text. Without these guiding sentences one cannot, so I think, ever understand Kafka's religious position. The hopefulness that lies in these and similar sayings of Kafka's must not be conjured away. Only by overlooking propositions like this, with their positive outlook, could one arrive at the point of placing Kafka in line with the "theology of the crisis"—with that religious tendency that sees between God and man, between man and the good deeds that are to be achieved by human strength, a yawning abyss that can never be bridged. It is significant that Franz, in a letter to me, draws attention to just those passages in Kierkegaard which explain not the powerlessness but the good moral strength and effective possibilities of mankind. Kafka quotes Kierkegaard with the introductory words, "And the following passage is *not* from the Talmud," which, when placed alongside my letter, is as much as to say,

170

"It corresponds with Jewish modes of thought; although it is to be found not in the Talmud but in Kierkegaard's books." He quotes the following great sentence: "As soon as a man appears who brings something of the primitive along with him, so that he doesn't say, 'You must take the world as you find it,' but rather 'Let the world be what it likes, I take my stand on a primitiveness which I have no intention of changing to meet with the approval of the world,' at that moment, as these words are heard, a metamorphosis takes place in the whole of nature. Just as in a fairy story, when the right word is pronounced, the castle that has been lying under a spell for a hundred years opens and everything comes to life, in the same way existence becomes all attention. The angels have something to do, and watch curiously to see what will come of it, because that is their business. On the other side, dark, uncanny demons, who have been sitting around doing nothing and chewing at their nails for a long time, jump up and stretch their limbs, because, they say, here is something for us, and so on."

While I lay special worth on the hopeful side of Kafka's work, which rejoices in activity, that is to say in the fundamental recognition of the fact that man, with his spark of reason, will, and ethical perception is not altogether the plaything of super-mighty powers, who judge according to other laws than his, which he does not understand and never can understand, faced with which he is lost, and only thrown unconditionally on God's mercy—the old problem of Job—while underlining then the position of human freedom in the case of Kafka, I do not of course wish to forget that this attitude of Kafka's is only an occasional flash, and that passages which describe man as powerless, crowd in on the reader in an overwhelming majority. But the propositions of freedom and hope *are there, too!* And if only *one* such proposition is found, in a religious thinker, it has the remarkable quality of decisively changing the whole picture of him. That's all I want to say, no more. These dispositions towards a more optimistic interpretation must not be neglected if one wants to read Kafka properly. In fact I think that just these gentle dispositions, wrung from all the endless bad moods and failures of a horribly difficult life, dispositions towards a "fight for the good against anything and everything," form the kernel, the best and the most characteristic part of Kafka's attitude as a thinker. *Just because the dispositions to faith were won from such a radical skepticism, they are in their truthfulness, refined by the ultimate tests, infinitely valuable and powerful.*

"Man cannot live without a permanent faith in something indestructible in himself," says Kafka. And adds, "At the same time this indestructible part and his faith in it may remain permanently concealed from him." Very significant is the following minor proposition which rejects the theism of the ordinary religious observance: "One of the forms in which this concealment may be expressed is the belief in a personal God." One might well say that skepticism and faith cannot be more intimately wedded than in this aphorism.

Kafka disputes with God as Job once did. He disputes about original sin, and Paradise Lost. He seeks, but fails to find the definitive word. He seeks a faith "like a guillotine, as heavy, and as light." But one thing he has become assured of in any case; quite independently of how we may judge God's attitude towards us—the attitude and the task of mankind is clear, it is activity in the service of the good so far as it is discernible by us. "Death is in front of us, rather like a picture of the battle of Alexander on the wall in the classroom. The point is to blur or even wipe out the picture *by our deeds while we are still in this life.*"

Compare with this an entry in the diary dated 11/11/1911 —to my feeling one of the most moving entries: "As soon as I perceive in any way that I have allowed evil conditions, for the removal of which I am really the right person, to go on their own sweet way—for example the extremely satisfied, but from my point of view desperate, life of Mrs. N.—for a moment I lose the feel of the muscles of my arms." There is a similar passage, May 1914, which reveals, however, a stronger emphasis on the limitlessness and complicated nature of all mortal things, which indeed so endlessly lead the

172

fight for the good into false paths (one could say, every great writer has made some facet of life clear, that no one had seen so clearly before him. And what has become clear through Kafka? The unclearness of life!):

"If I am not very much mistaken, I am getting nearer. It is as though there were a spiritual fight in a clearing in some wood. I penetrate into the wood, don't find anything, and through weakness, hasten out of it again; often when I am leaving the wood, I hear, or think I hear, the clash of the weapons of those fighters. Perhaps the fighters' looks seek me through the darkness of the wood, but I know only so little and such deceptive things about them."

Man's bewilderment is great. And yet, and yet—we let the "chariot," God's chariot, and the chariot of the good life, pass us by without getting in; one misses it only when one does not take things seriously. "Hold fast!" says that meditation which I believe to be the conclusive one. ". . . then you too will see the unchangeable, dark distance, out of which nothing can come except one day the chariot; it rolls up, gets bigger and bigger, fills the whole world at the moment it reaches you—and you sink into it like a child sinking into the upholstery of a carriage that drives through storm and night."

Kafka's fundamental outlook may be summarized in some such formula as this: almost everything is uncertain, but once one has a certain degree of understanding one never loses the way any more. It is Plato's doctrine in its purest form. For Plato, too, assures us in *Phaedrus* that for those who have once trodden the upper path, it is not ordained that they shall fall back to the lower one.

For all his mourning over the imperfection and intransparency of human actions, Kafka was convinced that there were truths which could not be assailed. He did not express this in words, but he did so by his whole behavior all his life. It was for that reason that in spite of all the depression he exuded, one felt infinitely well in his company. The "Indestructible" made its presence felt, Kafka's unobtrusively quiet but firm behavior was at the same time a pledge for the everlasting laws of love, reason, and kindness. He was admittedly limitlessly skeptical and ironic. But there was, for instance, for him no skepticism about the substance and heart of Goethe. Well then, after all not "limitlessly skeptical"? No, the limit was there—a very distant limit, but a limit nevertheless.

Belief in an absolute world—but we go astray, we are too weak, we do not grasp it. Next to his belief in the Absolute stands for Kafka his consciousness of human insufficiency. This feeling of weakness Schoeps explains by the special situation of the Jew today, who does not follow the traditional law of his religion. There is also an explanation from the Catholic side; the Jew who does not accept Christ. But as a motive in this feeling of weakness, we must not forget Kafka's many private, accidental failings and sufferings, beginning with his youthful impressions and the "education that went wrong"; they all condition the feeling of God's "farness" which expresses itself so insistently in his works. Through this one grasps real life and truth better than through theological interpretations. "To be near God" and "to live rightly" were identical for Kafka. As a member of a race without a country one cannot live properly. This almost realistically Jewish interpretation of Kafka, in which Zionism is accepted as a way of life of almost religious relevance, I shall endeavor to develop later on.

But let us first establish the general religious side.

The Absolute is there—but it is incommensurable with the life of man—this would seem to be a fundamental experience of Kafka's. From the depth of his experiences it takes on ever new variations; in the bitterest irony, in despair, in unexampled self-abasement, and in a tender hope that sings through all his savage skepticism, not often, but all the more unmistakably, here and there. The chief theme remains the enormous danger that we may lose the right way, a danger so grotesquely out of proportion that it is really only an accident—"*gratia praeveniens*"—that can bring us to the point of entering into "The Law," i.e. the right and perfect life, into

"Tao." How much more probable it is, on the contrary, that we miss the way altogether. "Once you have followed the false alarm of the night-bell—you can never put it right again." The eternal misunderstanding between God and man induces Kafka to represent this disproportion again and again in the picture of two worlds which can never, never understand one another—hence the infinite separation between dumb animals and men is one of his chief themes in the numerous animal stories which his works contain, not by accident. The same is true of the partition wall between father and son. This writer's gaze rests with the endless pity of understanding on everything that expresses incommensurability, and brings it into silent relation with the most fatal and greatest of all misunderstandings, the failure of man in the sight of God.

This perception undoubtedly has its kernel in the feeling that there is a world of the Absolute, Freedom from sin, Perfection—that is that which the faithful call "God." This feeling for the "Indestructible" was for Kafka an immediate certainty, at the same time—equipped as he was with the sharpest of eyes of the soul—he did not overlook a single one of the countless, wretched backslidings, not one of the sins, not one of the absurdities with which men embitter each other's lives, make each other's lives impossible indeed, and which cause them to wander farther and farther away from the fountain of life. A good life is prescribed for us, but we are incapable, through faults in our innermost being, of comprehending this life. For this reason the divine world becomes for us a transcendental territory, and in the truest sense of the words, strange, uncanny. To our ears the will of God sounds illogical, that is to say opposed to our human logic in a grotesque fashion. Since the Book of Job in the Bible, God has never been so savagely striven with as in Kafka's *The Trial*, and *The Castle*, or in his *In the Penal Colony*, in which justice is presented in the image of a machine thought out with refined cruelty, an inhuman, almost devilish machine, and a crank who worships this machine. Just the same in the Book of Job, God does what seems absurd and unjust to man. But it is *only* to man that this seems so, and the final conclusion arrived at in Job as in Kafka is the confirmation of the fact that the yardstick by which man works is not that by which measurements are taken in the world of the Absolute. Is that agnosticism? No; for the fundamental feeling remains that in some mysterious way man is nevertheless connected with the transcendental kingdom of God. Only the usual, flat, rationally understandable kind of connection it just isn't. And the terrible wound of doubt that Kafka's ever-fresh wit, and Kafka's ever freshly creating, bizarre fancy, deal our moral system, cannot be healed by phrases, by sanctimoniously lifting up one's eyes, and patching things up with evil, not by belletristic anointings, but only by a tremendous, mounting feeling for the positive that dares bid defiance to all this undisguised negation. To have registered the negative and fearfully defective sides of nature without veiling them in any way, and yet at the same time to have seen continually from the depths of his heart the "World of Ideas," in the Platonic sense—that was the distinguishing feature of Kafka's life and of his works, that was the thing that proclaimed itself to his friends, without a word being said about it, as a kind of revelation, peace, certainty, in the midst of the storm of suffering and uncertainty.

Perhaps there have been men who have had a deeper, that is to say, a less questioning faith than Kafka's—perhaps also there have been men with even more biting skepticism—that I don't know. But what I do know is the unique fact that in Kafka these two contradictory qualities blossomed out into a synthesis of the highest order. One might gather its importance into this sentence: Of all believers he was the freest from illusions, and among all those who see the world as it is, without illusions, he was the most unshakable believer.

It is the old question of Job. But Kafka stands almost completely on the side of man. That is how it is in the story, "Before the Law." The doorkeeper has deceived the man who demands admission, or he is too simple. To close the argument, K., to whom the legend is related, says, "It turns lying into a universal principle." It is true that that is also not
176

the last word. The priest argues against it, protests by word and deed. Thus the justice of the highest court (in his novel *The Trial*), the possibility of a good life in accordance with the divine command, "The Law" in fact, is not denied—but this possibility is not a certainty. Everything remains hanging in the air. Darkness and light hold the scales against one another. In what time is this "timeless" novel set? One minute before the creation of the world. Will it succeed, or not? A terrible fear of doubt, of uncertainty, fills one's heart.

What is the reason? Why man does not achieve the real, the true, that, with the best will in the world, he wanders from the path like that country doctor who followed the "false alarm of the night-bell"? Kafka, by the very nature of his being, was not inclined to give any promises, or any directions for the happy life. He admired everyone who could—he himself remained in suspense. But just this suspense would have been empty and bare, had he not felt the Absolute as something inexpressible (ἄρρητον) in himself. In his uncertainty one felt a distant certainty, through which alone this uncertainty is made possible and preserved. I have already said that this positive trait appears perhaps less strongly in his writings—and that is why they have been found depressing by many readers—than it was to be felt in his personal calm and serenity, in the gentle, considered, never hasty, character of his being. But also he who reads Kafka's works with care must again and again catch a glimpse through the dark husk of this kernel that gleams, or rather beams gently through. On the top lie distraction, and despair in that which is related—but the ease and minuteness of detail with which it is related, the "copy fever" which is in love with detail, that is, with real life, and with descriptions true to nature, the humor in the compressed structure of his sentences, which often has the effect of a short circuit, in so many tricks of style—the debtors "have become extravagant, and are giving a party in the garden of some inn, and others are breaking their flight to America for a little while to attend the party"—all this points, already *through the form alone,* to

177

the "indestructible" in Kafka and in the human-being-in-general that he recognizes.

When Kafka read aloud himself, this humor became particularly clear. Thus, for example, we friends of his laughed quite immoderately when he first let us hear the first chapter of *The Trial*. And he himself laughed so much that there were moments when he couldn't read any further. Astonishing enough, when you think of the fearful earnestness of this chapter. But that is how it was.

Certainly it was not entirely good, comfortable laughter. But the ingredients of a good laugh were also there—alongside the hundred ingredients of uncanniness, which I shall not try to minimize. I am only pointing out the fact that is otherwise so easily forgotten in studies of Kafka—the streak of joy in the world and in life.

What he reproached himself with was, in fact, just that his belief in life wavered, that life was not strong enough in him. And he admired the things of the country, an admiration expressed as early as in his (unpublished) youthful letter to Oskar Pollak: "Have you already noticed how the soil comes up to meet the cow as she is grazing, how intimately it comes up to meet her? Have you already noticed how heavy, rich, arable earth crumbles at the touch of fingers which are all too fine, how solemnly it crumbles?" It is still more clearly expressed in the diary he kept of his stay in Zürau, which says among other things, "General impressions of the farmers: noblemen, who have found salvation in their farming, where they have arranged their work so cleverly and humbly that it fits without omission into the whole, and will keep them safe from every wavering and sea-sickness until their happy death. Real citizens of the earth." But naturally his admiration did not stay confined to country folk alone. He writes in just the same style, 10/20/1913, in his diary, about a completely urban author, who was sure of his path: "Have just been reading the case of Jacobsohn. This strength to live, to make decisions, to set one's foot with joy in the right spot. He sits in himself as a first-class oarsman sits in his own boat, and would sit in any boat."

178

The scale of values that Kafka applied becomes clear from notes such as that. He loved an efficient vitality, but only one which stood at the service of what is good and constructive. (A twofold demand hard to satisfy!) He always found fault with himself for "never having learned anything useful." He complains in his diary, 10/25/1921, that "the current of life has never caught me up, and that I never broke away from Prague, was never put on to any game or trade." He often reproaches himself with coldness, incapacity for life, lifelessness, as we frequently find in his letters, and in the last chapter of *The Trial*. The two black mysterious bailiffs only carry out a sentence that has already been carried out. As they lead K. away, they form together with him "one unit, such as almost only lifeless matter can form." He is dead already: that is to say, dead to real life. That is the real reason why the ghostly appearance of Fräulein Bürstner has such a paralyzing effect on him. He wants to see her, not because he promises himself any help from doing so, but "in order not to forget the warning that she holds for him." K. had not married, remained a bachelor, had allowed himself to be terrified by the reality of life, had not defended himself against it—that is his secret guilt, which had already, before his condemnation, shut him out from the circle of life. "There would be nothing heroic about it if he did resist," is therefore the final conclusion: "if he were now to make difficulties for the gentlemen [the bailiffs], if he tried now by defending himself to enjoy the last appearance of life." K. died of weakness in living, is already dead from the beginning of the book—from the moment of the arrest, which Kafka must have written in a kind of trance, in a moment of clairvoyance, or did there exist then, in 1914, the tight-fitting black uniforms with buckles, pockets, buttons, and belt? Admittedly weakness is a relative idea, and if you translate the novel back into the autobiographical from which it came, then one must not forget that Kafka's life can only be considered as tainted with weakness when measured by the heroically moral, in fact monumental demands he made on himself. But what would not be weakness in this case? A feeling of this comes to life in the unbear-

179

ably moving passage at the end of *The Trial,* where "the responsibility for this last misdoing" is thrust off, where K. rears up, reaches after a far-away, unknown, indistinct person. "Who was it? A friend? A good man? Someone who sympathized? A man who wanted to help? Was it an individual? Was it everybody? Was there still help? Were there objections one had forgotten to raise? Surely there were some. Logic is, of course, unshakable, but it cannot withstand a man who wishes to live. Where was the judge he had never seen? Where was the high court before which he had never appeared?"

The old problem of Job.

Kafka's fundamental principle: pity for mankind that finds it so hard a task to do what is right. Pity, half-smiling, half-weeping pity. Not the fulminating excommunication of the "theology of the crisis" which knows so exactly where mankind has gone wrong.

Kafka's demands on himself were the most severe. Almost never did he believe he had come up to them. On the other hand, he was no "cultural critic" in the accepted sense of the word. For very much of what went on around him, many quite ordinary people he came into touch with seemed to him self-contained, admirable for their achievements and their strength, in fact absolutely blessed by God. In this there was a certain amount of truth, inasmuch as no one was so burningly conscious of the "distance from God" as he was. But in this consciousness of the distance, Kafka, in his humility, saw no virtue, but only uncertainty, that is, weakness. But as it was a preliminary condition of all life to feel the distance from God—from the perfection of a right way of life—clearly and without any veiling of ritual or mysticism, his praise and his admiration of the everyday man—the "pedestrian" as Kierkegaard describes him—often involved an extremely tender, unintentional, playful and at the same time touching irony. He gave the preference fictively to the victors of everyday life, simply out of the kindness of the superfluity of his wealth: "They know about the abyss as well as I do—and yet they balance gaily over it." But did they really know? The
180

joking hypothesis of the premise loosened up the personal tragedy of his life—was one of the roots of his entirely unique humor.

So Kafka's attitude is related to Job's attitude, and yet in many points is a quite different one. I cannot, as Schoeps and Margarethe Susmann do, trace this difference back in essentials to the historical difference between the stage of development of the Jewish race at that time and now.

In the first place the fact that Job from the very beginning appears a perfectly just man to others as well as to himself, whereas Kafka—with the reservations I have just made above —considers himself as a particularly imperfect one, demands a different approach to the problem.

In the question and charge laid against God, they are, it is true, at one with each other. It is the experience of incommensurability that is common to them both. The world of God's justice, and the world of human ethics gape wide asunder—the space for Kierkegaard's "Fear and Trembling" is created. Or as Kafka once expressed it in his diary: "It is not really and completely wicked for a tubercular man to have children. Flaubert's father was tubercular. The choice: either the child's lungs go for a penny whistle—very fine expression for the music the doctor puts his ear to the patient's chest to listen for—or it becomes a Flaubert. The trembling of the father while counsel is taken in empty space." Plumb the terrible hopelessness that lies in the phrase, "counsel is taken in empty space." It reminds one of that old demoniac hymn, which Kafka surely did not know, "*sederunt principes*." In the same way, Job does not mince matters; when he strives with God no expression is too strong for reviling God.

Job ix. 11–19. "Lo, he goeth by me, and I see him not: he passeth on also, but I perceive him not.

"Behold, he taketh away, who can hinder him? Who will say unto him, What dost thou?

"If God will not withdraw his anger, the proud helpers do stoop under him.

"How much less shall I answer him, and choose out my words to reason with him?

"Whom, though I were righteous, yet would I not answer, but I would make supplication to my judge.

"If I had called, and he had answered me; yet would I not believe that he had hearkened unto my voice.

"For he breaketh me with a tempest, and multiplieth my wounds without cause.

"He will not suffer me to take my breath, but filleth me with bitterness.

"If I speak of strength, lo, he is strong: and if of judgment, who shall set me a time to plead?"

That is exactly the same judge to whom K., in *The Trial*, cannot fight his way: or again, the gentlemen of the Castle, who don't allow themselves to be spoken to, who always put forward a screen of courts of appeal which have no responsibility and which do very wicked things.

In the Book of Job:

"If the scourge slay suddenly, he will laugh at the trial of the innocent.

"The earth is given into the hand of the wicked: he covereth the faces of the judges thereof; if not, where, and who is he?

"If I wash myself with snow water, and make my hands never so clean;

"Yet shalt thou plunge me in the ditch, and mine own clothes shall abhor me.

"For he is not a man, as I am, that I should answer him, and we should come together in judgment.

"Neither is there any daysman betwixt us, that might lay his hand upon us both.

"Let him take his rod away from me, and let not his fear terrify me:

"Then would I speak, and not fear him; but it is not so with me."

The solution in the Book of Job comes about later through God's answer out of the whirlwind, "Where wast thou when I laid the foundations of the Earth?" But thereby only the heteronomy between God and man is strengthened. Thereby divine right would be differentiated from human right *toto coelo*. To cap everything the Book of Job ends with a hymn-like description of two beasts, two monsters, "Behemoth and that Leviathan" whose beauty, so completely removed from humanity, is praised. "He maketh a path to shine after him; one would think the deep to be hoary—He is a king over all the children of pride." Really magnificent. But the paradox that God's yardstick is not man's remains unanswered. By human standards, God appears to be unjust—the wound remains. Job, it is true, finds some way of accommodating himself to this "Beyond Good and Evil."

Not so Kafka. His charge, at the same time, goes one step further than Job's, although one might think that were hardly possible. This is the step: "Behemoth and that Leviathan" have no ethics that man can fathom, but they are praised in an aesthetic sense, as God's works, magnificent to look at in their strength. Now with Kafka the "Court" is, in addition, dirty, ridiculous, despicable, corrupt; it sits in rooms in a suburb, works in a stupidly bureaucratic way, is treated in fact as aesthetically inferior. The intention of both writers is, of course, the same. The heteronomy of God is to be described—something that cannot be measured by men's standards. So far efforts have been made to describe this heteronomy solely by an endless exaggeration in the direction of the positive side: more light than one can imagine, greater, stronger than is bearable by human powers of comprehension. Kafka makes comprehensible the difference in kind of the perfect world, by fitting it out with negative characteristics. Already, with Job, the world of God—as that of his monsters—is radically opposed to the world of man, but it is at least on the grand scale. With Kafka it is seen besides to be petty, rough, trashy—this too is only a symbol for its being different, its being opposed. The world of perfection seems so disgusting to man; man is just forming a wrong judgment, that is all. This fact is thereby expressed with the boldest consistency—and the world of perfection remains, of course, for all this deliberately abusive picture of it, just as un-

183

affected, just as fundamentally incapable of being affected, with Kafka as with Job.

But Job comforts himself with the idea that God and man cannot be brought to the same levels. Kafka, however, does not comfort himself. And that shuts him out of the line Job—Kierkegaard—theology of the crisis. That brings him back to the Jewish creed, in one sentence of which, "Our God is one God," I see the strongest spell against all attempts to attribute to God ethical laws fundamentally different from those of mankind. God, the world of perfection, of the Platonic "highest good," is under the same laws as we are, our morality runs towards this goal, without, it is true, our being able to comprehend the goal; but the path that leads to it we can comprehend, and we refuse to recognize any heathen-divine nature-ethic, which would really be heteronomous to it. In that probably lies the deepest ground for the commandment in the Bible that we may not make ourselves any image of God. The theology of the crisis—in fact, Job already—Kierkegaard's Abraham-conception already—easily fall into the danger of deducing an unmoral or nature-moral God from the difference in kind between God and man, between the perfect and the finite, to imagine God as a negro fetish that bares its teeth. But, "Thou shalt not make any graven image." Even Behemoth and that Leviathan do not say the last word on the nature of God. God *did* create man "in His own image"—the humane teaching of the Old Testament to which the great Thomas Aquinas found the way back after the pessimistic errors of Augustine: *Signatum est super nos lumen vultus Tui, Domine*. Thus, too, Kafka sees no heteronomy between God and man, but only indistinctness, an admittedly almost desperate complication, caused by intermediate courts full of malice and poison, which thrust their way bureaucratically between, and continually hinder the Good.

In spite of all these intermediate courts which take up so much room in his writings, in fact sometimes rob life of all its pleasure, he writes sentences like the following, which
184

are full of hope and love, full of a comfort born at a heavy cost through a thousand sufferings:

"It is not a denial of the premonition of a final delivery when the imprisonment remains still unchanged the next day, or is even made more severe, or even if it is expressly stated that it will never come to an end. All that *can* be, much rather, the necessary basis for a final delivery."

"He is of the opinion one has only once to find the way over to the Good, and one is immediately saved, without paying any attention to the past, and even without paying any attention to the future."

Kafka saw the world of the Absolute before him, not beyond redemption, and not barred to us. Hope—for us, too! That he once expressed the opposite opinion is not conclusive enough to counterbalance the many "entries" into the Absolute which he recognized over and over again, and which I have taken it on me to describe in this biography as possibilities, which frequently recurred, of the right profession, the right marriage, and so on. For it seems to me that just this is the most important point in the presentation of a man who is motivated by religion; to point out the cramp irons that this man recognizes between the visibly finite world and the perfect world that lies beyond, to show where they are to be found, whether he has perhaps denied them altogether, and avoided them, or has only accidentally missed them, but in principle knows them and has striven to get at them, to experience them.

On March 15, 1922, Franz read me the beginning of *The Castle*.[1]

[1] He used to come to Prague, at this time, only temporarily and for short periods. In 1919 he lived for a few months in Schelesen near Liboch, at Stüdl's boarding-house; alone at first, then in winter with me. A second unhappy tale of love and betrothal began there, but came to a speedy end. He wrote the "Letter to My Father." His stay in Meran falls in the year 1920, as well as a love affair that went very hopefully for a short time. Many letters from this period are extant. That winter he tried to find in the Tatra Mountains, in a sanatorium at Tatranské Matliary, a cure for his illness, which was becoming more and more acute, and sometimes led to the severest crises. There he found a friend

In *The Castle* an exhaustive description is given of how a certain type of man reacts to the world, and in so far as every man feels an element of this type in himself—exactly in the same way that Faust, or Don Quixote, or Julien Sorel is hidden in each of us, whether it be as a predisposition, as a yearning, or as a component part of the ego—so Kafka's *Castle,* for all the individuality of the character it describes, is a book in which everyone recognizes his own experiences. Kafka's hero, whom he calls simply K., in autobiographical fashion, passes through life alone. He is the loneliness-component in us, which this novel works out in more-than-life-size, terrifying clarity. But at the same time it is a very special nuance of loneliness that is treated—and this, too, we know deep down in ourselves, feel it sometimes in quiet moments rising to the surface. K., namely, is a man of good will through and through; he doesn't wish for his loneliness, and is not proud of it, but would gladly be an active member of human society, would like to play his part in an honest way, would like to fit in; he strives after a useful career, wants to marry, wants to found a family. But everything goes wrong with him. One notices more and more clearly that the chilly layer of isolation that surrounds K. is nothing accidental—it is also no accident that the old-established inhabitants of the village in which K. had wrought a dwelling-place for himself shut themselves up against him, and that in his efforts to find contacts he hits upon just that family of farmers which is spurned by all the others. But the riddle as to why K. cannot make himself at home is not solved. He is a stranger, and has struck a village in which strangers are looked upon with suspicion. More is not said. One feels at once that this is the

in Dr. Robert Klopstock, a fellow-patient and a doctor. He coughed a great deal, suffered from high temperature and shortness of breath—Kafka, whose beautifully constructed phrases and magnificent sentences are distinguished by such long breaths. In the same way cruel nature let Beethoven and Smetana grow deaf, and many a painter go blind—just the organ which has been best developed is destroyed. Of the exact period in which Kafka wrote *The Castle,* I cannot inform my readers. Only the date of its first reading aloud is fixed on the evidence of my diary—it is probably not far from the beginning of his writing it.

186

general feeling of strangeness among men, only it has just been made concrete in this one special case. "Nobody can be the companion of anyone here." One can take this making-concrete a step further. It is the special feeling of a Jew who would like to take root in foreign surroundings, who tries with all the powers of his soul to get nearer to the strangers, to become one of them entirely—but who does not succeed in thus assimilating himself.

The word Jew does not appear in *The Castle.* Yet, tangibly, Kafka in *The Castle,* straight from his Jewish soul, in a simple story, has said more about the situation of Jewry as a whole today than can be read in a hundred learned treatises. At the same time this specifically Jewish interpretation goes hand in hand with what is common to humanity, without either excluding or even disturbing the other. The general religious interpretation I have endeavored to give in the appendix to the published version of the novel. Here are a few pointers on the relation between the novel and the lot of the Jews.

The first meeting with the farmers is immediately characteristic. K. has got lost in this village that is strange to him. He is tired. He sees an old peasant. "May I come in for a while?" asks K. The peasant mumbles something indistinctly. Immediately K. takes this as an invitation and enters the cottage. Later it turns out that the person who let him in is weak in the head. The remarkable legal claim on which the Jews in the Diaspora built up their "right to settle" occurs to one as a parallel, when one has entered into the spirit of this half-accidental "tolerance" which K. claims. It is very much the same a few pages before that. K. has asked the extremely unfriendly schoolmaster whether he could come and see him some time. The schoolmaster's answer is, "I live in Swan Street, at the butcher's." The author comments, "That was, it is true, rather giving an address than an invitation," but nevertheless K. says, "Very well, I shall come." Already in this little introductory scene one sees the position of the "gentiles" with their calm rejection, and that of the Jew with his obligatory friendliness, pushfulness, indeed importunity, described with shatteringly objective melancholy. This is a

187

peculiarity of Kafka's style: melancholy which seems to force itself out from an objective—not a subjective—arbitrariness.

But let us get on! In the cottage K. is shown immediately that he is not at all welcome to the people in it: that he is disturbing them in the middle of very intimate household tasks—washing the floors and the clothes, feeding a baby. At a pinch, they allow him to sleep there a little. Then he is bowed out. A "silent, slow-thinking man, broad-built, and with a broad face too," comes up to him. "You can't stay here." The Jew is not always thrown out rudely or on legal quibbles. But the thing goes with the inevitability of a law of nature, without passion, under compulsion. "We don't want any visitors." K. appeals to the fact that they had invited him, that he is going to have a proper post here as a land surveyor. Whether there is any truth in this story of an invitation, or whether K. only imagines it, that is the point on which the whole novel really turns—here again the parallel with the Jewish problem is easy to sense. Now, in this first chapter the simple man of the people gives the provisional answer which more or less corresponds to the attitude of instinctive anti-Semitism: "[Whether they want you] . . . that I don't know. If you've been asked to come, then you're probably needed, that is an exception, but we, we little people, stick to the rule, and that you can't blame us for." K. tries still to get quickly into conversation with a girl who is in the room, but "at once K. had one of the men on each side of him, dragging him towards the door, silently, but with all their strength, as though there was no other way of making him understand. The old man was pleased about something or other as this took place, and clapped his hands. Even the washerwoman was laughing with the children, who were suddenly yelling like mad things." The scene, which is the eternal fate of Jews, sounds like a very impartial rewriting of the saying, "It doesn't matter, the Jew will be burned." Arguments have no place in the debate about Jews which the world conducts with us: "Silently, as if there was no other way of making him understand."

The hostile village splits itself up for Kafka into two strata

188

—the village, and the castle that dominates it. In order to settle in the village, he needed permission from the castle. But the castle barred itself against him, in the same way that the peasants turned their backs on him. The castle, in the peculiar symbolic language of the novel, stands for divine guidance, the village and its peasants stand for "Mother Earth." For women attract K.—through them he hopes to get an entrance into the families and to find firm ground under his feet. In just the same way his work is a connection with the earth, a taking-root. As soon as the prospect of a girl from the place and of a job opens up for him, he thinks he has won the game, and he lulls himself with the dream that he will be able to walk about among the people of the village "indistinguishable" from them. The whole passage breathes the illusionary spirit of the psychology of assimilation: "Only as a village laborer, removed as far away as possible from the gentlemen of the castle would he be in a position to achieve anything in the castle. These people who were still so suspicious of him would begin to speak to him when he had become, not of course their friend, but still their fellow-citizen, and once he was undistinguishable from Gerstäcker or Lasemann—and that would have to happen very quickly, everything depended on that—then all paths would be opened to him at one stroke, and so on." K.'s reflections follow the familiar lines: to reach God through the community, out of the coalescence with a natural form of life to draw religious strength. But K. might very well be able to explain this mystery rationally—to live it to the depths (in these strange surroundings) he was not able. "I have been here quite a long time and am already feeling a little deserted," he complains to the schoolmaster. "To the peasants I don't belong and to the castle I don't either, I suppose." "Between the peasants and the castle there is no difference," the schoolmaster corrects him. And that, too, again sounds like a paraphrase of a well-known saying, a saying of the Psalms, "How can we sing the Lord's song in a strange land!"

The difference between K. and the natives in the passage given below displays the familiar features. On all sides the

Jew comes up against the old customs—he becomes a nuisance without wishing to be one—at the same time he has the feeling he knows everything better than the people on the spot, he would like to make the whole thing simple, more practical than they do, but they, in their incredible self-will, remain unapproachable. In numerous scenes Kafka shows with superior irony what unsuspected powers of resistance the outmoded and distorted arrangements of the village and the castle develop to oppose the intruder. "You are not from the village, you are nothing. But unfortunately you are something after all, a stranger, a person who is superfluous, and always in the way, a person for whose sake one has continual vexation, a person whose intentions are obscure—for all that I don't in fact at bottom reproach you. You are what you are. I have seen too much in my life already not to be able to bear the sight of this, too. But now just think what you are really asking for. . . . You have been in the place a day or two, and already you think you know everything better than the people who live here. I am not saying that it isn't possible once in a while to get something done even in the teeth of every rule and tradition, but then it certainly doesn't come about in the way you are going on, by saying no all the time, and sticking to your own opinions."

It is the same thing with the chairman of the parish council, who expresses his fundamental dislike of K. in a slightly different tone, but just as conclusively. "You were engaged as a surveyor, but we have no work for you here. . . . Nobody is keeping you here, but, after all, that is not throwing you out. . . . Who would dare to throw you out, Land Surveyor? The lack of clarity of the preliminary questions already guarantees you polite treatment. Only, to all appearances, you are over-sensitive."

In the long history of the sufferings of Jewry, we have heard all these notes before. K. comes to grief in the most pitifully ridiculous way, despite the fact that he went at everything so earnestly and conscientiously. He remains alone. Over all the painful situations this novel takes us through, over all the undeserved misery hangs, invisibly visible, the motto, "This is not the way to do things. A new, a quite different way of taking root must be sought."

In a still unpublished fragment from the year 1914, Kafka describes this fundamental feeling still more sharply. "I came once in summer, towards evening, to a village where I had never been before," is the opening sentence of a short story that covers fourteen quarto pages, but is then, alas! broken off. "On every side in front of the farmhouses one saw old and lofty trees. It was after a shower; the air blew fresh, I was so well pleased with everything." A door in the wall is opened. The children of the tenant farmer were peeping out to see who was passing by so late in the night. The narrator is startled, but is given information by a passer-by. "To a stranger everything may easily seem odd," he apologized, with a smile. The narrator would like to stay the night in the village, looks for an inn, is under observation. The man he first spoke to says to his wife, "I just want to see what this man is going to do here. He is a stranger. He is running around here in a quite unnecessary way. Just watch!" And Kafka goes on: "He was talking about me as if I were deaf, or didn't understand his language." An uncanny conversation follows with the married couple. The stranger is given a night's lodging in their house. Everything takes place in an atmosphere of half, or complete, unexpressed hostility. "If putting me up gives you even the faintest trouble, then tell me so frankly, I am not at all insistent on the point. I shall go to the inn; it's all the same to me." "He talks such a lot," said the woman softly. "It could only be meant as an insult; well, they answer my politeness with insults then; but she is an old woman, I can't defend myself. And it was just this defenselessness perhaps that was the reason why this remark of the woman's which I could not answer back had a much greater effect on me than it deserved. I felt some kind of justification for some kind of fault found with me, not for the reason that I had spoken too much, for really I had said only what was absolutely necessary, but for some separate reasons which touched my existence very nearly." Finally there is a description of how the stranger, without wanting to, disturbs the

191

children in their sleep by his clumsiness and misunderstanding, turns the whole house upside down.

The negative aspect of the Jewish problem, the indefensibility of the Jewish position is also demonstrated in the story, "Josephine the Songstress—or The Mice-Nation," the last finished work of Kafka's, and one which he himself destined for the printing press. To what particular people this picture of the baited, helpless host of mice most nearly refers need not be expressly stated. How the vanity of the star, of the literary man, of the leading "personality" asserts itself even in the midst of the deepest anguish of the people: this extremely ironical presentation of the protagonist who believes the world has waited for him alone, for his word of salvation that he and only he could utter, unhappily applies also to a phenomenon which is particularly common just in the Jewish factional and the Jewish literary world—the man who thinks that he alone was chosen, and with sneering superiority dismisses as unimportant, or hardly takes any notice of, anything that anybody else advises, does, or says. (Kafka himself is an example of the opposite type, that is, modest and humble, and has none of those "gestures of a savior" about him. He went, or so I think, almost too far in this direction. It is open to argument how far the unfavorable conditions of his life were responsible for his occasional self-depreciation and whether without it he would not have risen to the rank of a great, historically effective prophet of true religiosity.) Don't misunderstand me! The position of the helpless mice is simultaneously that of weak humanity in the battle against the demons of Evil. The vain prophet is to be found among other peoples too. And only in so far as the position of helplessness, as well as of the irresponsible, conscienceless "famous man" stands, in the case of the Jews, under the dazzling searchlight of the distress of the Jewish masses and of the Jewish soul, is it an especially sharp portrait in miniature, a symbol of the general sufferings of mankind presented in the form of a caricature.

In "Josephine," however, the road leading to a positive solution is indicated, and it seems to me not a matter of indifference that this happens just in the last work Kafka finished. Josephine the singer defies and hides away from her people, who have so warmly admired her art, indeed have regarded it as indispensable, and now the story says, "But the people, quietly, without showing any disappointment, imperiously, a mass relying on itself, which even if appearances speak against it, *can absolutely only make gifts, never receive them, not even from Josephine, goes on in its own way.* For Josephine, however, there can be only the downward path. The day will soon come when her last squeak has sounded and is heard no more. *She is a tiny episode in the eternal history of our people, and our people will get over the loss."* The incorporation of the individual in the fate of his people, his active participation is demanded. The reader of this biography will find sufficient points to show how Kafka, in his special, Jewish case, tried to find the link with the people. The last chapter also adds a few indications of this. Of course Kafka did not believe that a geographical change of address was sufficient; he regarded a change of heart as equally to be demanded. Both must be changed, both were equally necessary. Order in one's soul—as well as a normalization of the outward conditions of life.

Now one might ask why Kafka expressed this only in his diaries and letters, and never expressly in his literary works, why, as a writer, he expressed himself solely, allegorically or symbolically, in parables.

First one must recognize the peculiarity of Kafka's way of thinking, which went on in images, and not in discourse. Even in conversation, in a debate, the image prevails. In the diary, too, the inexpressibly lovely lyric passages—one of many: "Dreams come along, they come up the river, on a ladder they climb the quayside. One stops, one talks to them, they know so much, only where they come from, that they don't know . . . why do you raise your arms instead of folding them round us?"

Furthermore, one must not confuse "allegory" and "symbol." Kafka never is allegorical, but he is symbolical in the highest sense. An allegory is created when one "says some-

193

thing else" for something. This "something else" in itself is of little importance. The anchor, which stands for hope, in its character as an anchor, does not interest us in the least. It is all the same what color, what shape or what size it is. That is why, as a pure hieroglyphic sign, it stands so unequivocally, and sharply silhouetted, for "Hope." But Andersen's "Tin Soldier," who expresses perhaps a good, patient, loving heart, and many other things as well, running into infinity, touches us also through the personal story of himself, the tin soldier, in all its detail. The tin soldier is no more an allegory, but a symbol. The symbol stands on both levels at the same time, on the level which it describes by suggestion, and on the objective, real level. It unites the two levels in a peculiar way, and, what the Greek word also expressed, throws them together mixed up with one another—and this is such a way that the deeper one penetrates into the individual case with all its details about the tin soldier, the clearer one sees the universal. The *Marquise von O.* deals with faith between parents and child, but behind it, and high above it stands the question of faith in general, faith in the order of the world. Why then did the writer not say straight out the universal that he wanted to say? Because it cannot be said to the end, because it stretches into infinity. In the special case which he relates the writer gives only the starting point of an infinite process. Allegory takes the opposite path, presents the end of such a process, presents it in clear outline as a plaything—the mark of a tired soul. Symbol on the other hand is the bursting forth of a soul, is a matter of the tensive power which allows the individual case to send a ray into the infinite—and at the same time, according to the point at which one takes a cross section of the ray, one finds the affairs of the individual, of the people, or of mankind dealt with. And all this, too, simultaneously, with the same words, and in one single situation.

Behind all Kafka's scenes this infinite vista opens out. But the scene itself, too, the plain narrative, from which the ray shines, is full of love of nature and faithful to nature, of fine observation that is never boring—in this connection one ought
194

perhaps to read—but there are thousands of examples—the scenes of office life, which have been so thoroughly experienced, or of the rivalry between the clerks in *The Trial*. Only a man who loves life on the deepest foundation tells a tale in such a way. There is not a word that the presentation does not lend new color to, not a word that is meaningless—this special mastery of style is not merely aesthetic, it is a moral phenomenon, it is a result of Kafka's peculiar honesty. This would already be a great thing were it only a question of a simple realistic presentation. But the happenings he describes mean, with Kafka, himself in the first place, but they mean also at the same time *not only* himself. A ray shines out from every detail, pointing to the eternal, the transcendental, the world of ideas. In every great work of art one finds the eternal shining through the mortal forms. In the case of Kafka, however, it has apart from that become a formal principle of his writing; one simply cannot any longer separate content from structure, so intimately have they united.

CHAPTER VII

THE LAST YEARS

"THERE is no one here who wholly understands me. To have one person with this understanding, a woman for example, that would be to have a foothold on every side, it would mean to have God"—this is what Kafka wrote in his diary in 1915. It seems that this happiness did come his way at the end of his life, and that the outcome of his fate was more positive and more full of life than its whole previous development.

In the summer of 1923, Franz was staying with his sister and her children in Müritz, the Baltic seaside resort. There he chanced upon a holiday colony of the Berlin Jewish People's Home, which, founded by Dr. Lehmann, had filled him, as well as myself, with hope. Right at the beginning of the work, which has now spread widely and nobly in Palestine, he took a lively interest in it, and had at one time persuaded his fiancée F. in Berlin to take part as a voluntary helper in the work of this Home. Now, many years later, on the beach he meets children from this Home, plays with them, gets to know their teacher, goes to social evenings with them. Once he notices a girl in the Home's kitchen. She is busy scaling fish. "Such gentle hands, and such bloody work," he said with disapproval. The girl was ashamed, and had some other work allotted to her.

That was the beginning of his friendship with Dora Dymant, his life's companion.

Dora Dymant, who must have been nineteen or twenty at that time, came from a very much looked-up-to Polish Orthodox Jewish family. For all the respect she bore her father whom she loved, she couldn't stand the constraint, the narrowness of the tradition—a similar case to that of the actor Löwy, who combined a great respect for his parents with the realization that he could not continue to follow in their foot-steps. Dora escaped from the little Polish town, and found jobs first in Breslau, then in Berlin, and came to Müritz in the employ of the Home. She was an excellent Hebrew student. Kafka was studying Hebrew with special zeal at that time—of the papers he left behind, the papers filled with Hebrew exercises are not much fewer than those covered with literary works in German.

One of the first conversations between the two ended in Dora's reading aloud a chapter from Isaiah in the original Hebrew. Franz recognized her dramatic talent; on his advice and under his direction she later educated herself in this art.

Franz came back from his summer holiday full of high courage. His decision to cut all ties, get to Berlin, and live with Dora stood firm—and this time he carried it out in-flexibly. At the end of July he left Prague, after offering suc-cessful resistance to all his family's objections. From Berlin he wrote to me for the first time that he felt happy, and that he was even sleeping well—an unheard-of novelty in these last years. He was living with Dora in the suburb of Steglitz, first of all at 8 Miquel street, at Hermann's. There was writ-ten the comparatively happy story, "A Little Woman." The "little woman-judge" who lives her life in constant anger with her own "ego," which is really a stranger to her, is none other than their landlady. She must have put a lot of dif-ficulties in the way of the young couple. Six weeks later, therefore, we find them in 13 Grunewald street with Dr. Rethberg, a lady doctor, in a villa about whose loveliness Franz used to rave, although he had only two modest rooms in it. There I went to see him as often as I came to Berlin—three times it must have been in all. I found an idyll; at last I saw my friend in good spirits; his bodily health had got worse, it is true. Yet for the time it was not even dangerous. Franz spoke about the demons which had at last let go of him. "I have slipped away from them. This moving to Berlin was magnificent, now they are looking for me and can't find me, at least for the moment." He had finally achieved the ideal of an independent life, a home of his own, he was no longer a son living with his parents, but to a certain extent himself a paterfamilias. It is obvious that Kafka was not at all striving after a paradox, an ideal in principle unachievable —like Kierkegaard, like the "theology of crisis," but—and this is the decisive factor—that he wanted an intelligently fulfilled, good and proper life, that he stood more perhaps on the side of Martin Buber, who, in rejecting Kierkegaard, the solitary, from principle, says of living together with a wife, "Marriage is the exemplary bond, as no other bond does, it carries us into the great bondage and only as bondsmen can we enter into the freedom of the children of God— yes, woman stands in dangerous rapport with the finite, and indeed, the finite is the danger, for there is no greater threat to us than that of remaining tied to it, but just on this danger is our hope of salvation forged, for it is only over the finite fulfilled that our human path leads to the infinite" (Buber, "The Question for the Individual," 1936). In this sense I saw Kafka on the right road, and truly happy with his life-companion in the last year of his life, which, despite his frightful illness, perfected him. He was working with pleasure, read "A Little Woman" aloud for me, wrote *The Burrow*, from which he also read some passages aloud to me. When I introduced him to the manager of the publishing firm "Die Schmiede," he agreed, without much need of long arguments to persuade him, to the publication of four short stories as a title for which he took the name of one of them, "A Hunger-Artist." From all these circumstantial indications of his interest in life, I then later gathered the courage to regard as no longer valid his written instructions to me—written long before this period—which forbade the publication of any of his posthumous papers.

It was not only to me that Franz seemed to have found salvation in his whole existence, to have become a new man— from his letters you can see his good spirits and the firmness he had finally won. Take, for example, the following letter to his sister:

198

Dear Valli

The table is standing by the fire. I have just moved from the fireplace because it's too warm there, even for my back which is always cold. My oil-lamp burns wonderfully, a masterpiece of lamp-making, and of shopping—it has been put together out of bought and borrowed little bits—not of course by me—how could I manage a thing like that! You can light it without taking the lamp glass and the globe off; really there is only one thing wrong with it, it won't burn without oil; but after all the rest of us don't do that—and so I sit down and take out your dear letter, now so old. The clock is ticking, I have got used even to the ticking of the clock, I don't hear it very often, besides, and that generally when I am doing something particularly praiseworthy. In fact the clock has certain personal relations to me, like many things in the room, save that now, particularly since I gave notice—or, more accurately, since I was given notice, which is a good thing from every angle, and, moreover, a complicated affair it would take pages to describe—they seem to be beginning to turn their backs on me, above all the calendar, about whose mottoes I have already written to father and mother. Lately it is as if it has been metamorphosed. Either it is absolutely uncommunicative—for example, you want its advice, you go up to it, but the only thing it says is, "Feast of the Reformation"—which probably has a deeper significance, but who can discover it?—or on the contrary, it is nastily ironic. Lately, for example, I was reading something and hit upon an idea as I was doing so that seemed to me very good, or rather full of significance, so much so that I wanted to ask the calendar's opinion on it—it's only on such accidental occasions that it answers, in the course of its day, not like, say, by tearing off a page of the calendar punctually at a fixed time—"Even a blind dog finds something sometimes," it said. Another time I was horrified at the coal bill, whereupon it told me, "Happiness and contentment are the joy of life," in which there is admittedly together with the irony an offensive insensitivity: it is impatient, it can't wait any longer for the day I leave; but perhaps it is only that it wishes to

199

make parting easy for me. Perhaps under the page giving the date of the day I leave there will be a page which I shall no longer see on which is written, "God has told each loving heart, the day will come when we must part." No, one should not write down everything one thinks about one's calendar, "He is only a man, like yourself, after all."

If I tried to write you about everything I come into contact with in this way, I should of course never come to the end, and it would give the appearance that I am leading a busy social life, but in reality it is very quiet where I am, yet never too quiet. Of the excitements of Berlin, bad and good, I know very little; more of the former, of course. By the way, does P. know what you say in Berlin when you are asked, "How are you!" Oh, of course he'll know it. You all know more about Berlin than I do. Well at the risk of repeating an old, old joke, from the point of view of fact it is after all always topical, the answer is "Rotten $\times$ the index figure." And this one—a man is talking enthusiastically about the physical culture festival at Leipzig: "What a tremendous sight when the 750,000 athletes march in!" The other answers, counting up carefully, "Well, that's nothing, after all—three and a half peace-time athletes." [1]

How are things—this is no longer a joke any more, but I hope not something sad either—in the Jewish school? Have you read the paper by the young teacher in "Self-defense"? [2] Very well-intentioned, and zealous. I have again heard that A. is doing very well, and Miss M., they say, has reformed the whole of gymnastics in Palestine. You must not be too annoyed at old A.'s head for business. After all, it was already a tremendous thing to take the whole family on his back and cart them over the sea to Palestine. That so many of his kind do it is no less a miracle of the waters than Moses in the Red Sea.

I thank M. and L. ever so much for their letters. Remark-

[1] A reference to the inflation of the mark which had accustomed Berliners to divide all figures by a huge divisor, according to the index figure posted each day.

[2] *Selbstwehr*—the organ of the Zionist movement in Prague.

able how their handwritings, if you compare them, convey not perhaps the differences in their characters, but almost their corporal differences; at least so it seems to me in this last couple of letters. M. asks what about her life interests me most. Well, what she is reading; if she still dances. Here, in the Jewish People's Home, all the girls learn rhythmic dancing, free of charge, of course—and if she still wears glasses. I am to send Anny G.'s love to L. A dear, lovely, clever child, L., that is to say, but so is Anny—she is learning Hebrew hard, can almost read already, and sing a new song. Is L. making progress, too?

But now it is high time to go to bed. Well, I have been with you almost a whole evening, and it is so far from Stockhaus lane, to Miquel st.—Love . . .

The frightful winter of the inflation period has begun. It is that which really killed Franz, so I think. Every time Franz goes from our quiet suburb to Berlin, he comes home "as if he were coming back from the field of battle"—so Dora tells me. The sufferings of the poor touch him to the heart; he comes back "ash-gray." "He lives with such intensity," says Dora, "that he has died a thousand deaths in his life." But it is not sheer pity; he himself must also endure great privations, because he stubbornly insists on managing on his tiny pension. Only in the worst case and under great pressure will he accept money and parcels of food from his family. For by doing so he feels the independence he has won with such difficulty is threatened. Hardly has he earned a few pence through his contract with the "Schmiede" publishing house, than he thinks about paying back his "family debts," and expensive birthday presents—from the family who is worrying desperately about him he keeps the true state of his affairs back as long as he can. There is a shortage of coal. Butter he gets from Prague. When he heard that his sister was a member of a Prague Jewish women's club which was sending gift parcels to Berlin, he gave her the addresses of people he knew who were without means. "Not to let anything slip— for the money for sending things like this generally runs out

201

pretty quickly. I am sending the addresses straightway; could send many more of course, the supply will not run dry." Next to some of the addresses he put the note "Kosher." Then he happened to catch sight of one of these parcels, and criticized it, saying, "There it lay in front of us, deadly serious, without the faintest smile in the shape of a slab of chocolate, an apple, or something of that sort, as much as to say, 'Now live a few days longer on groats, rice, flour, sugar, and coffee, then die as best you can, we can't do any more for you.'" Thus it was never possible to satisfy his fine feelings.

So long as his health lasted he used to attend the Institute for Jewish Studies in Artillery street. He attended Professor Torczyner's and Professor Guttmann's introductory lectures on the Talmud. He read the easier Hebrew texts. It was only for the sake of these courses that he came regularly from his suburb into Berlin.

Between Christmas and the New Year he went through several severe attacks of fever, but recovered again. In February he moved to Zehlendorf, and his landlady this time was the widow of Carl Busse the author. He lived a retired life. Very seldom visitors came from Berlin—Dr. Rudolf Kayser, Ernst Blass.

The rise in the cost of living began to worry him. "If you cut yourself down to lodgings—over-magnificent lodgings, I admit, I shall give one room up next month—and food—excellent, I admit, conjured up out of two methylated spirit stoves and an improvised Dutch oven—which may perhaps also be an unwarrantable extravagance in comparison with the man my former landlady was always telling me about who cooked everything without exception in his bed—if you live in such simplicity you can just get along, also only with the help of your father and mother and sisters, it is true, but if anything out of the way happens, then you suddenly see that everything is impossible. Once I called in a doctor, Mrs. L. recommended me a relative of hers, a famous professor. Luckily he didn't come himself, but only sent an assistant, a young man not yet thirty; he couldn't find anything more than a temperature, and ordered nothing for the time being except to stay in bed and wait. For this visit he asked twenty marks, that is, 160 Czech crowns. The worst thing is, however, that this price is not only somehow justified according to the scale of fees—nobody ever asks more than his proper fee here—but that it also fully corresponds with the rest of the prices; everything is so dear, you must earn gold marks if you want to live here; I am already sometimes beginning to think I must give up the struggle against Berlin prices, and think of Schelesen, Vienna, and Lake Garda."

When one went to see Franz, he mentioned his troubles only in a jocular way. Thus he once worked out for me a plan for taking, together with Dora, who was such an excellent cook, some small restaurant where he would make himself useful as a waiter.

In the end it was impossible to shut one's eyes to the fact that Franz's bodily health—despite his spiritual equilibrium, which continued—was getting worse. One of his sisters went to see him; then I came back from Berlin and warned an uncle of his, a doctor, who went to Berlin and confirmed my worst fears. On March 14, 1924 I was in Berlin for the first night of *Janáček* (Jenufa) at the State Opera of Berlin, and on the 17th I brought Franz back to Prague. Dora and Dr. Klopstock had brought him as far as the station. A few days later Dora followed him.

Now that Franz was living with his father and mother again, he felt it, in spite of all the tender care that surrounded him, as the shipwreck of all his plans for being independent, as a defeat. Now he wanted me to go and see him every day. Other times he had never spoken so energetically, had always been extremely considerate towards the piles of work that overwhelmed me. This time he spoke as if he knew we should not have one another much longer. "Come tomorrow again at this time," he said with a certain amount of sternness almost.

As he grew worse and worse, he had to be taken to a sanatorium.

"All my terrors surpassed on the 10th of April," stands the entry in my diary, "by the news that Kafka has been sent

203

back from the Wiener Wald [Vienna Forest] sanatorium, to the Vienna clinic—tuberculosis of the larynx discovered. The most fearful day of disaster."

The only car to be had for the journey from the sanatorium to Vienna was an open one. It rained and blew. The whole journey through Dora stood up in the car, trying to protect Franz with her body against the bad weather.

Robert Klopstock, too, proved his great love and loyalty. He broke off his studies in Berlin—which were later to lead to important research results in the field of the treatment of the lungs—and devoted himself exclusively from that moment on until Kafka's death to looking after his precious patient. These two, Dora and Dr. Klopstock, now referred to themselves playfully as Franz's "little family"; it was an intimate living together in the face of death. Franz himself knew he was desperately ill, but was, as I was able to sense when I went to see him once, full of hope and courage. He seemed to be unaware of the imminent danger.

In the Vienna clinic—under Professor Hajek—he was not getting on well. All efforts to get more considerate treatment for him—a separate room, for example—were in vain. For a few days he even had to lie in a bed next to a dying man, and he told me afterwards, with great admiration, of the patience of the priest who waited on at the dying man's side with words of comfort, until the last moment, when all the doctors "had run away long ago." I wrote letters to influential people in Vienna, Werfel intervened energetically on Franz's behalf, but the Professor just as energetically explained that he could not look upon Kafka as anyone else but the patient in room number so-and-so.

Dora and Robert Klopstock finally succeeded in having Franz transferred at the end of April to the friendly, light sanatorium in Kierling, near Klosterneuburg. Here is an extract from a letter of Werfel's to me: "Professor Hajek maintained the only chance for Kafka was to stay in the hospital, because there all the medicines and treatments were ready to hand. He put up a direct struggle against letting him go." In Kierling, in a lovely room filled with flowers and looking out on the green countryside, cared for in every way by his two faithful friends, Kafka spent the last weeks of his life—so far as the pains he suffered allowed it, patiently and cheerfully.

Professor Neumann and the university lecturer, Dr. Oskar Beck, came from the hospital to Kierling. I shall quote a few lines from a letter the latter wrote to Dr. Felix Weltsch, on May 3: "Yesterday I was called to Kierling by Miss Diamant. Dr. Kafka was having very sharp pains in the larynx, particularly when he coughed. When he tries to take some nourishment the pains increase to such an extent that swallowing becomes almost impossible. I was able to confirm that there is a decaying tubercular action which includes also a part of the epiglottis. In such a case an operation cannot even be thought of, and I have given the patient alcohol-injections in the *nervus laryngeus superior*. Today Miss Diamant rang me up again to tell me that the success of this treatment was only temporary and the pains had come back again with all their former intensity. I advised Miss Diamant to take Dr. Kafka to Prague, since Professor Neumann, too, estimated his expectation of life at about three months. Miss Diamant rejected this advice, as she thinks that through this the patient would come to realize the seriousness of his illness.

"It is your duty to give his relations a full account of the seriousness of the situation. Psychologically I can quite understand that Miss Diamant, who is looking after the patient's interests in a self-sacrificing and touching fashion, feels she ought to call a number of specialists to Kierling for a consultation. I had, therefore, to make it clear to her that Dr. Kafka was in such a state, both with regard to his lungs and with regard to his larynx, that no specialist could help him any more, and the only thing one can do is to relieve pain by administering morphine or pantopon."

In the last few weeks he was ordered to speak as little as possible. He used therefore to communicate with us by writing messages on slips of paper, a few of which are in my possession. On one of them he writes, "The story is going to have a new title, 'Josephine the Songstress—or The Mice-Nation.'

Sub-titles like this are not very pretty, it is true, but in this case it has perhaps a special meaning. It has a kind of balance." He thinks of his father a great deal, of hearty eating and drinking. He tells Dora, "When I was a little boy, when I couldn't yet swim, I used to go sometimes with my father, who also can't swim, to the place reserved for non-swimmers. Then we used to sit together naked at the buffet, each with a sausage and a pint of beer. Father generally brought his own sausages with him, because the sausages at the swimming-pool were too dear. Just try and imagine the picture properly—this enormous man, holding a little, nervous bag of bones by the hand, how we used to undress, for example, in the little dark cabin; how he would then drag me out, because I was ashamed; how he tried then to teach me the little bit of swimming he pretended he knew, and so on. But the beer afterwards!" Although he was a teetotaler and a **vegetarian,** he knew how to appreciate the pleasures of beer, wine and meat, used to take a sniff at drinks sometimes, and praise their wonderful aroma—one wasn't quite sure whether ironically or honestly; quite towards the end he certainly did drink beer and wine again, once or twice, and was enchanted. "Don't you have the feeling that Leonhard has a glass of Pschorr in front of him when he is dictating?" he writes on one of his conversational slips (making a reference to some Leonhard or other which is not clear to me). Pictures of vital strength are in the majority: "My cousin, he was a magnificent man. When this cousin Robert, he was then about forty already, used to come towards the evening—he couldn't come earlier because he was a lawyer, had a lot to do, what with his work and his pleasures—well, when he used to come, about five o'clock in the afternoon, to the swimming-pool on the Sophie Island, he threw off his clothes with a few flicks of the hand, jumped into the water and threshed around in it with the strength of a beautiful wild animal, gleaming from the water, with his eyes sparkling, and then was off again like a shot towards the weir—that was magnificent. And half a year later he was dead, tortured to death by doctors. A mysterious disease of the spleen which they were treating
206

principally with injections of milk, in the consciousness that it was no use." He writes a lot, too, about his condition, about needs of the moment, pills, bandages. He asks for "a top hat like this made of water." In between words like "sons of the kings," "into the depths, in the deep harbors." He is tired, full of impatience. And then again: "Max has his birthday on May 27." "Often offer the nurse wine." "Here it is nice to give people a drop of wine, because everyone is a little bit of a connoisseur, after all." "That is a pleasure, to give someone something that gives him pleasure certainly and honestly at the moment you give it him." "One must take care that the lowest flowers over there, where they have been crushed into the vases, don't suffer. How can one do that? Perhaps bowls are really the best." On Sunday, May 11, I went to Vienna to see Franz once again. My journey was preceded by a curious scene. When I got to my editorial offices Saturday afternoon, they shouted to me, "Telephone! Immediately! There's a woman just calling you up from Vienna!" Without waiting to take my overcoat off I dashed into the telephone booth. It was Dora, who greeted me with the words, "You rang me up." I: "No, I've just arrived this moment." DORA: "Prague rang up, the *Prager Tagblatt* was speaking, that's why I asked for *you*." In spite of all my efforts to clear it up, the affair is still unexplained, because while it is true the *Prager Tagblatt* often rings up Vienna, it never rings up Kierling. Further, none of Kafka's sisters had rung Kierling that day. In a remarkable fashion, the whole journey after that lay under the shadow of death. Just as I was about to leave the house I was told that a young man in the flat below ours was lying on his death-bed. In the train a woman dressed in black spoke to me, whom I didn't recognize immediately. It was the widow of the minister, Tusar, and she told me all about her husband's death and her own unhappiness. In Vienna I spoke to no one, but went straight from the station to the hotel, and from the hotel to the station. Early in the morning I took the first train to Klosterneuburg, and from there to Kierling. I stayed till the evening, traveled to Vienna, and the next morning back to Prague. In the forenoon Franz had been quite fresh; despite all the doctors' testimony, his position didn't seem hopeless to me. We spoke about our next meeting; I was planning a journey to Italy which was to take in Vienna again. The first thing Dora told me, and Franz bore her out—he was not allowed to speak a lot—was the remarkable story of his wooing. He wanted to marry Dora, and had sent her pious father a letter in which he had explained that, although he was not a practicing Jew in her father's sense, he was nevertheless a "repentant one, seeking 'to return,'" and therefore might perhaps hope to be accepted into the family of such a pious man. The father set off with the letter to consult the man he honored most, whose authority counted more than anything else for him, to the "Gerer Rebbe." The rabbi read the letter, put it on one side, and said nothing more than the single syllable, "No." Gave no further explanation. He never used to give explanations. The miracle-working rabbi's "No" was justified by Franz's death, which followed very soon afterwards, and Franz, too, took his letter from Dora's father, which had arrived just before I did, and more or less formed the topic of the day for the "little family," as a bad omen. He smiled, and yet he was affected by it; we made efforts to put other thoughts into his head. But shortly afterwards Dora took me to one side and whispered to me that that night an owl had appeared at Franz's window. The bird of death.

But Franz wanted to live; he followed the doctor's instructions with an exactitude I had never observed in him before, and without protest. Had he got to know Dora sooner, his will to live would have become stronger sooner, and in time. That is my impression. The two suited one another quite marvelously. The rich treasure of Polish Jewish religious tradition that Dora was mistress of was a constant source of delight to Franz; at the same time the young girl, who knew nothing about many of the great achievements of Western culture, loved and honored the great teacher no less than his dreamlike, curious fantasies, which she entered into easily and like a game. They often joked together like children. I remember, for example, how they used to dip their hands together in the same wash-basin and call it our "family bath." Dora's care for the invalid was touching; touching too was the late awakening of all his vital energies. Dora told me how Franz cried for joy when Professor Tschiassny—when he was in the last stage already—told him things looked a little better with his throat. He embraced her again and again, and said he had never wished for life and health so much as now. Let me contrast this with the journey we made together to Schelesen in November 1919, from which I remember two things. Kafka was talking about Hamsun's *Growth of the Soil,* and explained in detail how in this novel, partly even against the author's will, everything evil comes from the women in it—further, as the train stopped somewhere, in tones of the deepest despair, "How many stations there are on the journey to death, how slowly it passes!" And now, in *articulo mortis,* he would have known how to live and wanted to live.

Franz Kafka died on June 3, on a Tuesday. The body was brought to Prague in a sealed coffin, and on June 11, at four o'clock, was placed in the grave in a well-chosen site of the Jewish cemetery of Prague—Straschnitz, on the outer side of the cemetery, near one of the main gates. When we got back to the house of mourning in Franz's home in the Old Town Square, we saw that the great clock on the Town Hall had stopped at four o'clock, and its hands were still pointing to that hour. Franz's father and mother were later laid to rest in the same grave.

I was able to get the following details of Franz's last hours mainly from Dr. Klopstock's account.

Monday evening, Franz was feeling very well; he was jolly, showed great pleasure in everything that Klopstock had brought back from the city with him, ate strawberries and cherries, smelled them for a very long time, enjoyed their fragrance with the double intensity with which he enjoyed everything those last days. He wanted people to take long drinks of water and beer in front of him, because it was impossible for him to do so; he enjoyed the others' pleasure. In the last few days he talked a lot about drinks and fruit.

On Monday, too, he wrote the last letter which his parents were to get from Kierling, which I quote below—a document full of self-control and a child's love for his parents, which may be compared with the letters Heine wrote to his mother from his final sickbed, in order to prevent any feeling of uneasiness from troubling her. The letter runs:

Dearest Father and Mother
Well, these visits you write to me about sometimes. I think it over every day, because for me it's something very important. It would be so lovely, we haven't been together for such a long time, I don't count being together in Prague, that was just upsetting the household, but being together a few days in peace in some beautiful district, only I can't remember when that was really, a few hours once in Franzensbad. And then to drink a "good glass of beer" together, as you write, from which I see that father doesn't think much of this year's wine, in which, as far as the beer is concerned, I agree with him. Apart from that, a thing I often look back on now during the heat, there was a time once when we often used to be beer-drinkers together, many years ago, when father used to take me with him to the public baths.

That and much more speaks for your coming, but there's a lot that speaks against it. Now, first of all, father would probably not be able to come because of the difficulty with passports. That, of course, robs your visit of a lot of its sense; but above all mother, whomever else she may be accompanied by, will be far too much thrown on me, dependent on me, and I am still not very beautiful, not worth looking at. The difficulties I met with in the beginning here in and around Vienna, you know; they got me down a little; they kept my temperature from subsiding quickly again, which all helped towards my getting weaker later; the shock of the larynx business weakened me at first more than it deserved to in reality.

Now for the first time I am working myself out of all these weaknesses with the help of Dora and Robert, and how great that help is you cannot imagine so far away—where should I be without them! There are still troubles, as for example a cold on the stomach which I caught in the last few days, and which has not yet quite gone. All that works together, so that in spite of wonderful helpers, in spite of good air and food, and a bath of fresh air almost every day, I am not yet quite better, in fact, on the whole, am not even in such a fit state as I was the last time I was in Prague. On top of that take into
210

account that I may only talk in whispers, and that not too much, and you will be glad to put off your visit. Everything is beginning to go well. Lately a professor found a real improvement in my larynx, and if I can't altogether believe this extremely kind and unselfish man—he comes out once a week in his own car and charges almost nothing for it, so his words were after all a great comfort to me—everything is, as I said, beginning to go well. But the best of beginnings are nothing if I can't show visitors—and especially such visitors as you would be—great, undeniable progress, progress that can be recognized even by the lay eye, it's better to leave it. Well, then, shan't we leave it for the moment, dear father and mother?

You mustn't think you could do anything to improve or enlarge on the treatment I am getting here. It is true that the owner of the sanatorium is an old and sick man, who can't be bothered with the thing very much, and my dealings with the very unwelcome assistant doctor are more on friendly than on medicinal terms; but in addition to the occasional visit of a specialist, Robert is there, above all, never stirring from my side, and instead of thinking about his examinations, thinks of me with all his might, and then there is a young doctor in whom I have every confidence—I have to thank Arch. Ehrmann for him and for the professor I mentioned above—and who comes after all not in a car, but modestly three times a week by train and "bus."

On Monday (and apparently also on Tuesday morning, which however I hardly believe) Franz was working on the first proofs which had arrived shortly before of his last book, "A Hunger-Artist." He gave orders for changing the order of the stories, showed some temper with the publisher, who had not paid sufficient care to this or that instruction. Dora once said very rightly, "Really he demanded a great deal of respect towards himself. If one met him with due respect, everything was all right, and he didn't care a thing about formalities. But if one didn't, he was very annoyed." At midnight he fell asleep. At four o'clock in the morning Klopstock was called into the room by Dora, because Franz "is breathing badly." Klopstock recognized the danger, and woke the doctor, who gave him a camphor injection.

Then began the fight for morphine. Franz said to Klopstock: "You have always been promising it me for four years. You are torturing me; you have always been torturing me. I am not talking to you any more. I shall die like that." He was given two injections. After the second he said, "Don't cheat me, you are giving me an antidote." Then the words I mentioned before, "Kill me, or else you are a murderer." They gave him pantopon; he was very happy about that. "That's good, but more, more, it isn't helping me." Then he went slowly to sleep. His last words were about his sister Elly. Klopstock was holding his head. Kafka, who was always terribly afraid he might infect someone, said—imagining it was his sister he saw instead of his doctor friend—"Go away, Elly, not so near, not so near," and as Klopstock moved away a little, he was satisfied, and said, "Yes, like that—it's all right like that."

Before this last scene he made a brusque gesture of dismissal to the nurse. "So brusque as he never was ordinarily," Klopstock told me. Then with all his strength he tore off his icepack and threw it on the floor. "Don't torture me any more, why prolong the agony." As Klopstock moved away from the bed to clean some part of the syringe, Franz said, "Don't leave me." His friend answered, "But I am *not* leaving you." Franz answered in a deep voice, "But I am leaving you."

I want to quote from a letter that Klopstock wrote on June 4 from Kierling, without altering his characteristic, odd grammar. "Poor Dora, oh we are all poor, who is so utterly poor in the world as we—she is whispering without stopping; one can only make out, 'My love, my love, my good one'—I promised her that we should go and see Franz again this afternoon if she would lie down. So she lay down. See him, 'who is so alone, so quite alone, we have nothing to do, and sit here and leave him there [1] alone in the dark, uncovered— O my God! My love'. . . and so it goes on. What is happening here with us—I say always so 'us,' we called ourselves, you see, 'Franz's little family,' is indescribable, and should never be described. Who knows Dora, only he can know what love means. So few understand it, and that increases pain and

[1] In the mortuary.

suffering. But you, won't you, you will understand it! . . .
We don't yet know at all what has happened to us, but slowly,
slowly it will get clearer and clearer, and more painfully
dark at the same time. Particularly *we* don't know it, who
have him still with us. Now we are going there again to
Franz. So stiff, so severe, so unapproachable is his face, as
his soul was pure and severe. Severe—a king's face from the
oldest and noblest stock. The gentleness of his human existence has gone, only his incomparable soul still forms his
stiff, dear face. So beautiful is it as an old marble bust."

I must add finally that the voices of Hugh Walpole, Hux-
ley, Bennett, André Gide, Hermann Hesse, Buber, Thomas
Mann, Heinrich Mann, Werfel, and many others in German,
French, Dutch, Czech, Polish, Italian, and Hebrew, in Eng-
land and America, united in explaining Kafka's importance,
and that his works have appeared in all these languages, and
awakened admiration.

Postscript—I closed the first (German) edition of this biography in 1937 with the above words. Now, in 1947, one
can hardly survey the gigantic essay literature that is concerned with Kafka. This literature contains, alongside isolated comments which are correct, very many absurdities
and contradictions. But Kafka has struck root in some few
spirits. In them his pure light continues to burn. Kafka's art
has also in other respects been formative of style in many
points, without its religious depth and power to convert
being clear to everyone who thinks that he is influenced by
Kafka or who writes about him. In fact one often has the
impression that here and there only the externals of Kafka's
methods have been imitated or analyzed, but not his essential endeavor, which is perhaps beyond the reach of some
who write so much about him and his art. If humanity
would only better understand what has been presented to it
in the person and work of Kafka it would undoubtedly be in
a quite different position; for which reason the attempt to
deal effectively with Kafka's aims cannot be regarded as
completed by this book either.

CHAPTER VIII

NEW ASPECTS OF KAFKA

FEW writers have been subject to the fate which was Kafka's: to remain almost utterly unknown during life, after death to be rapidly lifted to world fame.

In the case of Franz Kafka, this fate cannot be considered so cruel, since he was a man utterly indifferent to fame. Writing was for him "a form of prayer" (as he put it in one of his diaries). His efforts were directed toward inner perfection, toward a stainless life. It was not that he did not care what the world thought of him; rather, he simply had not time to worry about it. For he was wholly occupied with the striving for the highest ethical pinnacle a man can attain—a pinnacle which in truth scarcely can be attained. He was filled with a drive, intensified to the point of pain and semi-madness, not to brook any vice in himself, any lie, any self-deception, nor any offence against his fellow men—this passion for perfection often took the form of self-humiliation, since Kafka saw his own weaknesses as though under a microscope, magnified to many times their size. How he despaired of himself on account of these weaknesses, longing as he did for intimate fusion with the Pure, the Divine, which in his aphorisms he described as the "Indestructible." This ideal preoccupied him throughout his life. In this sense Kafka, of all modern writers, is the one most closely akin to Tolstoi. "Man cannot live without a lasting trust in something indestructible within himself"—in this sentence Kafka formulated his religious position.

After his death it was not easy to find an important publisher who would undertake to bring out a posthumous edition of Kafka's work. I had to go to a different publishing house for almost each successive volume. I tried to interest a few prominent personages in these works. Gerhart Hauptmann wrote to me that he had unfortunately never heard the

214

name Kafka. Today one can scarcely open any issue of a German, French, English, American or Italian literary review without encountering that name.

Now that the personality of Kafka has more or less entered the common domain, we are faced with the inevitable distortions of his image. These we can confidently pass over, and rest our faith in that "Indestructible" of which Kafka himself spoke. In other works, we are confident that, with the passage of time, the proper outlines of that complex personality will emerge of their own accord.

Nevertheless, it is gratifying that even today the right and essential features of Kafka are occasionally portrayed—the more so when witnesses come forth who once had personal ties with Kafka. Thus I recently received *Erinnerungen an Kafka* ("Recollections of Kafka"), written by a friend of Kafka's (Friedrich Thieberger, now in Jerusalem). Thus also Frau Dora Dymant,[1] who was Kafka's companion during the last years of his life, recounted a great deal about the time she spent with Kafka.[2] Much of what she said in public and private during her all too brief stay in Israel was written down by Felix Weltsch. In addition we have what Marthe Robert has written concerning Dora, and a remarkable book by Gustav Janouch. The special value of this lies in Janouch's having written down Kafka's conversation during his lifetime.

In the preface to his book, and in the Notes and Explanations of the Appendix, Janouch has related a bit of his own story, the genesis of the *Gespräche mit Kafka* (*Conversations with Kafka*),[3] and the varied fortunes of the manuscript. Here I should like to tell how the manuscript came to me, and point out what it contributes to our knowledge of Kafka's life for the period beginning March 1920—the time at which Janouch met Kafka.

In May 1947—eight years after I had left my birthplace of

[1] Died in London, August 1952.
[2] *See* J. P. Hodin, "Erinnerungen an Franz Kafka." *Der Monat,* I, 8–9. Berlin 1949.
[3] New York 1953.

Prague for good—I received a letter from that city which began: "I do not know whether you will still remember me. I am that musician of whom you wrote in the *Prager Tageblatt* shortly before your departure, and the person who arranged Florian's publication of the Czech edition of Franz Kafka's *Metamorphosis*." My correspondent went on to ask whether he might send to me his "diary entries on Franz Kafka," for which he was seeking a publisher. "Franz Kafka represents my youth—and much more. So you can imagine my suspense," Janouch wrote in a second letter to me.

The manuscript arrived after a considerable delay. Then, due to the fact that I was then overburdened with work, it lay around unread for a rather long time. At last my secretary, Frau Ester Hoffe (to whom I am infinitely indebted for her assistance in sifting through and editing Franz Kafka's papers), took it upon herself to look into the manuscript. She read it, and informed me that it was a very valuable piece of work. Now I too read it, and was stunned by the wealth of new material I encountered—which plainly and unmistakably bore the stamp of Kafka's peculiar genius. Kafka's appearance, too, his manner of speech, his expressive and yet delicate way of gesticulating, the very movements of his facial muscles, were reproduced in the most vivid manner. I felt as if my friend had suddenly returned to life and had just entered the room. Once more I heard him speaking, saw his animated, shining eyes resting upon me, felt his quiet, pained smile, and was deeply stirred by his wisdom.

Shortly afterwards came Dora Dymant's visit to Israel. She visited me often, and on one such visit I read to her from Janouch's manuscript. It affected her as it had me; she too recognized Kafka's inimitable style and his way of thought in all the conversations that Janouch had preserved. She also was shaken by the feeling of having again encountered Kafka.

Thus the genuineness of the material is supported by two witnesses; unexpectedly a third soon appeared. Kafka's *Letters to Milena* were edited by my friend Willy Haas.[1]

[1] New York 1953.

These letters had lain for more than two decades in the safe-deposit vault of a Prague bank; I had not known them at all. Now I read these letters. To my mind they belong among the most significant love-letters of all time and will ultimately take their place beside the ardently humble letters of Julie de l'Espinasse. There were several passages in them referring to that shy young poet Gustav Janouch who worshipped Kafka, brought him his first poems, engaged him in discussions—and was quite a bother, for Kafka's mind was upon entirely different ideas and passions at this time. The whole circumstance of the conversations which Janouch describes, and which he of course sees from only one side, contains a goodly portion of irony when seen from the other side, and in different perspective. But that very fact helps to confirm their authenticity.

Janouch, incidentally, turns up in the 1937 edition of this biography, although as a dim shadow, or rather: in the figure of his father. In Chapter III I mention that Kafka made friends of his colleagues in the office of the Workers' Accident Insurance, "even with some of them who were very simple or very confused" (*see* p. 86). I mention, for instance, a man who was the author of an "extraordinary memorandum." I have found this memorandum among my papers, and it now lies on the desk before me as I write. The memorandum begins with the words, *Nos exules filii Evae in hac lacrimarum valle.* The imaginative and eccentric author was none other than Janouch's father. At that time, I had actually made the acquaintance of both the father and, somewhat later, the son. The noble personality of Janouch's father and the story of his unfortunate mixed marriage emerge incidentally from the pages of Gustav Janouch's book, and next to the overpowering figure of Kafka form a poignant secondary motif. (*Cf.* on this Kafka's note about Janouch's father in *Letters to Milena,* p. 155.)

For Kafka himself, the whole period of his association with Janouch was fatefully determined by Milena. Janouch met Kafka at the end of March 1920. In Kafka's diaries there is a gap from January 1920 to October 15, 1921; the notebooks or pages covering this period are missing. On October 15, 1921 Kafka's first note indicates that he had given all his diaries to Milena. It is possible that he destroyed the very parts that refer to this great love episode. After Kafka's death Milena brought the diaries to me, along with the manuscripts of Kafka's novels *Amerika* and *The Castle,* which she had in her keeping, and which were intended for me. Milena's letter referring to this matter is the next to the last in the group of letters reprinted below. Kafka's notes on Milena, to whom he referred in the diaries as M., were contained in the part of the diary which I found elsewhere (in the little room in his parent's apartment which Franz occupied temporarily). These notes run to May 1922. The passionate relationship, which at first meant a summit of happiness to Kafka, soon took a tragic turn. I have a letter of his in which he implores me to prevent Milena from visiting him again.

Kafka's private affairs, then, were not of the happiest at the time of the conversations with Janouch. The young man could not know this. Kafka spoke only in allusions of the great sorrow that was preoccupying him at this time. For the most part he talked in the detached and philosophical terms of a sage surveying world events, the struggles of nations and classes, as well as religion. That fact may convey some notion of the tremendous self-control that Kafka exercised in almost every situation of his life—except when he sat down to write in his diary, or when he spoke with his closest intimates.

Kafka's talk, as Janouch has transmitted it, bears the unmistakable signs of Kafka's style in speech, which if possible was even more concise, more pregnant, than the style in which he wrote. Kafka was absolutely incapable of saying anything insignificant. I have never heard a shallow phrase fall from his lips—not even when he spoke of the most commonplace things. For him—and for the person with whom he happened to be speaking—the commonplace simply did not exist. And yet he never hunted for witty and epigrammatic turns of phrase; it all came effortlessly. If he had nothing vital to say, he preferred to keep silent.

In the earlier version of this biography I passed over this

218

entire period with which Janouch deals. Since Milena was still living at the time, I felt obligated to practice discretion. In the meanwhile we have learned a good deal more about this remarkable woman from Margarethe Buber-Neumann's book, *Als Gefangene bei Stalin und Hitler* ("A Prisoner under Stalin and Hitler"). We have heard of the spiritual force and encouragement Milena radiated toward everyone she met, and of her death in a concentration camp. Kafka characterized her dominant trait as "fearlessness" (Diary, January 18, 1922). For further insight into her nature we now have Kafka's letters to her, and the epilogue by Willy Haas, a tribute to a truly great woman. And in a certain sense radiations of her personality are also present in Janouch's account, although her name is never mentioned there. For much of what Kafka said to Janouch can be understood, can be heard with the proper resonance, only when we consider that Kafka was at that time beginning to think the Jewish problem through with particular intensiveness, and that in Milena he loved a Christian Czech—both of whose girl friends, incidentally, were married to Jews. Milena's husband was Jewish also. That fact led to violent conflicts with her father, an intensely nationalistic Czech prominent in politics. Kafka, thrown into a milieu so entirely new to him, faced with a challenge to his inmost being, and confronted with such vital decisions, thought long and hard about the Jewish problem and came to deeper insights into it.

After reading these *Conversations* with Janouch and the *Letters to Milena,* it became clear to me that this theme is at the bottom of *The Castle,* that prodigious ballad of the homeless stranger who vainly strives to establish roots in the home of his choice.

Quite aside from all the wider meanings, the universal religious allegory implicit in *The Castle,* this biographical factor must not be overlooked. We find significant clues to it in the Janouch material. Further confirmation comes from Milena's letter to me, from things she said in her talks with me, and from my own notes on that period in Kafka's life. In *The Castle* we may find Kafka's relationship to Milena mirrored with peculiar skepticism and bitterness. The actual events which perhaps served to rescue him from the crisis are rendered in an especially distorted form. Milena, represented in the novel in the extremely caricatured figure of Frieda, takes decisive steps to save Kafka (K.). She lives with him, sets up house with him, and remains cheerful and resolute despite poverty and renunciation; she wants to be his forever and by her devotion lead him back to the naiveté and immediacy of true life. But as soon as K. accepts and takes the offered hand, the old ties which formerly bound the woman assert themselves: (the "castle," the populace, society, but above all the mysterious Klamm, whom we must regard as an exaggerated and demonized image of Milena's legal husband, from whom she could not completely break away emotionally). The dreamed-of happiness quickly comes to an end, since K. will not put up with half a loaf. He wants his Frieda for himself alone, no longer constantly dominated by the emissaries of the Castle, the mysterious assistant and Klamm. She, however, betrays him and turns back to the realm of the Castle from which she came. It becomes evident that K. is far more fervent than Frieda about his determination to achieve integral salvation. She is content with a mere token of salvation, or at any rate yields too quickly to disillusionment. In our talks together Milena explained that her husband's interest in her revived when he learned that Kafka was his rival and wanted to marry her.

The parallels between novel and experience could be carried much further. If we do so carry them, the self-tormenting, self-castigating trait in K. emerges strongly. In the novel he represents himself as a swindler who alleges that he has been called to assume a certain post. Milena's girl-friends, who advised against the connection with Kafka, enter the novel in a mighty metamorphosis, becoming the mythic figure of the "landlady," who has the qualities of one of the Fates. She represents, as it were, the chorus of a Greek tragedy. The curious jealousy and contempt of Frieda for Olga in the novel may be seen as a counterpart to the attitude taken by Milena toward J. W., to whom Kafka was engaged at the time. As we see by Milena's letters, she insisted that Kafka break completely with J. W. and her family. Kafka obeyed her, albeit with a protest against the sharpness and injustice of her command.

The pariah-like character of Olga's family also had its correspondences in reality. There are a great many other such realistic building blocks to be found in *The Castle*—which makes us admire the novel all the more when we realize how the structure as a whole towers so high above all these building blocks. Out of the prosaic facts of his own situation the writer's imagination constructed a vast, twilight edifice, gloriously transcendent. I do not believe that we should overestimate the importance of biographical details for the genesis of a work of art; on the other hand, if we refuse to give them their due, we are prone to come to false conclusions.

The Castle, then incorporates the thoughts and feelings both of the *Conversations* and the *Letters to Milena.* Kafka was engaged on this novel during 1921 and 1922. The first date I have for it is March 15, 1922, when Kafka read aloud to me large sections from the beginning of his current work. The motif of the book, however, had appeared long before in his diaries (for example, June 11, 1914: "Temptation in the Village"). Kafka's experiences in Zürau in 1917 shaped the milieu of the novel. I have even been able to demonstrate the connection between the substance of the novel and his early reading of the fine Czech novel *The Grandmother,* by Božena Němcová, in which there is the theme of an alien castle ruling over a village.[1] The letters to Milena also contain an allusion to this classical Czech writer. These facts, however, are incidental. The image of the castle may have preexisted in Kafka's imagination. Nevertheless, it took the meeting with Milena to fill Kafka's soul with the turbulent content which fired him into writing his final great work. Kafka's letters to Milena, her letters to me, and Janouch's recollections provide indispensable documentation for the period of Kafka's life in which *The Castle* was being composed—documentation which is all the more important be-

[1] "Some Remarks on *The Castle,*" at the end of this volume.

cause Kafka's diary stops completely during the writing of the novel, and is relatively meager for the few years he had yet to live.

Milena's eight letters to me, which I publish here for the first time, provide profound insights into the whole relationship between her and Kafka, seen from her point of view. Thus they afford an essential supplement to the picture of this love-affair which is painted in the *Letters to Milena*.

The first letter is dated July 21, 1920. It, like the second, was written in German, of which Milena had an imperfect command. Letters 3 to 6, which are of far greater significance, and into which Milena poured the whole of her passionate personality, are in the original written in her elegant Czech. As her relationship to Franz faded, Milena's manner toward me became more reticent; thus in her last two letters she returned to German, in which she sounded more conventional than when she was expressing herself in Czech.

Frau Milena Jesenská was an excellent writer—and not the only one in her family, incidentally. The other Jesenská was her aunt, if I am not mistaken, who because of her chauvinistic Czech attitudes and philistine outlook was held in distaste in our circles. Milena, on the other hand, was a regular contributor to the liberal Prague daily *Tribuna*, a newspaper that had been founded by Jews who felt themselves to be Czechs—radical assimilationists and opponents of Zionism, that is. It had developed into a paper highly respected in literary circles, to which many of the best Czech writers contributed. For a long time Milena's articles were a regular Sunday feature in this newspaper. They constituted a kind of "letter from Vienna." I can still see the eagerness with which Kafka would hasten to a newsstand to see whether the latest issue contained something by Milena Jesenská. She wrote accounts of life in Vienna, social gossip, reviews, fashion reports, columns on events of the day, and general psychological observations. Kafka could not find sufficient words of praise for the subtlety, liveliness and winning style of these articles, which he was wont to compare with the letters and travel pieces of Fontane, one of his favorite authors. He was
222

always reading aloud to me long sections of these newspaper articles. I must confess that none of the descriptions he so highly praised made any particular impression upon me, and none of the articles has stuck in my memory. But the fault may well be mine. Kafka's literary appreciation was certainly not merely the result of his love for the author; it was based upon an objective evaluation of her literary qualities. His judgment in literary matters was always trenchant and highly original; he seldomed erred. Wherever he did, we can be sure that he was attacking, in a self-castigating manner, aspects of the author which he believed to be faults of his own. One example of such a strikingly misguided judgment is his comment on Grillparzer's "The Poor Fiddler" in the *Letters to Milena,* p. 96f., where he actually speaks of the "dilettantish and affected" quality of that work. To my mind, this comment is entirely unjustified—and moreover runs counter to Kafka's own enthusiastic opinion of "The Poor Fiddler" in his diary and in conversation. Here he was led astray by exaggerated self-identification with the author.

The correspondence between myself and Milena began with a matter which at first glance seems somewhat strange. I had heard of the case of an unfortunate man who had been held for many years in the Weleslawin sanatorium for nervous diseases; his family had reasons for wishing him to remain there. I had been urged to do what I could to rescue this person from imprisonment. As it happened, Kafka had told me that Milena had once been in this institution, and had met this Mr. X. I therefore wrote to Milena, asking her for information about X. I knew the lady, though only casually; I had frequently met her in the company of Werfel, and also of the poet Paul Kornfeld. She lived in Vienna, I knew, and was married to Ernst Pollak, a friend of Werfel's.

The marriage was known to be extremely unhappy. This man Ernst Pollak, gifted, versatile, highly cultivated, active as a philosopher (in the field of logic), widely known as "Pollak the Expert," exerted an uncanny power over Milena, and over other women as well. It is interesting to compare his character with Klamm in several passages of *The Castle.*

I knew that Milena had married Pollak against the opposition of her entire family; perhaps, in fact, her own enforced stay at Weleslawin had something to do with the family's efforts to put an end to the relationship. At the same time that Pollak was involved with Milena, he had an affair with a very beautiful, intellectually inconsequential woman in Vienna, who was incidentally allied to or married to another man. After the marriage to Milena, Pollak ostentatiously did as he pleased, showing no consideration for Milena's feelings—and she seems to have suffered a great deal from his ruthlessness, but at the same time to have loved her suffering. She had to earn her own living and was even reduced to doing occasional porter-service for travelers at a Vienna railroad station in order not to go hungry. Her millionaire family in Prague steadfastly refused to provide any support for their "prodigal daughter."

Such was her unhappy state when Franz met her. During the first half of 1920 he had gone for his cure in Meran. When he returned to Prague, I scarcely recognized the quiet Franz I knew—so joyously and tempestuously did he speak of the days he had spent with Milena in Vienna. He wrote her several letters a day, and received a great many letters in return, but far too few to suit him. Telegrams flew back and forth. How often Franz begged me to come to his office in the Accident Insurance Institute to help him pass the long hours during which he waited for a telegram from Milena. I saw that his health, already shattered by his grave disease, was deteriorating alarmingly under this inward stress. As my friend's faithful second—in the days of my own great love, later on, he was to perform the same service for me—I pleaded with Milena that she remember his illness and treat him with utmost consideration. Milena's second letter refers to that. The tone of the first letter, was still relatively calm and impersonal. The major subject under discussion was the affair of Mr. X. However, this too is intimately connected with Kafka and throws a bright light upon my friend's humanity, for it was he who had begged me to champion the man's cause. At any rate the two of us still had the strength in those days to take upon

224

ourselves not only our own tribulations, but also the sufferings of a third person. Nevertheless, to this day I can hear
like an evil omen the echoes of our footsteps in the corridors
of the insurance company. Ordinarily, Franz only spent mornings in the office—that was ordeal enough for him. But now
he also spent the afternoons there, for at any moment a telegram or special delivery letter from Milena might arrive.

Milena's first letter to me begins as follows:

My dear Doctor:
You ask me for some proofs that an injustice is being done
to Mr. X. in Weleslawin. Unfortunately I can give you very
little definite information that would be adequate for official
channels, although I should be extremely glad to do so. I was
in Weleslawin from June 1917 to March 1918, lived in the
same villa, and all that I could do for the poor man was to
lend him books a few times and get myself locked up a few
times; for he is not allowed to talk to anyone and if it is seen
that he is talking to anyone, even about nothing at all and in
the presence of an attendant, everyone is locked up and the
attendant is dismissed.

There follows a description of the desperate state of the in-
carcerated man. One interesting sentence, perhaps contain-
ing elements out of Milena's own experience, reads:

Psychiatry is a frightful thing when it is misused; everything can be abnormal and every word is a new weapon for
the tormentor. I would be willing to swear that Mr. X. could
really live differently and in the world. But as for proofs—I
can't prove anything.

My efforts for Mr. X. were unsuccessful. But that matter
belongs to a later period. The final part of the letter itself
concerned Franz, whom Milena usually called "Frank."

I have one more great request to make of you, Doctor. You
know that I can never find out from Frank how he is; the dear
225

fellow always will have it that he is "fine" and that he is super-healthy and super-calm, so to speak. I want to plead with you, really plead, *plead*—if you see or if you feel that he is suffering, that he is physically suffering on my account, please write me about it at once; I won't tell him that I have heard it from you and I will be a little calmer myself if you promise me. I don't know how I will help him in that case, but I know for certain that I will help him. Frank says everyone must "love you, be proud of you, admire you." I assure you that I do all that and thank you in advance many times—for one thing for knowing that I can rely upon you.

In my reply I did not conceal the fact that Kafka's condition had gravely worsened lately. On July 29 Milena wrote to me:

I was really greatly alarmed; I did not know that Franz's illness is so serious. He was really well here; I didn't hear him cough at all; he was brisk and cheerful and slept well. You thank me, dear, dear Max; you thank me instead of reproaching me for not having come to him long since, for sitting here and only writing letters. I beg you—I beg you, don't think badly of me, don't think I make things easy for myself. I am tormented to pieces here, all despairing (don't tell Frank!) and don't know what to do or where to turn. But that you write that Frank does have something from me, does get something out of me, something good—really, Max, that is the greatest happiness there can be. Frank will certainly go somewhere[1]—I'll do everything I can, and if there is no other way I'll come to Prague myself in the fall and we will send him away, won't we? And I hope too that he will be quiet there and in good spirits. I—must I say it—I'll do everything to see that it's so.

The story of my marriage and my love for my husband is too complicated for me to tell now. Only, the way it is, I cannot leave now—perhaps I cannot at all. I—no, words are too

[1] This sentence refers to my constant urging that Kafka give up his job and go to a sanatorium. Not until the end of 1920 did he make up his mind to take this necessary step.

226

silly. But I am always looking for a way out for myself, always a solution, always what is good and right. Please, Max, do believe that I won't let Frank suffer; please believe me that that is more important to me than anything else in the world.

You are with him now and you must tell me at once if there is anything to tell; you will be strict and truthful with me, won't you? I feel a little easier today because I have you, because I am no longer so much by myself.

Please, when you come back, write to me about the practical details of the trip (what about the office, for example) and all that, how and what is needed for it, and above all if the doctor really offers a hope that he can get well. But what am I writing—all that is unimportant. The main thing is that he goes away; he will do it, certainly he will.

Many, many thanks. I am really deeply grateful. Your letter was so good to me. Forgive me for calling you Max—Franz does it and I am already accustomed.

Many regards,
Milena P.

The beginning of the third letter refers to one of my books, which Milena praises highly. She then continues, writing in Czech this time:

I would have to spend many days and nights replying to your letter. You ask how it is that Frank is afraid of love and not afraid of life. But it seems to me that the matter is otherwise. For him life is something entirely different from what it is to everyone else. Above all, for him money, the stock market, foreign exchange, a typewriter, are utterly mystical things (and they are that in fact, only not for the rest of us). To him they are the strangest enigmas, toward which he has an attitude altogether different from ours. Is his work as an official, say, anything like an ordinary job? For him the entire office—including his own part in it—is something as mysterious and remarkable as a locomotive is to a small child. He does not understand the simplest thing in the world. Have you ever gone to a post office with him? After he has filed away at a telegram and then, shaking his head, picked out the window he likes best, and after he has tramped from one window to the next, without in the least understanding why and wherefore until he finally stumbles on the right one, and after he has paid and received his change—he counts up what he has received, finds that he has been given a crown too much, and returns the crown to the girl at the window. Then he walks slowly away, counts his change again, and on the last step down to the street he sees that the returned crown did belong to him after all. Now you stand helplessly beside him—he shifts his weight from one foot to the other and ponders what he ought to do. To go back is hard; there is a crowd at the windows upstairs, "Then let it be," I say. He looks at me in utter horror. How can you let it be? Not that he cares about the crown. But it's wrong. There is a crown too little. How can a thing like that be ignored? He talked for a long time about the matter; was very dissatisfied with me. And variations of that incident would be repeated in every shop, in every restaurant, in front of every beggar. Once he gave a beggar two crowns and wanted to have one back. She said she had no change. We stood there a good two minutes thinking how to regulate the matter. Then it occurred to him that he could let her have two crowns. But no sooner had he taken a few steps than he became very annoyed.[1] And this same person would unhesitatingly, with enthusiasm, filled with happiness, at once give me twenty thousand crowns. But if I were to ask him for twenty thousand and one crowns, and we had to change money somewhere and did not know where, he would seriously consider what he should do about the extra crown which I was not supposed to receive. His constraint with regard to money is almost the same as his constraint toward women. Likewise his fear of his job. I once telegraphed, telephoned, wrote, implored him in God's name to come to me for a day. At the time it was very necessary for me. I cursed him and railed against him. He did not sleep for nights on end, tormented himself, wrote letters full of self-abasement—but he did not come. Why? He had been unable

[1] Cf. Kafka's letter to Milena about this episode, p. 113f.

to ask for some days off. He had not been able to bring himself to say to the director that he wanted to come to me—this same director whom he admires from the bottom of his heart (seriously!) because he can type so fast. And to invent some pretext or other—another horrified letter. What did I mean? Was he supposed to lie? Tell the director a lie? Impossible. When you ask him why he loved his first fiancée, he answers: "She was so good at business."[1] And his face begins to shine with sheer respect.

Ah no, this whole world is and remains mysterious to him. A mystical enigma. Something that he cannot afford and that, with a pure, touching naiveté, he esteems because it is "efficient." When I told him about my husband, who is unfaithful to me a hundred times a year, who holds me and many other women in a kind of spell, his face lit up with the same reverence it had held that time he spoke of his director who types so fast and is therefore such an excellent person, and as it did the time he spoke of his fiancée as "good at business." All such things are alien to him. A person who types fast and a man who has four mistresses are just as incomprehensible to him as the crown piece at the post office and the beggar's crown piece, incomprehensible because these things are alive. But Frank cannot live. Frank does not have the capacity for living. Frank will never get well. Frank will die soon.

[1] These words are in German in the original letter. There is a fundamental misunderstanding on Milena's part here. That is evident from a letter of Kafka's (*Letters to Milena*, p. 79) which he sent to her at the same time as Grillparzer's *"The Poor Fiddler."* He was sending her the book, he wrote, because Grillparzer "looked down on us in the park . . . because he is so bureaucratic and because he was in love with a girl who was good at business." Kafka was of course referring to the "poor fiddler's" girl, a person of upright, competent nature, capable of coping with all the vicissitudes of life. In his own peculiar, ironically admiring and yet at bottom really admiring phraseology, Kafka summed her up as "good at business." Kafka's first fiancée was that too: not "good at business" in a banal or pejorative sense, but upright, clear, energetic, dominating life by her own force. In other words, she possessed qualities for which Kafka had the highest esteem and which he wrongly (though not *wholly* wrongly) thought were lacking in himself. Thus Kafka, referring to the novel, was saying that he considered persons like the fiddler's girl "good at business." Milena, however, missed the reference and took the word in a literal sense.

For, obviously, we are capable of living because at some time or other we took refuge in lies, in blindness, in enthusiasm, in optimism, in some conviction or others, in pessimism or something of that sort. But he has never escaped to any such sheltering refuge, none at all. He is absolutely incapable of living, just as he is incapable of getting drunk. He possesses not the slightest refuge. For that reason he is exposed to all those things against which we are protected. He is like a naked man among a multitude who are dressed. Everything that he says, that he is and in which he lives cannot even be called truth. Rather, it is such a predetermined state of being in and for itself, stripped of all trimmings that could help him by distorting life—distorting it in the direction of beauty or of misery, no matter. And his asceticism is altogether unheroic—and by that very fact all the greater and more sublime. All "heroism" is lie and cowardice. One who conceives his asceticism as a means to an end is no true human being; the true human being is one who is compelled to asceticism by his terrible clarity of vision, purity and incapacity for compromise.

There are very intelligent people who also do not wish to make any compromises. But these put on rose-colored glasses and see everything in a different light. For that reason they do not need to make compromises. For that reason they can type rapidly and have women. He stands beside them and looks at them in astonishment, looks at everything, including the typewriter and the women, in equal amazement. He will never understand it.

His books are amazing. He himself is far more amazing....
I am very grateful to you for everything. The best regards. When I come to Prague, I may call upon you, may I not? Cordially.

The next letter, undated, is one wild cry of despair. Milena had received Kafka's letter from the Tatra Sanatorium, in which he broke off their relationship. She quotes what he had written to her: "Do not write and let us not see each other."

The reason for this break is obvious. Milena was prepared

to come and be with Kafka for a while. But she was not prepared to leave her husband and live permanently with Kafka. Kafka refused to be content with a surrogate marriage, for he regarded marriage as a sacred coronation of life, a common fate to be shared with wife and *children*. Perhaps at that time, given Kafka's deteriorating health, it would no longer have been sensible to think of marriage. Only accomplishment of the impossible, the irrational—only a miracle could save him. Kafka sought this miracle, and later—in Dora Dymant— some rays of it came his way. But Milena, with her earthy character, could not give it to him, much as she tried, close as she came to the thing which would have shattered all barriers. "Am I at fault or not?" she asked me in the distraught letter in which she herself had scratched out or made so many lines illegible. She wanted me to tell her whether she, too, was only another of those women who could not save Franz.

Here is the whole letter:

Dear Doctor,

Forgive me for not writing in German. Perhaps you know enough Czech to be able to understand me. Forgive me for burdening you. I simply don't know what to do—my brain is no longer capable of taking in any impressions, forming any thoughts; I know nothing, feel nothing, understand nothing. It seems to me that during these last months something utterly horrible has happened to me, but I do not know much about it. I do not know much about the world in general; I only feel that I would kill myself if I could somehow get into my mind the thing that keeps slipping away from my mind.

I could tell you how and why and wherefore all this had happened; I could tell you all about myself and about my life. But what would be the use—and, moreover, I don't know—I just keep holding Frank's letter from Tatra in my hand—a deadly plea, and at the same time a command: "Do not write and let us not see each other; I ask you only to quietly fulfill this request of mine; only on those conditions is survival possible for me; everything else continues the process of destruc-

231

tion." I do not dare to write a word, a question, to him; and I don't even know what I want to ask you. I don't know—I don't know what I want to know. Jesus Christ, I would like to press my temples into my brain. Only tell me this one thing—you must know, you were with him lately: Am I at fault or am I not at fault? I beg you, for God's sake, don't write comforting things to me, don't write that nobody is at fault, don't write me any psychoanalysis. I know all that, believe me, I know all that sort of thing that you could write to me. I trust you, Max, in what is perhaps the most difficult hour of my life. Please understand what I want. I know who and what Frank is; I know what has happened, and I do not know what has happened; I am on the verge of madness; I've tried to act, live, think, feel rightly, guided by conscience; but somewhere there *is* a fault. That's what I want to hear about. Of course I don't know whether you can possibly understand me. I want to know whether I am the kind of person who has made Frank suffer the way he has suffered from every other woman, so that his sickness has grown worse, so that he has had to flee from me, too, in his fear, and so that I too must get out of his life—whether I am at fault or whether it is a consequence of his own nature. Is what I am saying clear? I *must* know that. You are the only person who may know something. I beg you, answer me, please answer the absolutely naked, simple truth the brutal truth if it must be so—what you really think. [Three lines scratched out.] I shall be very grateful to you if you answer me. That will be a certain point of departure for me. Furthermore, would you please let me know how he is? For months I have heard nothing from him. [Two lines scratched out.] My address: M. K., Wein VIII, Postamt 65, Bennogasse. Forgive me; I cannot recopy the letter; I cannot even reread it. Thank you.

Milena

The next letter is couched in a somewhat quieter tone. It is plain, however, that her inner stress is still very great. Here is the text:

Thank you for your kindness. In the meantime I have to some degree come to my senses. I can think again. Not that that makes me feel any better. You may be absolutely sure that I will not write to Frank. How could I! If it is true that people have a task to fulfill on this earth, I have fulfilled this task at his side very badly. How could I be so immodest and harm him when I have not been able to help him?

What his terror is, I know down to the last nerve. It existed before he met me, too, all the while he did not know me. I knew his terror before I knew him. I armored myself against it by understanding it. In the four days that Frank was with me, he lost it. We laughed at it. I know for certain that no sanatorium will succeed in curing him. He will never become well, Max, as long as he has this terror. And no psychic strengthening can overcome this terror, because the terror prevents the strengthening. This terror does not refer to me alone, but to everything that lives shamelessly, also to the flesh, for example. The flesh is too exposed; he cannot bear to see it. That was the thing I was able to dispel, that time. When he felt this terror, he looked into my eyes, and we waited a while, just as though we could not catch our breath, or as though our feet hurt, and after a while it passed. Not the slightest exertion was necessary; everything was simple and clear; for example, I dragged him over the hills on the out-skirts of Vienna, I running ahead, since he walked slowly— he tramped along behind me, and when I close my eyes I can still see his white shirt and tanned throat, and the effort he was making. He tramped all day, up and down, walked in the sun, and not once did he cough; he ate a fearful amount and slept like a log; he was simply healthy, and during those days his illness seemed to us something like a minor cold. If I had gone to Prague with him that time, I would have remained what I was to him. But I had sunk both feet so firmly, so in-finitely firmly into the ground here; I was not able to leave my husband, and perhaps I was too feminine, too weak, to want to subject myself to this life, which I knew would mean strict-est asceticism for life. But there is in me an insuppressible longing, a raging desire for an altogether different kind of life

233

from the one I lead and probably will always lead, for a life with a child, for a life that would be very close to the soil. And probably that weakness won out in me over everything else, over love, over the desire to take flight, over my admiration and again over my life. You know, whatever one tries to say about that, only a lie comes out. This one is perhaps the least of the lies. And then it was already too late. Then this struggle in me came too plainly to the surface, and that frightened him off. For that is the very thing he fought against all his life, from the other side. With me he would have been able to find peace. But then it began to pursue him even with me. Against my will. I knew very well that something had happened which could no longer be thrust aside. I was too weak to do the one and only thing that I knew would have helped him. That *is* my fault. And you too know that it is my fault. The thing that you all call Frank's non-normality—just that is his greatest trait. The women who were with him in the past were ordinary women and did not know how to live except as women. I rather think that all of us, each and every one of us, is sick and that he is the only well person, the only one who sees rightly and feels rightly, the only pure person. I know that he does not resist *life,* but only *this kind of life:* that is what he resists. I I had been capable of going with him, he could have lived happily with me. But only now do I know all that. At the time I was an ordinary woman, like all women on the face of the earth, a little instinct-ridden female. Hence his terror. It was perfectly right. Can this man feel anything that is not perfectly right? He knows ten thousand times more about the world than all other people in the world. That terror of his was right. And you are mistaken; Frank will not write to me of his own accord. There is nothing he could write to me. In fact there is not a single word that he could say to me in this terror of his. I know that he loves me. He is too good and chaste to stop loving me. He would feel guilty if he did. He always thinks himself the guilty and weak one. And yet there is not another person in the whole world who has his tremendous strength: that absolute, irrevocable, necessary drive toward perfection, purity, truth. That is how it is.

234

I know down to the last drop of my blood that that is how it is. Only I cannot bring this knowledge fully into my consciousness. When that does come about, it will be frightful. I dash through the streets, sit at the window whole nights through; often my thoughts skip like little sparks when a knife is honed and my heart hangs inside me as if it were stuck on a fishhook, you know, a very thin little hook, and it pierces me so and gives a very thin, terribly sharp pain.

As far as my health is concerned, I've reached the end, and if anything is sustaining me, it's happening against my will; probably it is the same thing that has kept me going so far, something extremely unconscious, an involuntary love of life. Recently, somewhere at the other end of Vienna, I suddenly came across an array of tracks—imagine streets stretching on for miles, like a great oblong pit—and down below tracks, red lights, locomotives, viaducts, freight cars—it was such a horrible black organism; I sat nearby and it was as though something were breathing. I thought I should go mad for sheer grief, longing and terrible love of life. I am as lonely as the mute are lonely, and if I speak to you of myself as I do, it is because I am vomiting out the words; they rush forth entirely against my will, because I can no longer keep silent. Forgive me.

I shall not write to Frank, not a line, and I do not know what is going to come of it all. In the spring I am coming to Prague and will call on you. And if you write to me how he is from time to time—I cannot cure myself of the habit of going to the post office daily—I should be very glad.

Thank you once more.

M.P.

One more request, a very ridiculous one. My translation of the books *The Trial, Metamorphosis, The Stoker, Contemplation*[1] will be published by Neumann—Edition Cerven—in the same format as Charles Louis Philippe's *Bubu of Montparnasse*—you surely know the book.

[1] Identical with "Meditation" in *The Penal Colony*, New York 1948, pp. 21–45.

Now I am finished with it—in these last months it devoured my heart and brain; it was ghastly, to be so abandoned and to work on his books—but Neumann wants me to write "a few words to introduce him to the Czech reading public." Jesus Christ, am I to write about him for people? Furthermore I simply do not have the ability to do so. Won't you do it for me? I don't know whether you may not have political objections—Červen is Communistic, but the series of books is non-partisan. Neumann is so cordially glad to be bringing out the book and is looking forward with such pleasure to its publication—but of course your name would then be on it—would that bother you? If not, I do beg you to write three or four pages—I'll translate them and include them as a foreword. I once read something of the sort of yours—an introduction to Laforgue—a very, very fine piece. Would you do that for me? I'd be so grateful. The book must come out in the best possible way, don't you agree. The translation *is* good. And your introduction would certainly be good. Please, if you have no political scruples, do that for me. Of course it would have to be something informative for the Czech reader. But don't write it just for the public, but for itself, as you did that Laforgue preface. Where you love, you are sincere and very clairvoyant. And then the way you say things is very, very fine. It would have to be very soon, Max; please do it for me. I would like to appear before the eyes of the world with this book as perfect as it is possible to make it—you know, I have the feeling that I must defend something, justify something. So please.

And say nothing to F. We will surprise him—all right? Perhaps—perhaps it will give him a little pleasure.

A lengthy pause in the correspondence between Milena and myself seems to have ensued, as the beginning of the next letter indicates. I have no recollection of whether the book translated by Milena was actually published, or of what became of my preface. I have no copy of the book or the preface. The other preface mentioned by Milena referred to a translation of Jules Laforgue's *Pierrot* which I did together

236

with Franz Blei, and which exerted a considerable influence upon Kafka and upon the early poems of Werfel.

Here is Milena's sixth letter:

My dear Doctor,

Forgive me for answering you so belatedly. I got out of bed for the first time only yesterday; my lungs have about reached their limit; the doctor gives me only a few months more if I do not go away at once. At the same time I am writing to my father; if he sends me money, I shall go, though where to and when I do not yet know. First, however, I shall certainly come to Prague and shall take the liberty of calling on you to find out something more definite about Frank. I shall write you again when I arrive. But please, I insist upon this, do not tell F. anything about my illness.

I have no idea when the book will appear—evidently in winter. It will be published by K. St. Neumann, Borový Publishers, as a volume in the Červen series, Stefangasse 37; perhaps you could ask him if you may publish the preface independently before it appears in the book. There is little paper and money; everything takes a long time: I did not want to cut anything from your preface. (It is so fine.)

I have the impression that you are somehow annoyed with me. I don't know why I had this impression—just from that letter. Forgive me the "analyses" of Frank; it is shameful and I am ashamed that I allowed myself to do that; but I sometimes feel as though I must press my brain together with the palms of my hands to prevent it from exploding.

Thank you for everything, and *auf Wiedersehen.*

Yours,
M.P.

The two last letters from Milena belong to the first few months after Kafka's death. Kafka's only actual meetings with Milena were the "four days" in Vienna and the brief, unfortunate encounter in Gmünd which precipitated the alienation between the two. In *The Castle,* too, harmony between the two lovers is of brief duration. And after their first night

237

of love we read: "He was too happy to have Frieda in his arms, too troubled also in his happiness, for it seemed to him that in letting Frieda go he would lose all he had." Immediately afterwards, difficulties begin, interspersed only by rare episodes of trustfulness. Concerning the second time K. and Frieda are together, the fourth chapter pronounces (right at the beginning) a fearful malediction. I have already said that the version of the love affair as given in the novel is to be regarded as a bitter caricature. Reality was more generous and merciful than the novel's picture of it; he felt compelled to distrust and denigrate his own emotions. Reality gave to Kafka those moments of happiness that shine forth from the glorious pages of the first letters, gave him the letters (unfortunately destroyed) of Milena and his own rapturous cries of gratitude. The climax lay between the "four days" and the second stay together. Probably Milena also visited Kafka later on in Prague, but these were only sick visits; when Kafka spoke to me about them, he said that they had been on the whole painful and disturbing, although he continued to appreciate the salutary influence that Milena's personality exerted upon him. A meeting in Marienbad, of which Haas speaks in the epilogue to Milena's letters, did not in fact take place; the diary note of January 29, 1922 refers to an episode of many years past, the meeting with F. in Marienbad in July 1916.

The reader will feel, I think, the force and passion of Milena's nature in the letters I have quoted *in extenso*. These letters form a valuable complement to Kafka's own letters to her, all the more valuable since, as I have indicated, other direct documents of that period are lacking.

Here now are the two last letters to me (originally in German). The first was written on her father's letterhead, which would suggest that a reconciliation with her family had taken place.

Dear Doctor,

I am returning the book to you, with thanks. Please forgive me for not visiting you. I scarcely think that I could talk about
238

Franz now, and you surely will not wish to talk about him with me either, now. I'll let you know when I come to Prague in September, if you permit. Please remember me with friendship and give my cordial regards to your wife whom I once probably wronged, without wishing to do so. If you are able, would you kindly arrange for my letters to Franz to be burned; I confidently entrust them to you; though the matter is not important. His manuscripts and diaries (which were absolutely not meant for me, but date from the time before he knew me, approximately fifteen big notebooks) are in my possession and at your disposal if you should need them. That was his wish; he asked me to show them to no one but you, and only after he died. Perhaps you already know parts of them.

With warmest greetings, I remain

Your friend,
Milena Pollak.

July 27, 1924

Dear Doctor,

I cannot come to Prague to hand over the manuscripts to you, much as I should like to do so. I have also not found anyone to whom I can entrust them, and still less do I dare send the notebooks by mail. I shall try to postpone my trip to Prague until October, by which time you will presumably be back and then I can give you everything personally. I shall also ask you to obtain my letters from Kafka's family; you would be doing me a great kindness. I personally do not want to ask them for anything; I never got on well with his relatives.

Many, many thanks—I look forward to seeing you in Prague after October 1. If you do not intend to be in Prague then either, please write me, to Vienna, when you will be returning from Italy.

Sincere regards,
Milena Pollak.

Thereafter I had many talks with Milena, and also received Kafka's manuscripts from her.

It can be a catastrophic mistake to try to analyze Kafka by the rules of simplistic psychology. The following facts, with which I became acquainted only a few years ago, bear this out.

In the spring of 1948 the musician Wolfgang Schocken[1] who was then living in Jerusalem, wrote to me disclosing the fact that Kafka had fathered a son. As evidence he showed me the letter of a certain lady, M. M., who had been a close friend of his. In 1948 the lady was no longer living, and the child had been dead more than twenty years. The particular tragedy of this episode lies in the fact that Kafka never had the slightest inkling of the existence of the boy, who had lived until he was barely seven and died before Kafka himself. The child's mother, a very proud woman, independent both intellectually and materially, given to withdrawal out of sensitivity, may have had inhibitions about confiding in Kafka, for the brief relationship had been followed by a lasting alienation. I knew Frau M. M. casually, but had no idea there had been any friendship between her and Kafka. In fact, on the basis of what Franz had told me, I had rather thought the relationship a more or less hostile one. In Franz's diary there are hints that point in the same direction. In any case, M. M. was a person of consequence, successful, strong-willed, uncommonly intelligent, possessing a broad, wide-ranging view of life.

The effect upon Kafka would almost certainly have been enormous, had he learned that he was the father of a son. It would have exercised a beneficent influence on his development. For there was nothing he more fervently desired than children, no potentiality within himself of which he had greater doubts than this, that he could become a father. Everyone who has read his journals has been touched by those passages in which Kafka expresses his longing to be a father, to sit beside the cradle of a child of his own. Fulfillment of this desire would have seemed to him a confirmation of his worth from the highest court of appeal. He would have felt ennobled—just as he always regarded his lack of offspring

[1] Not related to the publisher.

as a special disgrace, a sentence of guilt that had been pronounced upon him. Perhaps that child, had Kafka taken loving charge of it, would have been strong and well; perhaps
the self-assurance it would have brought him might have
saved Kafka's own life; perhaps my friend would be sitting
beside me today, instead of my writing away into a vacuum.
But since that is not what happened, it must at least be admitted that in this matter life has composed a story that
amazingly resembles the wanton cruelties and complexities,
the ironic bitternesses, in the works of Kafka.

Frau M. M. went to Prague to visit Kafka's grave. At that
time she met my informant in Prague again. A long time afterwards, on April 21, 1940, she sent him a letter (she was at that
time in Florence and he in Israel), which contain these crucial lines: "You were the first who saw me in Prague in great
distress, oppressed by premonitory fears. And even then your
music-making in your friends' disordered room, and those
short walks through the magical city, which I loved more
than you suspected, helped me to get over terrible anxieties. I
had gone to visit the grave of the man who meant so very
much to me, who died in 1924; his greatness is hailed to this
day. He was the father of my boy, who died suddenly in
Munich in 1921, just before he reached the age of seven. Far
from me and from him, from whom I had already had to part
during the war and then did not see again—except for a few
hours—because he was prey to a fatal illness in his homeland,
far from us. I have never spoken of all this. I believe this is the
first time I have told anyone the story. My family and my
friends did not know, only my later employer. For that reason
he was so kind and awfully decent to me. I lost a great deal,
everything when this good man died in 1936. But now I do
not sorrow so much over any of this, for they have escaped the
sufferings of these times." For a number of years Frau M. M.
had always spoken in so special a manner of Kafka and
Kafka's work that my informant is convinced that this passage in the letter can only refer to Kafka. Soon afterwards
Italy entered the war, and the correspondence between M. M.
and my informant had to be broken off.

The visit to Prague had taken place in the shadow of the seizure of power by the Nazis in Germany. M. M., who lived in Berlin, rightly spoke of premonitory fears. She fled to Switzerland, to Israel, finally to Italy.[1] The last word my informant had concerning her came from the British Red Cross, dated May 16, 1945. The report read: "Mrs. M. M. was taken away from S. Donato di Comino, Frosinone, by the Germans in May 1944, together with other Jewish people living in the district. We regret that at the present time there is nothing more we can do." Through further investigation it has been ascertained that M. M. died at the hands of a German soldier, who beat her to death with the butt of his rifle. I have followed up all the trails which my informant has so kindly suggested to me. They led to several persons in Florence, to the San Giorgio and Jennings-Riccioli pensions. There was some slight prospect of locating the belongings of M. M., which included many letters of Kafka's. Max Krell, the writer, who lives in Florence, hunted down every clue for me. But nothing came of these efforts. It is possible that Kafka's letters are now in the possession of a certain E. Pr. who had obtained an emigration visa to Chile for M. M.

We have never discovered what name was given to the boy who was Kafka's son, what he was like or in what way he died. Few persons have left behind so slender a trail as this child of Kafka's.

Kafka's aphorisms I have set aside from the body of his work and presented as a separate branch of his writings.[2] Not only are these statements short and self-contained but, by their content and mood, they reveal another side of their author. In them Kafka lays stress on the "Indestructible" in man, on faith and positive trust in God. His narratives, on the other hand, give free rein to all his doubts and uncertainties.

[1] Another informant, independent of Wolfgang Schocken, has now corroborated the story; in Florence Frau M. M. told him a great deal about Kafka and her child, also about the "Berlin woman." I am tracking down further clues.

[2] *Great Wall of China*, New York 1946, pp. 263–307; *Dearest Father*, New York 1954, pp. 34–48.

In the narratives Kafka shows how man is confused and misses his way; in the aphorisms he exerts himself to define what the way is, and there are intimations that man is not doomed to confusion. Naturally, we cannot create an artificial separation between these two visions which Kafka expressed simultaneously. Among the aphorisms, too, there are many that make one catch one's breath for sheer sorrow and perplexity. On the other hand, the novels are irradiated with glimpses of hope, not merely pictures of hopelessness. Kafka is always the whole Kafka. Still, we may with some vadidity affirm that the "Kafka of the aphorisms" tends more to be a helper and teacher, while the Kafka of the tales and novels tends to be the victim of doubts and self-torment. How, we may ask, did it happen that these two aspects of a single spirit divided themselves, with greater or less distinctness and consistency, between these two genres? One answer might be that in the narratives, letters and diaries Kafka let himself go, yielded, surrendered without reserve to his angels and demons. In the meditations, on the other hand, in the aphorisms and in certain letters, he attained self-control, and an attitude of manly command. He was no longer the sport of the forces of tragedy and absurdity, but took a stand against them, in affirmation of an imagined or real universe around him. In this mood he could write the crucial passages in which the freedom of man's will is pitted against the machinations of destiny, grace against damnation. He could issue a call to humanity to put an end to the "Alexandrine Battles," to usher in an era of peace, and to place hope in those seemingly submerged powers which call out from the depths: "'Nevertheless, you mute, marching, pushed and shoved souls, you men trustful to the point of savagery, nevertheless we will not abandon you, not even in your greatest stupidities—especially not in them." Through the chaos and the nihilism, manifest in Kafka's world, there sounds softly but unmistakably the note of love for the human creature who will "nevertheless" not be abandoned—so runs the promise—by the divine powers; he will become a blessing.

CHRONOLOGICAL TABLE

1883	Born in Prague, July 3.
1893–1901	Attendance at the German State Gymnasium.
1901	Beginning of university studies at the German University in Prague; in Munich for a time.
1902	Plans for studying at the Export Academy in Vienna. Beginning of correspondence with Oskar Pollak. Summer in Liboch (Schelesen).
1905–1906	Summer in Zuckmantel. April 1, 1906: Unpaid probationer in the office of Dr. Richard Löwy, Prague lawyer.
1906	June: doctorate at law. Summer in Triesch with his uncle, the "country doctor" (Dr. Siegfried Löwy). October 1, 1906 to October 1, 1907: Practice at the criminal court in Prague; later at the civil court.
before 1907:	"Description of a Struggle" and "Wedding Preparations in the Country" written. Other youthful works (lost).
1907	October: Takes position with the "Assicurazioni Generali."
1908	Begins work at the Workers' Accident Insurance Institute.
1909	Two sections from "Description of a Struggle" published in *Hyperion*. September: At Riva and Brescia with Max and Otto Brod.
1910	Beginning of the Diaries. Yiddish theater troupe. October: In Paris with Max and Otto Brod.
1911	Business trip in January and February (Friedland, Reichenberg). In the summer: trip to Zürich, Lugano, Milan and Paris with Max Brod. Then Kafka alone at sanatorium (Fellenberg's Naturheilanstalt) in Erlenbach, near Zürich. Travel diaries.
1912	Novel "The Man who Disappeared" (*Amerika*) begun. Summer at Weimar with Max Brod, then alone at Jungborn in the Harz Mountains. Meets F. B. on August 13. On August 14 manuscript of *Contemplation* (*Meditation*) sent off to Rowohlt publishing house. *The Verdict* and *Metamorphosis* written.
1913	*Contemplation* (*Meditation*) published by Rowohlt (January). In May publication of *The Stoker*. Garden work in Troja near Prague. Trips alone to Vienna, Venice, Riva.

244

1914	Berlin, end of May. Engagement. Preliminary study for *The Castle* (Diary, June 11). Trip to Hellerau, Lübeck, Marienlyst (part of this trip with Ernst Weiss). Outbreak of the war. Additional responsibilities in regard to brother-in-law's factory. Breaking of engagement. Work on *The Trial*. *In the Penal Colony* written.
1915	Meeting with F. B. again. Work on *The Trial*. Trip to Hungary with sister, Elli. Fontane Prize.
1916	At Marienbad in July with F. A number of country doctor stories written.
1917	Apartment on Alchymistengasse, then in the Palais Schönborn. Further work on country doctor stories. Second engagement in July. September 4: Diagnosis of tuberculosis. Sharing apartment with sister Ottla in Zürau. September 12: leave from duties at office. Kierkegaard studies. Aphorisms (octavo notebooks). Second engagement broken in December, at Prague.
1918	Zürau. Prague, Turnau. Schelesen. *The Great Wall of China* and *The Bucket-Rider* written.
1919	*A Country Doctor* published by Kurt Wolff. Fräulein Julie Wohryzek (Schelesen). Prague *Letter to His Father*. In Schelesen with Max Brod. *In the Penal Colony* published.
1920	Meran. Sick leave. Milena Jesenská (Vienna). Back at office in Prague. Arrival in Prague, July 5. End of the year in the Tatra Mountains (Matliary). Robert Klopstock.
1921	Tatra Mountains, Prague. Milena.
1922	Spindlermühle. In February back in Prague. March 15 read aloud from *The Castle*. In May last meeting with Milena. From end of June in Planá on the Luschnitz with his sister Ottla. Prague.
1923	July in Müritz. Dora Dymant (Diamant). Berlin. Schelesen. End of September with Dora in Berlin-Steglitz. Zehlendorf. *The Burrow, Josephine,* possibly *Investigations of a Dog*. The four stories of *The Hunger Artist* sent to press (Die Schmiede Publishers).
1924	Berlin until March 17. Prague. Departed for the Wiener Wald Sanatorium April 10. Prof. Hajek's clinic in Vienna. Then sanatorium in Kierling, near Vienna, with Dora Dymant and Robert Klopstock. Death on June 3. Burial in Prague.
1952	Death of Dora in London (August).

INDEX